Find 'Em & Keep 'Em:
A Guide to Attracting the Right Partner

By Michael Santonato

Published by BurmanBooks Media Corp.
260 Queens Quay West
Suite 1102
Toronto, Ontario
Canada M5J 2N3

Interior design: Lara Vanderheide
Editing: Nicolette Hernandez

Distribution:
NewLeaf Distribution
401 Thorton Rd.
Lithia Springs, GA 30122-1557

ISBN: 978-1-927005-47-7

Printed and bound in The United States of America

Dedication

To all the wonderful loves of my past, the current one I am with, and any future ones that await, in this lifetime or the next.
Thank you for everything you have helped me achieve and understand. It has made me the person I am today.

I thank you, and I love you for it.

Every moment was a gift and I cherish them all.

Michael

Table of Contents

INTRODUCTION - WHY READ THIS BOOK?

If you're single and looking to be in a great relationship, you should read this book. This is a bold statement know, especially for the first line of a book you've never heard of. Here's why: this is a straight up guide to be the kind of person you want to be, meet the kind of person you want to meet, and have the kind of relationship you want to have. If this book is in your hands or on your screen, it's for a reason. Only your unconscious mind and higher self knows what that reason is, it guided you here after all. Maybe you need it, maybe it's time for you to be in a relationship maybe it's time to change the current relationship you are in. Maybe it's time to start off your life on a new path or maybe you need to break some bad habits. This book will do all that for you.

I can completely and confidently say I can help anyone find a great partner and keep a great relationship. It's something I've done my whole life with ease and a little focus. I've been teaching people how to do it for the last several years and I can teach you if you take this book and apply what's inside of it. Heck, if you apply 60% of it, you'll get what you want. Can you do that? Do you know someone who could really benefit from it? If the answer is yes, then take it home and give it to them. If no, then put the book down and I thank you for picking it up. If you bought this book then 1) Thank you! 2) Congratulations 3) Lets begin!

This book is for anyone looking to find themselves in a relationship in the near or not too distant future. How do I define a relationship? An ongoing interaction between two people, while exchanging affection and care for each other.
Not necessarily in marriage and not necessarily 'The One' either. That's a conversation for another time--Chapter 9 to be exact. My intention with this book is that you use it for whichever relationship you desire. If you are looking for love, use this to find love. If you are looking for the one, use it to find the one. If you're just looking for a great connection with someone, and someone to spend time and have fun with, then by all means, you can use it for that too.

This book provides a process to enhance your love life and personal life. I know that might sound amazing to some, but I can wholeheartedly say, not only because the process outlined in the book works, (it has been created, crafted, and tested by myself and by others again and again and again) but because, by buying this book, you will enter *a certain space,* a *mentality* if you will. Upon entering this space you will begin to emit a specific energy, a vibration if you will. In this vibration, the signals, and energies will transmit throughout the world to find the right partner and increase your overall experiences in a loving relationship (a very small act, but a significant one). Don't judge these words just yet, if you're skeptical, I will prove this later.

By taking this book you are making a choice to enter *into* that space. Think of it this way, when you enter a restaurant, you take on the behaviours, thoughts, attitudes, and actions that demonstrate you being in a restaurant, or of one who is looking to be fed. From that point on, you go into 'restaurant mode' (unconsciously of course) because you've done it so many times before. Your mannerism's change: you are polite, you are smiling, you tap into your taste buds, you tap into your appetite, your desire is awakened, and you become alert to the things you haven't eaten in some time. Your cravings go up, you prepare yourself to indulge, you become curious about the menu items, you consider the prices, and how much you want to spend. You might pay attention to the cleanliness, the last time the place was inspected and the grade they received on their health inspection. Prior to that, if you are walking down the street looking for a place to eat, you might look at the menu's posted outside, on the door or walls before you enter and consider the other options nearby and whether to actually step inside or not.

After you have decided that this place meets the needs of yourself or your group, you go in. Once you go in, you're in, and once you're in, you're eating. With this in mind I recommend that if you really want to work on your relationships, and you really want to find that right partner you've been wanting and waiting for, head to the exit with this book in hand right now (don't forget to pay on the way out!) As I said, the process works, but just by picking it up and taking it with you, it starts going to work on you already. Why? Because unconsciously, you have entered this space my friends. You will have stepped foot into the restaurant and the process of finding the right partner will have begun. Not bad for under $30?

This book is for all people out there who believe it isn't possible to have a great relationship, fall in love, and have it all like you see it in the movies. This is for those who haven't had great experiences, and who have given up, those who feel like "my time is up," "what's the point?" and "it's too late for me". This is for you, so you can see the way forward and experience the joys, the bliss, the love, the beauty, and the ups and downs that we have all seen, in loving another person. My hope is that you can achieve the magic that I have experienced, and helped others just like you experience. It is NEVER too late, and it's truly worth it all the way. Life is so enriching, in so many ways when you are in a great relationship with someone else.

This book is also for people who are looking to make their current relationship really great. Like really, really great! Maybe you had something really great with your current partner once, and now it has become routine. Maybe the spark is gone, maybe the communication isn't working. Maybe things have gotten off track. Put the tools in this book into practice, and I promise you can have it all back. With newness and excitement, you will be pleasantly surprised. I will give you everything I have got, I wouldn't want you to have anything less.

I believe this is a unique book because it isn't just another relationship book. However, it is another relationship book with something very different. It is a guide specifically based on having an amazing relationship in every way, in every sense of the word, from beginning to end. Most importantly we will start from the beginning with finding the right partner. That is the foundation. While I can speak to everything in a relationship, meeting someone amazing has been what I have been most able to help people find.

The other piece which is unique about this book is that I will be actively using and explaining the law of attraction and its validity, which science has proven is in fact, an actual law. (It has? Yes. It did? Yes. When? Recently!) We don't really need science for everything right? But for those of us who do, and we all do sometimes, I will back it up with recent discoveries and proof The other great thing about science is that it helps our logical mind understand things, for example, until Isaac Newton defined gravity, we knew that if I threw a ball in the air, it would eventually come down. We didn't need him to explain that to know that the ball would come down, but we're sure glad he did aren't we?

Now normally, only people who are willing to take responsibility for their lives can and do actively acknowledge the truth about the law of attraction. Those who have yet to accept 100% responsibility for their lives sometimes refuse to acknowledge this as true, and that's only because of the different state of mind they have. People who are successful, people who get what they want out of life *attribute themselves as being the sole cause* of their goals being realized (of course we all need help along the way, we can't do and learn everything ourselves). These people will often talk about the actions they took, the persistence they had, the focus, the friends who helped, and the luck they were also blessed with. If not luck, they might call it God, Allah, Source, The Universe etc.

After watching or reading The Secret you may have attempted to use it consciously. Now one of three things may have happened to you: 1. You got what you wanted and were amazed, 2. You didn't get what you wanted and you said, aw heck this doesn't work, or 3. You forgot to consciously use it over time and just left it out of your life.

Here is the thing, the law of attraction, like the law of gravity, works and is a law nonetheless that exists, whether you use it or are aware of it or not.
In this book, we will go deeper into the law of attraction. I've used it my whole life unintentionally at first, and then intentionally, and I've helped plenty of people use it as well. It won't all be about the law of attraction, it will be about what works and what doesn't work, plain and simple.

So let's get started.

PS: I'll ask you to make notes and do a few exercises throughout the book, so grab a pen and some paper. You'll be doing some writing. "But daaaad!" you say. I know. Don't worry, it's a good thing. When you write, you bring what isn't physical into the physical world. You are bringing a thought into

material form. First it manifests in writing, then it manifests in material form.

1
STOP TRYING TO FIX YOURSELF AND BE YOURSELF

Starting Out

So you're ready for a relationship! Why do you want a relationship anyway?

Really, what's the big deal? They are overrated aren't they? They're challenging, difficult, and they take time and energy, and of course, they cost money too! After all this they may not even work out for you! What the heck? Why not just stay at home and have your best friends, or the TV, your cat or dog fulfill all of your personal needs?

Okay, I know that was excessive. I want you to become present to the amazing joy of a loving relationship in your life. Think about it. What's in store? Better yet, what's possible when a great relationship is in your life? Magical and fun experiences, adventures, road trips, long talks, walks, sharing yourself and your life with another human being, breaking down barriers, crossing new lines together! You can laugh with side splitting humour, have moments of tear jerking happiness, and be part of a power couple! You get to know another person's family, and maybe fall in love with that family. You can appreciate and recognizing another's beauty, cherish them, being cherished by them and so much more! Don't forget the romance, the passionate, blissful, sensual Sex! You're in relationships in all areas of your life anyway, so why not have a relationship where you can create something extraordinary with another human being. You can have someone to kiss, make love to, hug like no one else's business, wake up to in the morning, fall asleep with at night and call home.

Some of my most favourite moments are falling asleep next to my partner after a long and busy day. When my head hits that pillow and she is there next to me, wow! What a breath of fresh air. And you know, my day definitely gets off to a better start when I take just a few extra moments waking up to hug and hold the one that I love.

Enough about me and my view, you must create this for yourself. Since you picked up the book and you're the one who wants the relationship, you must list your reasons. *Why do you want a relationship?* This is very important, because this is the basis for everything. That's why we start here. You must know for yourself the reason you are doing this. What are you doing this for? This is your purpose for reading this book, and the journey you are about to embark on.

For some of you it will be a big deal, maybe a bit tough. For others it may not be. Many people are here and in the position of being single, or they will be at some point in their lives. Maybe you're reading this to avoid a future struggle later in life. Maybe you're reading this now because you're having trouble finding a good person to share your life with. Maybe you're wondering why you're with the person you are with, or if they are 'right' for you. The funny thing is, there is no right and wrong. All that matters is why you picked this book in the first place. So go ahead, take a moment and list your reasons for wanting a relationship now.

Who are you?

*It's hard to **really** know someone, until you know yourself.*

Life is a discovery process. You are constantly learning and growing. At least you should be. Whether you believe it or not, you are always experiencing new things. The easy way to say it is, "every day is a new day". And it really is. Even if you feel like you are just going around in circles and repeating yourself over and over and over, you actually aren't. You ***are*** seeing new things, meeting new people, and creating new thoughts all the time. You will continue to do that, every minute of every hour of every day of your life. So life is a discovery process, and you are continually rediscovering yourself, and your reality, the reality that you experience now. And now, and now! Have you ever read these words before? Have you ever read this book before? If you have read it before, guess what? You are a different person this time around. How do I know? Because science has proven that your cells are changing, and are *completely different cells every 42 days.* That's right. You have a new body, a completely new cellular structure every 42 days! That's what's up. So if you are re-reading this book, (cool, good for you!) you will actually be getting something new, and something different this time around. The words will hit you with different depth, scope and magnitude. (While this book will not be overly scientific, you will see facts from science and spirituality from time to time, because I will be giving you the most current, relevant information available, even the stuff that isn't being shared in the mainstream). And it should be fun! It really should! You won't know what is coming, or what you'll experience along the way, and how could that not be fun?

Remember when you were young and you became excited when you learned something new? There were new stories you'd be able to tell all your friends the great things you did? Start allowing it to excite you. Why you might ask? Because otherwise you will struggle and stress about this whole process, and that will just make it hard on you and those around you. Dating is meant to be fun and exciting! So do yourself a favour and allow it to be! (If that really freaks you out, not to worry, we'll cover this more in a later chapter.)

Now from here on out, you want to start something new. Create something you haven't created before. Earlier, I asked you to create the reason you are doing this because it is absolutely vital. Earl Nightingale said, "Think of a ship leaving port. Imagine it has no destination. Where will it end up? Likely after heading to sea, it won't be long before it winds up derelict and shipwrecked. Now think of the ship that has a destination. It gets to the destination because it has a course that it has set and it follows that course." The same applies to you.

So who are you? Where are you going? Obviously you're male or female or you consider yourself transgender. And you're '__' feet tall and you have '____' hair and you weigh '___'. But apart from that, list some things about yourself that are not physical attributes. What do you like to do for fun? Why do you like to do it? Where do you like to go? What do you like to eat? What matters to you? What are your priorities? List some things about yourself now.

Why are these questions important? Your partner will want to know them. Oh yeah! Not only will you get asked those questions (and this might occur for some of you as basic) but I know that once you know the answers to these questions, you will start to find people who know their answers too. This is very important, and, there's a pretty good chance that some of their answers will be the same as some of yours. You see, when you define the things you want in life, you will move towards them naturally. You will do this subconsciously, consciously, and more importantly, your brain will begin to recognize these desires when you see them.

The great philosopher Plato said, 'Know thy self.' And Pythagoras said 'Know thyself, and thou shall know the Universe and God.' I agree with those guys and what they said, and I say, *"Know yourself, and you will know what you want. And better yet, you will find it."…* I know, hold your applause.

In the coming chapters, we will define what you want, who you want, why you want it, and where to find it. And then, my friends, it is only a matter of time until you find it. For some, it has happened in as little as 3 weeks.

Are you excited yet? You should be.

What are you?

You are energy, and spirit. Wait, what? What do you mean I'm energy and spirit?

Einstein proved everything in the universe is energy. I'm going to say that again because sometimes we need to hear it more than once: everything is energy. Yes, everything. Take a microscope and look at anything. Go ahead, anything! Water, paper, your skin, a blanket, it's all made up of the same stuff--energy. You see back in the day, scientists said, (who for some reason we regard as the only experts who can prove things. If you're a scientist, I truly apologize but it's true. Actually, it's a compliment!) 'Everything is made up of atoms,' and we believed them. Then technology improved, and they said, 'Everything is made up of electrons and neutrons, inside of atoms,' and we believed them. Then technology improved and they discovered protons, and we said, 'Oh, okay, that makes sense.' Technology improved again and they…. can you see a pattern developing here? Now we're at Quarks and after that 'particles. Well, the greatest advances and discoveries in science show, that everything is made up of energy, **the same energy is in everything**. This is the same energy, in everything all around us and it is all held together by vibrations. So basically, they discovered that everything is made up of the same stuff: vibrations, empty space, and energy.

Recently, science and spirituality have caught up to each other (spirituality and science actually used to be connected in people's minds many, many lifetimes ago back but then they disconnected and separated them for some weird reason I don't have time to go into) and that's why we're seeing some great things in quantum physics, the metaphysical world, and great movies and documentaries like "The Secret," and "What the bleep do we know?" (If you haven't seen these movies yet make a point of seeing them. It will help you discover more about what it takes to attract the right partner.) We now know that consciousness is spirituality and it is measureable.

Consider that you can be anything you want to be. You may have heard the saying, 'You can be, do, or have anything you want in life.' Well it's true. And it's *all about the way you're being right now.* You can literally *BE* any way you want. Go ahead and be excited. Go, put the book down and be excited. You can do it, I'll wait.

When I finish writing the last page of this book, I will be super excited! A dream will have come true! I will have written my book! However, it will only last for five minutes because after my jumping jacks and my dance to myself in the mirror (I have little shame) I will turn that excitement off. Why? Because I know it will have to go to the editor and take another 2 months before it is released. I will have to make several edits and adjustments all over the place. So I will realize this and then choose to turn it off and get back to work. But you, you can do it right now. You can be excited whenever you want.

Did you do it? Good. If you didn't, shame on you (just kidding). But really, think of something you're excited about. A new movie coming out, a date you're really looking forward to, or a vacation. Maybe you can be excited about a past moment in your life. You can feel it any time you want if it's in your memory. Did you just feel excitement? Good!

Now feel sadness. I want you to think about something that makes you sad--go ahead. Don't worry it's only temporary, I promise. Don't dwell on it for too long, but notice; did you just feel lonely? Did you pause and go somewhere else? Was it a little unpleasant? Did you remember someone who died? Someone close to you? A traumatic experience you witnessed? Okay, let's be done with that. Come on back now to your old self and smile.

Do you see what I mean? You can be anything you want to be, whenever you want to be. If you still doubt what I am saying, here is another example: feel pride. Feel immense pride! What are you proud of? What achievements are you happy to share? What do others recognize in you? What do you recognize in yourself? What have you accomplished? Did your chest just expand outwards? Were you able to go to that place of confidence, of knowingness, or self-assurance? Good! Great!

Now do you see what I mean? Remember this feeling and this moment.

And when I say you are a spirit. That's what you are. You are a soul, a spirit, inhabiting a body. You are not your body. And you are not your mind. You *have* a body. And you *have a mind,* but you are not those things. You are a spirit and energy, residing in a body. We are human beings, because we are being human… right now! We are spiritual beings, having a human experience. It is your being, your spirit that causes you to be alive. We'll cover the brain later, so don't worry about that for now.

However you choose to be is perfectly fine. You can be anything, and do anything, so don't worry or stress about how to act or be in front of another person. At least not yet, we'll cover that later too. Science has also proven that energy never dies, it only moves or transfers someplace else. Science has proven this and it was Einstein as well.

We got through that part with the technical bits! Now this next section will be much easier.

How should I behave?

How do you want to behave? Who do you want to be?

Since you are a being and you can be anything you want to be.... Who do you want to be in your relationship? What kind of man would you like to be for your woman? What kind of woman would you like to be for your man? Do you want to be chivalrous? Do you want to be kind hearted? Do you want to be romantic? Sexy? Flashy? Comfortable? A provider? A joy to be with? Do you want to be full of surprises? Would you like to be compassionate, considerate, forgiving, respectful, honest, integral, faithful and open? We'll cover some of the ideal qualities in a little while. These aren't "be all end all" qualities, and yet, they do make for an amazing partnership.

Ideally, you want to be some of those qualities I mentioned. Otherwise, your partner, if they have any self-respect, might leave you. And that's okay! Really, that is fine. Not everyone is a match anyway! You will want to discover for yourself your behaviours when you are with people. Go ahead and list some now. And if you need to, ask other people,

Golden Nugget

'How do I come across when we hang out together?'

(This is a huge tip! I will be sharing the big difference makers with this → *Golden Nugget* throughout the book).

Have fun with it. Ask the questions of those people in your circles, but ultimately, the goal is to be yourself! Be real to yourself and demonstrate what is real and authentic for you. What do I mean? I mean if you're a geek, be a geek! If you're a bookworm, don't hide it, be a bookworm! If you are a sappy romantic, then please, go ahead and be a sappy romantic. In any area of life, not just relationships, you need to own who you are. Be yourself, it is very important. People know when someone is being authentic, being real and true to themselves, and people know when someone is just going with the status quo, faking it, or trying to pull one over on someone. Besides, don't you want to be with someone who is really themselves, especially if we're talking about falling in love, or finding "the one".

My Characteristics – Strengths and Weaknesses

You have strengths and you have weaknesses, just like everyone else. Why should you know yours?

It doesn't matter how you view them: Good and bad, Strengths and Weaknesses, Positives and Negatives, everyone has them. No one is perfect. Let me say that again, **no one is perfect**. No one. Not you, and not your partner either. Everyone has something that they can work on. They might be perfect for you and you might be perfect for them. In fact, that is the goal but no one has something called perfection. Be honest with yourself and others, and list your characteristics on either side. What are your strengths and weaknesses?

Why do this? When something comes up that annoys your future partner, or you feel insecure, you can recognize and acknowledge with confidence, that it's just your strengths and weaknesses coming out. You've got to take the good with the bad. Now here's the cool part--what becomes possible is you can anticipate the breakdowns and frustrations that you have with your partner or yourself in your relationship. The complaints they have, the complaints you have, will likely revolve around these characteristics. Better yet, you can be responsible for it, when it comes up and that will make the difference (we'll cover how to be responsible in due time.) If it is a persistent issue, consider talking to someone about it, and maybe developing yourself in that area of your character.

If you go to a job interview and they ask you about your strengths and weaknesses, and you answer "I have no weaknesses" or something ridiculous like that, they probably won't hire you. Why? Because it is common knowledge that everyone has both strengths and weaknesses, and they will know you will be an arrogant ass, and likely a difficult person to work with. The same goes for your future partner. So that attitude is one that you need to drop immediately, and this way you can work things out more easily together.

Now, don't get me wrong, relationships aren't all rosy, all the time. In later chapters we will cover what it takes to have a happy, fulfilling, working relationship all of the time. It is normal that your future partner will disagree with some of the things that you do or that you believe in, so don't take it too harshly when they do. Otherwise things would be boring between you anyway. Remember, variety IS the spice of life.

So get to know your characteristics and list them for yourself and then own them. Ownership is the key to responsibility, and responsibility is powerful.

Loving Yourself

You can't really love someone, without loving yourself.

Wow, if this isn't one of the most important pieces of advice in the entire book! I'm glad we are covering it early because it is imperative that you love yourself. Period. Now, some of you will have this handled, and others will not.

Golden Nugget

But the thing is if you aren't in love with yourself, you won't be able to be in love with someone else.

If you are always finding faults in someone else, it's likely because you find a lot of faults within yourself. The majority of times, the people I work with who have trouble with love, have deeply rooted, unresolved issues with themselves, oftentimes dating back to childhood (we aren't exclusive here, everyone has this.) This is perfectly normal in our world and society, and very common everywhere. Some people say, "Everyone has baggage" or "Everyone has something going on." Well it can be very true. Where do we get taught to deal with our stuff? When do we get the tools to repair the damage done to our hearts, minds and souls? We don't. It is not taught in school. Your parents may give you some advice, but even theirs comes through a filter of their own stuff. You can get your computer repaired, you home repaired, your clothes repaired. But where can you go to repair and heal yourself? Thankfully, there are plenty of things you can do, in today's world to really resolve those issues for yourself. I highly recommend it (see my suggested resources at the back of the book, all my resources are either personally used or validated by me, and are oftentimes people in my life whom I trust.)

If you aren't happy with yourself, what makes you think you will be happy with someone else? Think about it for a second. What has you think you would be able to make another person happy if you can't first be happy by yourself? This may irritate and even offend some of you but we must deal with it if we want you to be truly happy in a relationship and in your life. Unfortunately, a lot of people get into relationships to try and fill a void of happiness that is missing in their lives, and they try to find a partner to fill that void. But that's all backwards!

In my opinion, and many other experts would probably agree, it is no one's job to make you happy. Now I'm not saying your partner shouldn't make you happy when you're together, absolutely they should! Think of all the great wedding day speeches where the bride and groom exclaim with joy, "You make me so happy!" It's wonderful! It really is, but it can't be the sole mission of your partner to make you happy. That's your job.

I was once in a relationship where I fell in love hard, with a wonderful girl. She still is wonderful and we still talk to this day. However, I didn't notice until the time we were together for 10 months that the basis of our relationship was about fixing a problem. I thought I had to make her happy. I was doing everything I could for months to try and help her **be happy**, and nothing worked. I was so exhausted

from trying to open and run a business in that same year that I decided and I was adamant we had to take a vacation after all that work (secretly, also because I hoped it would make her happy). We were sitting on the beach in Dominican Republic, an all-inclusive resort, where for a week, we got to abandon everything and forget about it all and bask in paradise, and yet... she wasn't happy. I sat there bewildered, 'Here we are away from it all, in paradise, and she still isn't happy? I don't get it!' Then it hit me like a ton of bricks. I understood then in that moment, that I thought it was my mission to make her happy. Anyone could see I was acting that way and doing everything I could just to keep some consistency in her smile. I don't remember when I took it on to be my job... but it was clear to me that I had done that at some point. Well guess what? When I got that it wasn't my job, I was free from that job. It isn't yours and it isn't anyone else's. The main lesson to learn here is that I took the job on myself, she didn't give it to me. I took it on, so I place no blame on her. I take full responsibility for it.
Happiness and love are connected. Happiness is a choice and so is loving yourself. The truth is, I stopped loving myself for a while when I was in that relationship towards the end. And once I realized that... well that just couldn't be not for one more minute.

How do you relate to yourself?

Understand how you think and feel about yourself - *How do you feel when you look in the mirror?*

This echoes on from the previous section. Take an introspective look into how you think and feel about yourself. Write down these questions and answer them.

What makes me happy?
Who makes me happy, and why?
What aspects of myself and my life do I dwell on?
What gets me down?
What stops me from going after my dreams?
What are my dreams in life?
What concerns do I have in life?

What really aggravates me?
Why?
What brings me peace?

Take notice of your thoughts. What comes up? I know this isn't everyday thinking, or everyday conversations you have with yourself. I want you to recognize that we are going on a journey together and it is okay for this ride to get bumpy at times. You know you're getting somewhere if you are finding yourself a little uncomfortable. That's okay. I'm here to help.

What I want you to know here is very important: **How you think and feel about yourself is how the world shows up for you. Your inner world is a reflection of your outer world.** You have heard this before, and this is true. When you take a look at these observations, take note of them, for this is how you will see people and react in the majority of your circumstances. Don't do anything with this for now, I just want you to be aware of it. You will see why later.

How do you relate to others?

Understand how you feel about other people.

This might sound silly, but your partner is another person. We as people judge everyone differently. Do we ever judge people! We are judgment making, observation stating, and opinion bearing machines! When you say things out loud it creates it in existence that much more for you and others. Maybe that's why we gossip so much! Because we want to be validated for the things we think, and say about other people. If you think you don't gossip, think again. I was once in a program where one of the assignments was to keep track of all the times I was gossiping in my day to day life. WOW! You'd be surprised, I know I was (and this was only the times I could remember it).

So it's good to know where you judge people and how you relate to them on a day to day basis. How do you feel about the average bear, the random stranger in the store, the person at the bus stop, or the coffee shop? I want you to really think about this. I want you to take this out there into the world. I do this with clients and they often come back surprised with interesting results. Your homework is to do this too. Commit to taking this on tomorrow, and put a reminder in your phone if you have to.

At first glance, you might feel like, "Yeah I feel good about people, I like people, I'm friendly, and I'm open." That might be the case… however, trust me on this one. Take stock, be aware over the next few days, of how you react to the people you meet, those that you know and don't know. When do you prejudge them? This is important because

Golden Nugget

The judgments you make and place on people, are the limits you place on your future partners.

Every assumption you make ladies and gentlemen prevents you from being aware of and open to a possibility for an amazing interaction! 'He's too rude', 'He's a weirdo', 'He's a jerk' or 'She's a bit stuck up', 'She's out of my league', 'She's not cool enough' are all thoughts and judgments that will limit your potential for meeting your future partner.

What's more, those thoughts and judgments you create in your mind are a signal that goes out which says 'I am a **no** to that kind of guy/girl,' or 'I am **not good enough** for someone who looks like that' and 'I am definitely a **no** to someone who acts **that** way!' And that just limits the whole purpose here. We are trying to open you up to other partners since the previous ones you met just aren't doing it for you.

You aren't intentionally creating limits and opportunities in your brain. But your brain is always working whether you want it to or not. Dr. Ron Ball says that "the brain creates a new pattern every 21-30 days" so for a certain duration of time there is a window where you can create a new brain pattern. Besides, your life will fill up with joy if you lessen the amount of judgments you place on others!

Why? Because you'll have so much more time and brain power to focus on and develop on the things you want out of life!

How do you treat yourself?

You teach people how you want to be treated.

One of the best public speakers I have ever seen, Lisa Nichols--a woman who is extraordinary--helped me overcome some major obstacles in myself. She says, "You are the demonstration for how people should treat you." This means that you act as a reflection of how other people will talk to you, react around you, and behave towards you. If you wonder why people treat you a certain way, it's because you have shown them that it's okay to do that. It's pretty simple. If you don't like the way someone is treating you, you have to tell them and show them that you accepted it before but that you won't anymore. Then they may test you, and they might test you again and again. They are checking to see if you really mean it. You will have to hold yourself to this new standard of respect and

treatment. These are called boundaries, something that we will cover shortly, which will be very important for our development.

Another one of my mentors Robert Chun used to say, "What are you a request for?" Actually he said, "Everything on this planet is a request for something. A door is a request to be opened. A chair is a request to be sat upon. A pen is a request to be written with. Just the same, a person is a request for something." (Are you a request for love or a great relationship? Are you displaying the emotions and behaviours of someone who wants to be loved?) You can be a request to be treated poorly, fairly, greatly or equally. A millionaire is a request for wealth, and maybe even opulence. I am a request for great people in my life. I am a request to be heard. If I'm not heard I feel abandoned. So what are you a request for? Make some notes in your notebook now.

The golden rule is "Treat others how you want to be treated." And think of Karma "What goes around definitely comes around." Why do you think that is? Really, by now, in today's day and age, we shouldn't be wondering this anymore. You don't need to look far to see how we are treating people, and how people treat us in return. I have an old friend who is certain that the world owes him something. Everyone owes him something: his family, his girlfriends, his co-workers, his bosses. Needless to say, he hardly gets along with anyone. There is confrontation everywhere in his life. He blames everyone around him for his problems, and is never satisfied. He rarely puts on a happy face, is mostly miserable and pretty much condemns all who cross his path. At the moment, everything is crumbling around him. Are you surprised by this? I'm not.

Can you see how important it is to realize how you treat others and treat yourself?

Your future is designed by your past

But only if you are repeating the past. Are you repeating the past?

What does a broken record do? Or what did it used to do, when people used that reference way back? It repeats, and repeats, and repeats. Well guess what? Everything works in cycles. Our respiratory cycle, the four seasons, day and night, and recently in 2012 the precession of the equinox; those were all just cycles. It was just part of a greater cycle of time it turns out so we're still here. Cycles bring new choices as well as repetition and prediction for future events. Cycles are necessary for our world and that doesn't mean they don't come with change. They do. The seasons are different in today's time than when you were younger. Depending on where you live, there might be more or less snow or sun in the winter or summer. So if nature can change that means you can change your cycles as well. Let us take a look at your cycles and patterns right now.

Recent scientific discoveries have discovered more of how the brain works and it is finally being shared by some amazing people and forward thinking organizations. I am going to sum up this incredible, life altering information in a few sentences so get ready(sorry, but this book isn't about the brain, however you can do your own research and use it to your advantage in your life). The brain is made up of pathways, neuronal pathways that are created by repeated based on your thoughts and observation patterns. And these patterns by the time you're age 25, are very, very, very ingrained into you and your every single thought and action. They shape everything from your behaviour, the way you speak, and the way you think and feel about everything. Think of a stream which starts from rainwater that drizzles down from your roof or a slope on your property nearby. If it lasts long enough, that stream of rainwater will ingrain itself into the earth, your soil, and create a pathway. And you can see this path more and more over time, as it develops. It leaves a mark, and it may stay there for some time unless it is tended to and repaired. Your mind is like that. Whether intentional or unintentional, the brain will create the pathways based on your repeated thoughts, actions and observations. So it's no wonder if once or twice something happens to you with a partner or a parent or even a coworker, and you start to think, 'this happens all the time.'

Now I'll explain it a little bit better, in the words of Ron Ball. "When you have any thought, the hippocampus part of your brain takes it, uses protein and turns it into energy. When you have a thought, the energy goes into the basal forebrain, with such force, these thoughts seem super powerful immediate and real! This thought fills your mind and body, whether it is with fear or joy, and it stays in your system for 24-48 hours. This will cause the thought surge to pulsate through you. And it feels so real, and in your body and your mind **it is real**. It seems so real, that if you don't change that certain observation or thought you have about someone or something, it becomes a part of your brain and your neural pathways (picture a tree and its limbs growing out from the trunk.) If you don't replace that thought, then nothing will block the protein synthesis that happens in your brain to make this thought **real**." When he said this, I realized when a thought becomes something you consider real, it then becomes a belief. And when you have a belief, eventually it becomes something you know (or at least think you know.) If you know it, in today's world, you're screwed. This is because the average individual is so stuck to their beliefs and what they think they know to be true, they often aren't willing to change, because why would they change when they **know it**. You then have no chance of creating something new. He continues, stating that "If you do block that thought pattern, with a technique like EFT, TFT, hypnosis or just consciously being aware of that thought and replacing it with a different thought that might serve you better, then you have a chance. This provides a chance to prevent that thought and that belief pattern to become real in your life. And you only have 24-48 hours to do this before it becomes pretty permanent.

Wow! What information! Take what you need from this, and apply it wherever you like. It can serve you in every area of life.

But know this.

If you are going around in circles, and many of the people I coach are, (this is why they come to me, to break the cycle) then you have to do something to get out of the cycle. You have to take notice of what your cycles are. Take notice of what personality types you keep running into, what relationships you have, and the events and circumstances you keep pulling into your life. If you are a man reading this, do you keep meeting women who are insecure and clingy in your opinion? Do you find you keep complaining about the women who are in your words 'needy?' (I hope that you can see that some people are needy, and that's okay. But even then, 'needy' is a point of view.) If you are a woman, do you have a past of getting into unsupportive relationships? Or simply unfulfilling relationships where the man takes, and takes and all you do is give? Do you feel like he puts you down, or doesn't encourage you to go after your goals?

Golden Nugget

Be mindful of your thoughts. Your thoughts create observations, and your observations are what dictate your actions.

Where do you avoid telling the truth?

We're all fibbers and liars at some point or another. Where do you hide the truth?

I bet you think you don't lie. I know I did. Everyone lies and it's okay! It is human nature. We have things we don't want to let others know about and we have skeletons in our closets for sure. The point is to be honest about them and let them go so that you can sleep at night. I once cheated on someone. It's not something I'm proud of. I eventually came clean and did my best to restore my integrity with my partner. It took months and months, and multiple conversations and attempts, and I've actually managed to make peace with her, after it happened. Now we are actually at a point where we have respect for each other and I have earned her trust and friendship once again.

I wouldn't be able to write this book if I didn't go through many, many situations in order to know what it takes to have a relationship work. I failed a lot, and I recovered from those failures, learned and grew from them. To be able to experience them and tell the truth about what myself and others encounter and how to really deal with it powerfully is what enables me to make a difference with my clients.

Some people are excessive liars, and excessive gossipers. But that only works for so long if you're looking to have a relationship work, as in **really work and last**, then you will have to be honest, and better yet, transparent. Married couples, happily married couples, are transparent with their partners, and they know that transparency is an absolute must. Why? Because when you are sharing your life with someone, you must realize that they are sharing their life too. You make the kind of commitment that means you will be together forever and that means sharing almost everything. I say almost, because even married couples need their own space and privacy sometimes. You need to tell your partner what's going on, what your concerns are, and what you're all about. We will cover more on this in the chapter on communication. But I also want you to know that at some point, after some practice this will be start to be a joy! You will begin to love getting your concerns out, sharing your dreams, your fears, and communicating your needs and expectations, because much good will come out of it! You'll see.

We also need to look into what is behind the lying? What is behind the secrecy?

What gets uncovered may be unpleasant. It may be ugly. There may be some skeletons in your closet as I mentioned earlier, and that's okay. We are all human, and to be human is to make mistakes and to have secrets. Do not worry about the judgments of others, it is only temporary.

But take a look at why that is.... really I encourage you to do so. I support you in doing so wholeheartedly. You do not have to bear that burden alone. In fact, it's important that you don't. Once you communicate and open up about your skeletons, (your secret that is) you can be free of it. In the situation above where I described I was keeping my infidelity from my partner, I was on edge and it lasted a few months. I was always concerned. It was in the back of my mind. When I communicated what I had done to her, I cried for about seven straight minutes. I'm not kidding. I cried and sobbed and bawled for seven minutes straight. I was shaking with immense shame and grief over it. I was more upset than she was. She just watched. I think she was surprised herself. But the thing is I felt so ashamed because I knew deep down, how much she cared for me and how great she was for me. We worked things out and are still friends, but if I kept it all to myself, I would have become convinced that I had to hide it because I would be judged or shunned, and that is not necessarily the case. In this situation what you might find is that you made up some similar thoughts all by yourself. You don't know how the other person will react, and that is a good thing, because that means all those things you think will happen are not real. How do you know? They haven't happened yet, and it can be made right.

Now I'm not just talking about cheating or being unfaithful, but still, the same principle applies. The worst thing I've seen is people overtaken by lies, insecurities and skeletons. Sometimes I've met people who keep so many secrets, and have so many skeletons, that they shake. Literally, people tremble and develop twitches. Their secrets and the things that they are hiding manifest in bodily responses such as excessive blinking, twitching, shaking, fidgeting, part of their jaw/teeth clicking, rubbing together feet/hands constantly etc. (makes sense no? The energy has to go somewhere.) It could be unpleasant for you and your potential future partner if you develop these habits. How do you get over it? Tell the truth, quit hiding, and be authentic. I don't have much to say other than that, because it is that simple. Once I came clean with my partner, I felt immense amounts of freedom as soon as that ugly monkey was off my back. At that point, I wasn't off the hook just yet, I had to be responsible for the impacts my actions had on her. This is something we all have to deal with. How do you do that? Claim and accept responsibility, and that's the part where you grow as a man or woman and develop some real maturity and character.

Where do you tell the truth?

Everyone wants the truth, but not everyone is able to tell it.

Why is the truth so important? Isn't that what we strive for? Don't we want that, need that, and look for that in our lives? From our parents, our siblings, our government, our educators, our justice system, don't we want the truth? Why should our relationships be any different? This might be a no brainer, but when you look at the previous section, it's pretty a darn needed component (I don't believe there is any such thing as an inherently bad person, although historically this assumption could be questioned). Hopefully even if you are a truthful person and most people are, you just discovered some places you could open up and be a little more honest with some people in your life, and that's a good thing. I'm sure they would appreciate you or acknowledge you for it in the very least.

Why would they acknowledge you? Because it takes something to be truthful! It really does. It takes courage. Just a little and yes sometimes more. If you're overwhelmed by this section, don't be. We are not talking about you being JFK or Martin Luther King or Bill Clinton here. You aren't going up in front of a nation and defending or confessing some accusation that others have made. While it would be absolutely incredible, you aren't exactly standing for a race or a generation against an onslaught of oppression. So relax. It is one person, or two, and it will pass. It is going to come and go, and the communication of your truth may result in more love. When I told my partner what I had done, I looked forward to the truth coming out, and eventually I got down to brass tacks. The pain suffered in the moment would not compare to the pain suffered over time, the longer I waited. What was at stake was honesty, love, and everything I actually respected her for. Don't you want your partner to be truthful to you as well? Well guess what, you will have to be first. That's right. If you're thinking, 'Why me first?' you've got the wrong thinking cap on my friend.

Golden Nugget

It starts with you. Everything starts and ends with you.

Take this on in your life and know the great power that you will wield. This way you have full control and responsibility for everything that happens in your life. You are no longer at the effect of circumstances or others, you are at cause in creating your life, and that is very powerful and compelling!

So if you're already telling the truth, and some of you are, then I acknowledge you! Make note of where you tell the truth in your life already and know yourself as great, and definitely special. I commend you because it takes courage, honour and love to do so. When you bring forth and muster the bravery and courage to tell the truth when we live in a world filled with untruths, your partner will thank you, your partner will love you more than you know, and your partner will respect for telling the truth even after the relationship has ended. If they never thank you, or never have thanked you, then I thank you! Yes you, I am thanking you right now. Because it can be a thankless job sometimes and my heart goes out to you.

When and where are you comfortable?

You need to know which situations you are most comfortable so that you can milk it

Take a look at when and where you are when you're in your element. Think of a time and place. Maybe it's while you are cooking a meal, or when you're going to see a theatre show, or getting together with friends. Heck maybe its playing cards? Think about yours. Mine is trying new things. I am very comfortable doing new things. I have done so many new things and tried so many new experiences, and expanded myself over the years that I am used to and very comfortable with the feeling of doing things I've never done before. I recognize the feeling of being in my element easily when I'm jumping into something new. Which is why you'll see me in anywhere from 4-8 courses, conferences or seminars each year. And I really enjoy it! I love meeting new people, learning new things, and trying to take new actions I've never taken before. So I am comfortable there, and I am in my element in those situations. I can forget about myself and my worries and just focus on what I'm doing in the moment. It's great! You know what I've noticed? This is where people get to know me best.

Now think of your comfort zone. Stop and take a minute. Stop now. Got it? Good. Think of a few situations or places where you are most comfortable. Now notice your behaviour, your body language, and the way you talk. Isn't it great? Aren't you comfortable there? At home? Free? At peace? Calm? All is well, yes? Good, now milk that. Get to know this part of yourself and bring people there. Show people this side of you. They will want to see it. This is the best of who you are. Be there, and know that people want to be there with you. People want to see you shine. It is when you are in your element and your prime. It is as if you could do anything in those moments, and nothing would matter. That is magical. That is perfect! That is exactly what you want your partner to see. And believe me, **your partner wants to see it too**.

Now you can't go there all the time. Imagine it and feel this great any time you want. But don't brag about it. That is to say, obviously don't verbally brag to other people in a 'you should like me because of this kind of way'. Don't exude that you are bragging too. That is just terrible and in bad taste. People can pick up on that and nobody likes that so don't do it. If others around you do that, they aren't the kind of partner you necessarily want either, because it is just inauthentic and inauthentic people get old fast. You can't be the center of attention all the time. You've got to step outside of your comfort zone as well and into the other person's. You've got to let them have their moment too.

Once you've identified that place, don't stay there forever. Grow yourself! Expand what that space is, and what it encompasses. What do I mean? Simply expand yourself. Begin to stretch yourself out of your comfort zone. Your partner wants to see you grow and chances are if you grow, they will too. Here is a key to a great relationship that could last forever.

Golden Nugget

Grow together! Keep growing as individuals.

I have found that sometimes people split up because they aren't growing in the same direction or at the same pace and one person can't keep up with the other. That can be a pretty valid reason.

Here's the thing, your partner wants to know there will be excitement and creativity and exploration afoot, and that it won't be boring. Whatever it is that you have working for you, you want to nurture and grow that aspect of yourself as well. Whether it is in the bedroom or in social settings, this is where you are at your best, so be the best, because that's a great thing! A great quote is "focus on your strengths and master them. Don't waste time on your weaknesses." Imagine if you can be even greater at what you already do which is great. If your partner already loves you for it, your partner will love you even more for it!

What makes you cringe or tick?

Know what freaks you out! And be prepared for it!

What are you afraid of? What makes you uncomfortable? If you can predict your fears, you can deal with them beforehand or as they happen. Imagine being on a date, or in a social setting, and you know you're going to feel awkward, or look bad. But right then and there you can do something about it, and control it or at least be aware of how you react. Make a short little list of some of the things that make you uncomfortable and a thing you can do about them if something come up. For example, what if you are fearful of insects, snakes, public performances, awkward moments, spilling or knocking over things. What can you do? You can avoid going to places like karaoke, or the petting zoo. Or you can face your fear and go to the zoo, pet some snakes and do more Karaoke and get over those fears! Another thing you can do is talk to your potential partner on a date about these things so that they are aware and they won't take you anywhere or suggest going somewhere you don't want to go. Or you can make light of those things have a great laugh about them! I highly recommend doing that for great fun and good conversation. You will make light of things and put each other at ease. So refreshing!

If you do get into a situation where you are uncomfortable or freaked out and depending on how you react, you might scare your partner away. You might have lost out on the opportunity for a possible wonderful partnership that could have unfolded. If that's the case, don't worry, you will want someone who can handle your uncomfortable side anyway. At the very least, you might not wonder what happened later on when you are single again or they aren't returning your calls.

As I mentioned earlier, it's a chance for you to grow and expand yourself. If something happens with your partner where it feels like the shoe is on the other foot, you will be able to understand what is going on with them. It will be an opportunity for you to **have compassion for them** when they are nervous, scared, or uncomfortable too. This will earn you major brownie points with them and/or their family or friends should they be nearby. This will actually blow some people away! How? If for example something happens like bird shit lands on them, or they fall off a go cart, bike, seat, help them out, have sincerity, compassion and genuine understanding for them (remember, we're all human and this could happen to you too!) Chances are, they will be **hugely impressed** and appreciate you for it, and increase the likelihood of being with them in the future. You will be remembered for this! This is the kind of thing that they go home and tell their friends about. A girl might say, 'You'll never guess what happened..... And this is what he did. Like, who does that?' And a guy might say, "She is a pretty cool chick, you know? She did that for me and not everyone would." Whoever it is, they will be very happy about it and share it with others, and I'm sure it will come back in kind.

Are you sexy?

Sexy is a Point of View, and an attitude

Everyone is and can be sexy at any time, whenever they want! How come? Because the quality of sexiness is inside of us. Being sexy is possible for anyone. Flip back to the beginning of this chapter when we talked about being anything you want to be. Being sexy is not actually outside of us, it is an attitude that is inside of us, despite what everything and the media will tell you. It's a feeling, an attitude, a way of being, and a state of mind. The brain is actually your most erogenous zone! Erogenous means especially sensitive to sexual stimulation. So go there to that place in your mind where you are sexy. Then go there in your body. Some of you may be able to pull this up on command, without practice and that's great! That's likely because you have been practicing your whole life. So go ahead, new or tenured, and be sexy. You can do it! Just like you can be angry, happy or grateful any time you want.

Now yes, looks are important! Don't be silly! You will be spending lots of time with this person, so you'll want to like what you see, and they will want to like what they see as well. But you should know that there is someone for everyone on this planet.

Golden Nugget

Again, there is someone for everyone on this planet.

How do you know? Because there are so many of us, seven billion plus! What is sexy? It so simple; sexy is a point of view, an opinion, a perspective. Remember the saying, "Beauty is in the eye of the beholder." Well the same goes for what is sexy. Many people find all kinds of different qualities, characteristics, and traits sexy. You don't have to look far in today's world to see all the different sexy people and who is attracted to them.

Have you ever looked in the mirror and seen how sexy you are? Have you ever smiled and felt great in your skin, knowing that you were hot? Do you like feeling attractive? I hope you have felt and known this sensation at least once. If you've felt it and known it once, you can do it again. I hope you do because someone somewhere will find you attractive. In fact, it's pretty likely that many people do already. You just don't know it or haven't considered it fully.

"Why is that important?" It will help you attract the right partner, and there's nothing wrong with that. That is the point! It's a game, it's a chase, and it is supposed to be fun! Sexy feels great! Sexy is confidence, it is focus, and it is **attractive as all heck**! It is a great experience and a joy in life to be sexy. Would you like to be irresistible? We will cover this more in the latter parts of the book.

For now, be happy, and be proud of yourself! You've made it through Chapter 1! Congratulations!!

Thank *you* for doing it!

2
FINDING A GREAT PARTNER

What kind of person do I want to be with?

My partner is…

Now that we're done with you, let us focus on them!
This is our next starting point, and this is where we will begin building upon your idea of who that person is that you want to have in your life. So tell me now, who is your future partner? What do they look like? What do they sound like? What do they like to do? Where do they like to go? What kind of people do they associate with? Where have they been? What do they wear? Most importantly, how do they make you feel? You will have to create this, if you haven't already. Maybe some of you have done that work, which is great! You may have seen this before or received feedback from friends to make a list of qualities of your future partner. This is a fun and absolutely great way to start to pull that person towards you. If you've already done it, pull that list out and refine it. If it is your first time doing this, go for it. Take out a clean slate of paper, and have at it. The thing is, you want to go somewhere with this. You want to envelop yourself in it and use your creativity, your imagination. Go into a mental sandbox and play. Go ahead and create that list of ideal characteristics and qualities your future partner has now.

Good, now how did you feel making that list? How did you feel when you saw yourself with that person or when you saw that person in your mind's eye? How do you feel right now? Are you smiling? Are you happy? Are you calm and are your shoulders relaxed? Take notice. This is great, and I'm happy for you as this is a vital step. If you aren't happy or relaxed about this, it's likely because you have doubt or disbelief. Well, guess what? That won't work and it won't get you anywhere. So what you'll have to do is tell yourself, 'Look I know I don't believe and I know I have doubts, but I want this to work, and I want this relationship to come to me! I deserve this, despite my doubts!' And do it again. Close your eyes and focus on this person. Allow them to appear in your vision. Allow them to show up in your mind. Allow the fog to be cleared, and bring yourself to a place where you can feel them coming towards you as if in a dream.

I want you to know this works. This is often one of the first steps my clients take, and it gets them into a state where they can begin to enjoy themselves in the process. This is a creative process. You are literally creating your partner out of thin air. Along with the work we will do in later chapters, he or she will appear. I have a friend, Jacob who a few years ago sent a bunch of us an email about his future female partner. He was single at the time, and he literally pulled everything from his desires and described what he wanted at the time in his partner. I saved the email and the list and I'm sharing it with you here:

- I will be with a girl who lights me up with her personality and sense of humor
- I will be with a girl who is committed to me for life and is committed to a life of ongoing personal development and spiritual expansion
- I will be with a girl who dresses sexy and sophisticated depending on the occasion
- I will be with a girl who communicates really well
- I will be with a girl who wants to expand her curiosity for adventure, whether it be travelling the world or spending a night out of town.
- I will be with a girl who takes care of her fitness, eats well, and has a passion for good food
- I will be with a girl who is silky smooth to the touch and smells amazing head to toe
- I will be with a girl who can meet new people easily and enroll them into our lives
- I will be with a girl who is financially independent
- I will be with a girl who is up to living a big life together
- I will be with a girl who values personal development.
- I will be open to knowing and loving her family as if they were my own

This is how descriptive your list should be.

You should know that a few months later my friend Jacob met Sandra on a plane coming back from Australia. They are still together two and half years later. We love Sandra and she is incredible. She is exactly as Jacob has described. Jacob is still head over heels for her, and she is stunningly beautiful and completely committed to him. Lucky guy! Is it luck at all? She has and is everything that he described above.

If you have any concerns at this point about this process, disappear them now. Everything from where to find them, how to approach them and how to have fun during the process will be covered in the coming chapters. I did promise that you would enjoy this, so please smile!

Next, start with your deal breakers. This is very important. These are the things that you won't negotiate on. What is it that your partner cannot have, or cannot be without? Must they be a non-smoker? A cat person? A Foodie? Do they have to be healthy, or health conscious? Do they have to be active in sports or fitness? Do they have to be able to converse about politics? Notice that they get a little more fickle as you go on. (Yes their political standing is fickle.) Try to keep them straight, as in 'no ifs ands or buts.' You will be the judge as to which ones are non-negotiable. This can be tricky, because there might be something for you here, to learn as a lesson.

Golden Nugget

Which not everything has to be as perfect as you think it does.

So these must resonate with your highest values. And yes we will talk about values later.

What is the result I want?

I'm doing this for…

You need to know what your motive is for finding this person and starting this relationship is. What is the result you want or the outcome of the relationship? Whatever your motive is, whether it be someone to marry, someone to share your life with, or to raise a family or just have fun with, it's all good in my books. That is why this book isn't called, 'Find your soul mate' or, 'Find your spouse' because not everyone is looking for that. And, we're all looking for different things at different points in our life. But you need to know what you're looking for right now. List three things you want to have as a result of this relationship. And see if you can keep writing and create a deeper, more authentic result or outcome.

Like we said in the last chapter, what is your goal? Also, you need to share this with your potential partners at some point. What? Yes, that's right. Your future partner needs to know what you're looking for. Although this may scare you, the earlier you share this, the better. Why? Because then you can filter through those who aren't looking for what you desire. This goes hand in hand with the truth, remember? I'll tell you this, many arguments in relationships occur because one person is expecting something uncommunicated or unrealistic from the other person. The other person is left upset, and confused in a state of bewilderment at times and asks, "How was I supposed to know?" "Why would you expect that from me?" In the interest of not only fairness, but also time and integrity, tell your potential love what it is you are looking for. That way they can make a decision if they are willing to, a) fill that need or, b) if they feel they are willing to take on this part-time job of being that person for you right now. I say its part time because the other part/responsibility belongs to you, although sometimes with exception, something unnatural actually comes out of it. For example, a friend of mine said to her current husband of six years when they started dating, 'Just so you know, this is only sexual.' They have been happily married for 6 years as of this writing and are one of the best examples of great parents and quality relationships that I know of. Who knows, a great relationship could have been my friends ulterior motive the entire time. I am willing to bet she was simply protecting herself with that statement. Why? Her previous partner was a father to her child and had left the picture, and the country!

I must address that there's nothing wrong just wanting a sexual relationship either. Some people do just want to have fun! In fact, I recommend this is 'out of your system' by your early-mid 30's if you aren't in a fully committed marriage/ relationship by then. Why? Because I hear plenty of couples and people who are in relationships that say, "If I was still your age" or, "If I hadn't settled down when I did…" but the most common thing I hear is a flat out, "Make use of your time now." All that can all be prevented as sometimes what's behind that is a form of regret or resentment or simple wisdom (mostly common amongst men) That can lead to other ugly things, and we want to prevent that. So there is no need to hide your sexual desires if that's all you're looking for. You just need to know and be straight about it with yourself and your partner.

Golden Nugget

There are an infinite number of possibilities in this world with people, and someone out there wants what you have.

Remember that, someone wants what you have and someone wants the same things that you want.

Imagine what will happen, (and this happens all the time) if all you're actually looking for is sexual relations and you don't tell your partner. You just do what some people do unfortunately and that is,"bang 'em and leave 'em." Well that's just terrible. You're leaving them with a world of confusion and hurt and potential upset. What if they actually liked you? What if they believed you when you said you wanted a relationship or something serious? That's a whole set of emotions they will have to process. You wouldn't want that happening to you now would you? Good, so don't do it to others.

Complete the past to create the future

Who were your previous partners?

It is absolutely essential to do this step if you want to guarantee yourself future success. I usually do this with clients after the previous exercise on creating your future partner. This next exercise allows you to wipe the slate clean now, before meeting your future partner. Don't even think about skipping this step if you skipped the previous one. Why? You take things from your partners and your partners leave things with you. When you share yourself with someone over a period of time, there are things that stick after they leave, they don't just disappear. So we're going to clean up the residue that your past partners leave on you.

Take a moment and think of any previous partners you have had recently. Some of you may have to go back six months or five, 10, or 15 years to recall a last partner, and who they were, or what they did. For many of you, that person will be right there, ready in your mind. By the time you were reading that last sentence, they were probably already right in front of your face! It is normal for people to have an impact on us like that, which is why I am taking so much time to create this book. Powerful partners and powerful relationships can last a lifetime in your mind, whether they be good or bad.

If when you were thinking about your previous partners you had negative thoughts, or negative emotions come up, then I want you to do something. I'm going to share something to you here.

I strongly believe that to create the future, you will need to complete your past. So here is an exercise you can do to complete the past relationships that happened in your life that you might be incomplete with.

How do you know you are complete? Your emotional attachment and bodily reaction to the thought of this person is as little as possible after completing this. You can be 'at peace with' or happy with things, the way they ended, and where they are now. This is something that my clients and friends receive a lot of value from and you can use it again and again, whenever they need to. Ready? Grab a blank sheet of paper. Write these answers out and then leave them for an hour and come back to them. Repeat twice. Who is asking you these questions is the person you are attempting to be complete with (i.e. someone wronged me and they are unavailable/unwilling to communicate). That "someone" is who is asking the questions.

Write out whatever comes to your mind, and be relentless. BE RELENTLESS about it. Use this exercise on an individual case by case basis i.e., one person in your life at a time. This is about you, and you moving on powerfully. This is not about them at all, so do not hold back. With everything that you write, try to be as vivid and fully expressed as possible. It will make the difference.
Who am I for you?
Who did you wish that I was that didn't show up?
What did I do that didn't go the way you wanted it to?
What didn't I do that I said I would do?
What did I say that affected/hurt you?
Look at what frustrates you most about us/it.
Why?
What did you enjoy about us?
What do you miss?
How would you have liked things to go?
What do you want to say to me that has not yet been said?
What part did you (the person writing) play in this?
What else is there?
What is the result/cost of all of this?
Note: None of this is possible unless you are willing to move on. IF you have done all of this and can't let go, you may not be ready. You can CHOOSE to be ready. ... I will say that again. YOU CAN CHOOSE TO BE READY TO BE COMPLETE. Stand inside of what freedom you will have once this is complete and go from there.

Do you want the same partners as before?

If you want your life to change, you have to change things in your life.

Great work on the previous exercise, by the way. That took something, I'm sure. It's not an everyday thing for people to do that kind of work. I want you to know that I know the courage it takes to do that.

This is your opportunity to create a brand new kind of person that you will be with in your future. Take a quick moment to flip back to your partners characteristics from before and see if anything changes. Don't spend too much time on this, but feel secure in your list after having done this.

Try not to repeat the past. I don't recommend it, it's unfair and unfulfilling for your partners to try and live up to an image of one of your previous partners that you're trying have them fit.

Now where do I find this person?

You CAN meet them anywhere, but the 'where' is the real key

Right now at this point in your life, where are you looking for a partner? Are you looking in the bars and clubs of the world? Well if you are, you probably aren't having much success. Why is that? People who go to bars and clubs typically are looking for one thing, to have a good time, or to have a good time (having sex), to have fun or hook up. People generally aren't looking for meaningful relationships at clubs and bars. Let's face it, bars and clubs are filled with stories of drama and excitement, but also temporary satisfaction. If you are having success at bars and clubs or have had in the past, great! Look back on those relationships for a second, did they last long? Were they fulfilling, meaningful? Did they add or subtract value to your life? Sometimes you meet them at a bar or a club and you're there with your friends for their birthday party! Sometimes that works out great! That's the funny thing, when you're least expecting it, or when you're focused on something else, you meet someone great who really stands out and/or sparks your interest. This is key, but we'll come back to that shortly.

Singles events? If you go to singles events, you will usually find two things: people who are looking for a quality person to date and potentially get into a relationship with (this is great If that's what you're looking for) and people who are just looking for sex. What, no! How come? People in these environments tend to use the setting to pick up people, and just pick up, nothing more. Who? Sadly, mostly men. I had a longtime friend whom I haven't seen for some time tell me at my first singles event, 'this is a great place to pull!' I said "Pull?

What's that?" Well never you mind, I won't repeat what he said. But ladies, you sometimes go for that guy subconsciously and you don't know why you do that. Even if you're actually looking for a relationship, you might be reading this and thinking, "How come that happens to me? Or, "How come I meet guys that only want to sleep with me?" Well sometimes as humans, we don't think so well. It is normal not to think *consciously,* that is human nature. So don't be upset with yourself, but do use this as an opportunity to redefine what you actually want and are committed to in life right now. That's why you picked up and read this book, good for you!

This is one of my favourite pieces here and one of the most fun parts of the journey, so please do consider having fun here.

Golden Nugget

You can meet your partner anywhere!

Most people are attached to finding the one, or their perfect partner, or the person they want to be with at a certain place and a certain time, and that's bull crap. Listen to me, you can and will meet your partner in the unlikeliest of places, and it will be wonderful. I promise you, if you allow it, and give up stressing on it, you can meet them anywhere and everywhere in your day to day life, and it will be thrilling and exciting! If you are out there living your life, and in the right frame of mind this is what you will find.

This is the method that I have chosen to work with my clients, and it works for them and personally, it has worked for me my entire life. I call it the 'natural organic method.' This is where you are out in the world, living your life, in your day to day, and you meet or are approached by someone without much effort. You and he/she are in the same place at the same time, not by much effort but by matter of happenstance. This is the way things line up for you when *you have done the work to line yourself up properly*. Now you or the other person must take some action, and start the interaction somehow. I'll get to that in a moment, but for now understand that this person could be anyone and anywhere. Someone you might not expect, at a time when you might least expect it, and someplace you may not expect. When you get into the state of mind that THEY ARE OUT THERE and it's only a matter of time, then it will happen easily and effortlessly.

Seek and ye shall find!

How do I meet them?

You can meet your future partner, or future partners (in case it doesn't work out with the next one) in a multitude of places. Here's some examples of instances in my life where I've met a wonderful woman or two and it progressed over dates and turned into a great relationship: at a bus terminal I met Carla, while waiting for the next bus to come. I met Amanda on a cruise ship, and I met Katherine at a high school reunion, and yes we went to high school together but we hadn't dated previously.

Here's the brilliant thing, you can turn any situation you find someone you may be interested in or attracted to into an opportunity to meet and have a great connection with that that person. If you pay attention, you will find that you are always in situations with potentially great people around you.

How did I meet Carla? At a bus terminal in a not so great part of town, I met her on a grey winter day. It was chilly outside. People were bundled up and frigid in the cold afternoon near the end of winter. We were both standing several feet apart, and we noticed each other a couple of times. We made eye contact and once or twice, a small but noticeable smirk crept up on her face as we did.

Golden Nugget

Making eye contact more than once or twice is a key connecter, and smiling is even better.

I was listening to music on my headphones, minding my own business and she was a reading a book, when a scruffy looking man, possibly up to no good came up to me and said in a loud voice "What's up man? What cha listening to?" (There was a substantial crowd of us at the outdoor terminal and why he picked me of all people, I don't know). I replied, "Hey man, it's all good!" (I was feeling good, and having dealt with plenty of confrontation in my life, it's pointless in my books.) He then asked, "Yeah? All good? Cool, let me hear it!" At this point, even though it had only been a few seconds, people nearby noticed (you know when you can feel the eyes of other people on you?) Well, one set of eyes I felt was the cute girl I had just caught eyes with seconds prior. Before I could reply a word to the man, he picked my headphones off of my head and started listening to be the judge himself. Instantly, he started grooving to the music, and really began 'vibe'ing' with it! Yes, my headphones were still attached to my mp3 player in my jacket! Some of the sets of eyes nearby were growing concerned, but with the situation as it occurred to me, I had no other option but to laugh out loud, and I did, hysterically! It helped

that off in the not too far distance, I could see the cute girl, having a little giggle herself.

When I saw she was laughing, I let out a big laugh, especially since the man was now *really* getting into it. I laughed harder and harder and just smiled and nodded with this brand new jazz man standing one foot away from me, grooving to my tunes. What made it so funny for me is that it wasn't Bob Marley, but Black Sabbath that I was listening to. A few seconds later, he finished and handed me back my headphones, smiled and just walked away. I laughed, she laughed, and other people nearby just looked on puzzled. Immediately, I knew, this girl was cool, and she had a great sense of humour, my kind of humour. I knew I had to talk to her. Guess what my opening line was, "Five bucks says you won't guess what kind of music I was listening to."

From there, the rest was history. We chatted and conversed and had a good time laughing about the situation overall. She was curious about the things the man was saying to me and what I said in return, since she couldn't hear it from where she was standing. I happily relayed the event with all the savoury details from my perspective to her. We got on the same bus and talked about the book she was reading and music in general. I asked her for her contact info as this was way too cool an event to pass up.

I have plenty of examples like this I could share with you. Some of them lead somewhere, and some of them lead nowhere. The thing is, you have to make the most out of an opportunity like this. You don't need some weird interference from a possibly homeless man to enable an interaction with someone you are interested in (although it does help). What I want you to know is once I connected with Carla on a real level, after something very real happened around us, the only thing left to do was be authentic. That opened up an authentic dialogue between us. Why does this work? Because the walls are down. Far too often our walls are up, and **to find someone great ladies and gentlemen, your walls have to be down and your ability to be open has to be expanded.** When I connected with Carla or others in my life you will see that you can get to know the other person authentically as well. Then you will have a shot at an authentic relationship, which we'll get to in another chapter.

The experience I just shared with you was a lot of fun for Carla and I. How did it happen? It happened because we made the best of a funny and odd scenario. That's just the kind of people we are, and that was the kind of partner we wanted.

You'd like to hear one more, wouldn't you? Okay, a fast one. I was on a cruise ship, my first one, and this one was special. This was a leadership cruise for leaders in communities. The ship was docked in Mexico and there was a party on the top deck. I had just been walking around the ship, coming from one part to another. As I rounded the corner of one side to the open expanse of the sun deck I saw a beautiful woman standing by herself at the railing, looking down towards the party below. In the distance behind her, there was another cruise ship parked right next to ours. It was big, bigger than ours! However, in my walk I noticed something. Our ship was partying the day away, having a band, dancing, people laughing and having a great time! Yet the bigger ship had several crowds gathered around on their railings and edges, watching us and staring at our party! It was a real sight to see! Here was this bigger boat, with more people on it, and they were admiring us! Instead of all the things they could be doing, about a hundred of their passengers were watching our party! I was walking in the direction of the wonderful woman and she had her back turned to the onlookers. Proud to be on the 'right ship' I said to her, "Hey, turn around for a second, check this out!" "Wow!" she said. I said "I know right?" And we both laughed together. I said "Isn't it great how they are checking us out and we're just partying away carefree?" From that great opening a conversation was born ladies and gentlemen. I'm very happy that event happened. It felt almost as if it were planted there for me to comment and take action.

The funny thing in this story is that I wasn't attached to any kind of outcome. I just had the perfect situation to bring what I saw as 'obvious' to attention and maybe make someone laugh in the process. These things happen anywhere and everywhere, **if you're aware of them.**

These events could happen at a coffee shop, at the bakery, at work, on your way to work, at the grocery store, at school, at a seminar, on the subway, on vacation, or on a plane ride as it unfolded with my friend Jacob in the last chapter. Now imagine if Jacob had this ideal person, this woman he was so attracted to, imagine if he didn't say anything to her? When you make your approach, allow the conversation to flow naturally and effortlessly. Have fun with it! The more fun you can have, the easier it will flow.

You can use the experiences I shared with you for yourself or you can scrap the whole thing and just be yourself and have your own kind of conversation. It doesn't necessarily have to be awkward, weird, or funny. Talk to people. Get out there. People are everywhere. You know the line, "There's plenty of fish in the sea?" Well that goes for men and women. Keep it fresh. I do not recommend scripting, it will sound terrible coming out of your mouth and it will be picked up by the other person as inauthentic. Be yourself, and be authentic, that is what I recommend most. It works, trust me.

What do you say to someone you might be interested in?

You only get one first impression

That's right. A first impression only happens once. Now you might think that that is unfortunate, and you might want to curse the part of the brain that creates and stores memory. It's not necessarily a bad thing. You get plenty of first impressions with people you meet! You meet people every day, and some people you've met before and don't even remember.

Katherine was one of the prettiest girls in High School. She had one of the best smiles too. She was shy, but cool. She was out there, but grounded. She was cute and humble. I liked her. How could I not by the sounds of her, right? Well I confided in a few friends that I liked her, and that was a mistake. Although she was approachable, I wasn't fully confident that she would receive my advances so well. So I decided to write her a letter (d'oh! Mistake # 2!) I gave it to a friend to give her on my behalf (mistake # 3) So, my friend 'lost the letter' and he told another guy as well for some reason, and it got ugly fast. I ended up asking her about it, if she received it, and she had no idea what was going on. Then of course I had to explain everything to her and that was an even messier mess! (Not a mistake. If I hadn't told her it would've cut the story and the possible future off here.) She held no grudges, saw no harm and well, nothing happened, we stayed friends and the possibility of a romance fizzled out, if there ever was a possibility. Then we graduated and I didn't see her for five years at a mini reunion some people put together.

She wasn't actually at the reunion. She was taking classes at the school and I saw her at the vending machine. "KATHERINE!?" I yelled. "Michael!?" "Hey!" She said. After the usual pleasantries and catch up conversations, it was "Hey remember that thing that happened with the letter?" I asked. "Yes, it was a disaster! I wanted to kill Jamie!" "What the heck was all that?" she said. "Who knows, it was such a mess!" I said. It helps that we were laughing the entire way through. Laughter makes a huge difference in being comfortable with things. I complimented her on her smile, which didn't change (still really great). We exchanged contacts and met for coffee a few times. Coffee led to lunches. Lunches led to dinners, and dinners led to one of the most amazingly romantic and deeply connected and sexually blissful relationships I have ever had. Katherine and I are still close after all we've shared. We are great friends and call each other when things get tough personally. We're very much there for each other and she is a very important person in my life.

So a good first impression is ideal, and if it doesn't go well, it's really okay.

Golden Nugget

You never know how it's going to turn out.

So like my examples in the previous section, start your conversation by stating something that is going on, potentially obvious even, in the situation around you (the common acknowledgement will be humorous for both of you.) Or, if it's someone you know, knew, or met before, say something about the past events or connections, and make a comment about it. You could also ask a question. Whatever you do, make light of it! Don't be so heavy and significant! You will be well received if things are light and fun! Sometimes you may make fun of yourself, or something (maybe even someone else nearby so long as it's not too damaging of the other person) with the kind of thing that someone can laugh at.

Ladies- men enjoy a woman who can have a good laugh at things, whether it is at themselves or a funny or awkward situation. Men want to make their ladies laugh and it helps if you do (wink wink). Also ladies, have fun with it, don't be so heavy or significant about it. If you take the approach or the joke lightly, then it will indicate to them that you are able to have fun! Men sometimes seek the

opposite sex to relieve them of their troubles and be a source of lightness in today's significant world.

Men, ladies enjoy a guy who can make them laugh. How you approach them in general is a display of your creativity and confidence, so have fun with it and go for it! Ladies want to feel taken care of, that you will put thought into things for them, so improvisation goes a long way, since it seems like you are thoughtful and caring, and you are! Good for you!

How will you receive their approach?

You are the other half of the equation

If someone comes up to you, male or female, and you aren't paying attention you might miss them! And they might be a great catch! You will never know unless you talk to them. Now it is likely that you might prejudge them as soon as they come up to you, but try not to do that. In fact, don't do that. You never know what kind of contribution that person could be in your life. If not for a potential partner, they could be a business contact, a friend, they could be able to help you in some way or know someone who could assist you and partner with you in some way. Or in general they could be someone to just have a great conversation with. What is the harm in that? This person could be the person you have been looking for or waiting for! This part about receiving their approach is very important, and it's dependent upon you!

Your reaction will determine what is next for you both, and what is next could be very exciting! Imagine a tennis game. You will be bouncing the ball back and forth if you want to play. Playing can be fun, enlightening, fulfilling, and as I said, exciting. Your job is to play the game and hit the ball, back and forth. Receive it well, and hit it back. That's it.

If you think of conversations like that, then it will be a lot more of an enjoyable process, where more can happen out of the interaction. You never know who that person might turn out to be. They could be your next big crush, next big date, fun fling, great relationship, great sex, or even 'the one.'

So what can you do? Laugh, ask a question, make a joke, comment on something nearby, compliment them without an agenda, say hello, thank them for something they may have done or are about to do, welcome them with kindness. Whatever you do, make it genuine. That is what will communicate.

The key is, to be open.

Golden Nugget

Be Open

If you aren't open to the possibility, or the opportunity of getting to know a new person, or at least seeing where 'it' goes, you will miss the boat. You don't stand a chance, (and neither do they) if you aren't open to what might come out of it. So please, do yourself a favour and make a commitment to being open, and if you think "But I am open" then my advice is to take it to a whole other level starting right now.

I would insert a section for you here, to list all the opportunities of possible partners that you may have missed, except WE'LL NEVER KNOW WHO THOSE PEOPLE WERE WILL WE? This is because they're in the past, and you have no idea what could have been. **That's okay, because right now, we're moving forward.**

The Give and Take

Remember this and your journey will be easier

Like any relationship 'the give and take' is very important. It's a balance that is very important to maintain, a balance between giving and receiving. While you may be thinking, 'this sounds like something I'll need later in the relationship phase,' HOLD ON. It is just as important at this stage (dating), and the sooner you learn it and implement it, the better things will be later on.

So what am I talking about? Reciprocal recognition, continuous appreciation, giving and receiving. These are all fancy names for 'share the love.' With your new partner that you are discovering and getting to know, share the love. What I mean is compliment them, make them feel good, do plenty of little things for them. Notice things about them. Tell them what you like about their character, the way they carry themselves, the habits they have. Let them know the things they are doing which you are enjoying. Do it in such a way, in a relaxed setting where it will be well received. Spread it out, don't say it all at once, or they might think you are obsessing over them which might hinder the whole thing. I would hope this is basic information, but some people just don't know it or don't do it yet.

Now ideally, they are doing some of this too, showing you some love. This would be a very good sign that things are moving along as they should and that they are into you as well. Your job here is to receive the compliments and admiration, and be flattered/thankful. Not even be flattered, but be a 'yes' to their flattery. This person does not have to say anything nice about you, and if they do, great. Sometimes it takes great courage for people to say things, so receive them well. It actually makes them feel good about what they are saying if you receive it well. If they are not saying good things about you, then maybe it's a sign to move on. You want to be with someone who can adore you and make you feel good. Receiving compliments and admiration feels good.

While you're giving and receiving compliments during the dating stage, you will be establishing a pattern within yourself to give in the relationship and receive during the relationship too. Now, some people just love to give, that's what they do, it fulfills them, and that's great! But even they need to be sustained by love. Some people, well they just love to take, take, take, and then take some more.

Don't be that person. That will not get you far... and it won't get you liked very much either. Friends might actually secretly dislike this part about you even now. Why? Because it's kind of exhausting to be around someone who wants to take without giving. The good news is, there is ALWAYS MORE LOVE TO GIVE. So go ahead and give it.

Are you someone who tries to force the outcome?

The difference between Honey and Vinegar

You can't force yourself into a relationship, not if you want to be in a good one.

Have you ever heard the saying, 'You get more flies with honey than you do with vinegar?' Have you ever heard the story of David and Goliath? Good. Well you might want to try using honey, instead of vinegar. That means being sweet and thoughtful instead of being aggressive and sour. Now, sure this is common knowledge and everyone knows this, but sometimes we don't do the things we know we should.

Some of us don't realize we do it, but after the first few dates our critical, fearful nature comes out. For men, when we aren't getting what we want, we can sometimes become aggressive, even hysterical, so much so we don't realize how we are behaving, and we lose sight of a lot of reason. We yell, scream, ignore, throw our hands up in a huff, and we give up on our partners. For women, when things don't go your way you tend to become really insecure (men's actions comes from insecurity too, don't worry) and you begin to worry, panic, and wonder a lot. You tend to ask a lot of questions, and want a lot of answers. You sometimes reach the point of obsession. These are forms of vinegar.

Using honey works, it really, really works. If people describe you as a go getter, and someone who makes things happen, that's amazing, so long as you are not forcing it and crushing people in the process. At this stage, trying to get things by force will only get you abandoned and wondering why they aren't returning your calls or why things didn't work out. Well, there's one place to look for the reason why.

With David and Goliath, David overcame Goliath by using one small, yet timely and accurately placed rock. He defeated this mammoth giant of a strong man, with one shot. What can you learn from this? By finding out your partners, or potential partners likes and dislikes and paying attention, and then utilizing your knowledge to buy a certain gift, complete a certain task or chore on their behalf you can seal the deal, and win their favour!

This goes for everything. Being too aggressive physically, (unless it's in the bedroom and its welcomed) in conversation, forcing a subject or a topic, trying to get something out of someone, excessive phone calling, or texting, going for the kiss one too many times... at some point you have to learn to take the message. Less or no communication at all is indeed a form of communication.

You'll get more with honey if you are being yourself, being authentic, and telling people what is really going on with you. Telling someone about a concern you have, something that's in the back of your mind, instead of trying to avoid it or beat around the bush, will get you a lot further with them.

Watch out for these signs!

What to avoid ladies and gentlemen

Here's a list of things to avoid when getting to know your new potential partner. Now don't go looking for them in every person you meet, (seek and ye shall find remember) but notice if they come up. If they do, ask a friend or a family member if you have any doubts or concerns.

Here's what to look out for (note: if this is you, then do something different immediately):

They still live at home... and they're 40+ years old. While some people go through circumstances and ups and downs in life, which is normal, if they've been there for some time, you might want to consider what is really going on. This could be an indication of poor finances, low ambition, laziness, and potentially deep family issues--something you might not be too keen about being a part of. However, if say they are taking care of their parents, or one parent due to health, circumstances etc. then don't worry. As I said, it's important to consider what is going on with them.

Too much communicating, especially in the early stages – such as a lot of texting, calling, emailing and excessive voicemails can be a nuisance. These are all signs of desperation. You see, in the beginning of a relationship you want things to flow, effortlessly and naturally. Someone who over communicates in the early stages is not a good sign for a relationship. If you're feeling overwhelmed, you can ask them to slow it down, take it easy, and that there's no rush. You don't have to rule them out immediately.

Beware of your own thoughts that you 'can change them.' People do change but 100% of the time, its only if they want to. If you have these thoughts, you are headed down a path of extreme exertion and manipulation, and no one likes to be manipulated.

If someone drinks too much – this is a big one and should be on your deal breakers list. If this is the case, definitely get out as fast as you can. This is not your problem to solve. If you try, you will be in for a long and destructive journey. Recommend them to get help and stay clear, this is connected to other deep personal issues.

If a person sleeps a lot – this might mean their life isn't too exciting, which will mean your relationship might not be either. Remember to ask about health.

When asking them what they do in their spare time, if the most common reply is watching TV, expect to be doing this a lot in your relationship. People's habits echo into other areas of life so don't expect the TV watching to stop just for you.

If he/she doesn't let you talk that much – If on the first or second date, you haven't gotten that many words in, don't expect to in the future. It will be boring and unfulfilling for you. You'll wish you weren't there.

If he/she is overly physical immediately – while this can be fun, and you might be thinking, "Hey, what's wrong with that?" Nothing really, but you can probably expect nothing more than a physical encounter or two at the most from this person, and nothing meaningful. There are exceptions to this rule. When you hit it off SO WELL, that the connection is sometimes so intense, a physical action is something you BOTH feel compelled to do. Please note: It is still risky to do this as you are giving yourself up easy.

If he/she doesn't want you to talk about your recent ex-girlfriend/boyfriend this is another warning sign. It's healthy to talk about a past relationship. It helps gives them a sense of where you were coming from. If they don't want you talking about those people, it's usually from their own insecurity and jealousy. Beware.

If he/she uses derogatory names to refer to all of their previous partners, run! While this is sometimes reality, maybe, as people can be some of these names, there is usually one common denominator in the scenario: Them.

They are obsessive about the way they look – male or female, being overly concerned with the way they look hides all kinds of insecurity. Some will say its confidence, but that's not necessarily true. What usually accompanies this is a lot of drama, and fussiness. You don't want those headaches.

Another flag is that they won't let you be yourself – don't mess around with this one. They want you to do things differently. They will literally tell you 'don't do that, don't go there, and I think you should do x.' If it's a situation or a problem you are discussing that's a bit different, but if they're insistent about the kind of person you should be, or what you should or should not do with your life, LEAVE.

How confident are you?

The qualities of confidence and why you must have them

They say you either have it or you don't. But being confident is easy. Go back to Chapter 1 and the section on being anything you desire at any time. Confidence is important for men and women. Women look for confident men, and men look for confident women.

If you're saying, "but I don't have any confidence!" Well no worries, we're going to get you some. Grab that pad of paper that you've been writing on. If you feel you already are confident, go ahead and grab it anyway, give yourself a boost. List some of your accomplishments and achievements. It doesn't matter if they're when you were 10 years old, 25 years old, or 45 years old, you did them. No one else did them, you did. It doesn't matter if you won at bowling, got a raise at work, a promotion, helped a total stranger with something, won a championship, or beat a regional record in track. Go ahead, be proud!

Now list some things you like about yourself, that others like about you, that you've done or can do that no one else can do. What are your talents and skills? Go beyond the resume. Sure what you have there is great, but go beyond that. Think of some of the things that other people appreciate about you and be proud of them. Be proud of your ability to do them, and to do them again, and again! Because you can! And you will! And that is confidence.

You have to own who you are. Who you are is someone special, someone different. You have unique strengths and abilities. Know yourself. Knowing that you are worth something, knowing you can do something without considering, "Can I do this?" Never mind how you look or how you appear to others. The world has enough of that going on. Think back to history and great people in the world. Never has life been defined by looks, it is always defined by character. You have character and confidence. Confidence is certitude, it's an attitude and it's attractive. Why? Because people want to be around confident people, period. Again, why? Because it makes them feel confident too. All that confidence is, is knowing who you are and believing in yourself.

back or not. Let me tell you, he lit up like a light bulb. When we had our session the next week, everything changed for him. He said he was "using it, loving it, and feeling free of worry!" When people returned his call or message, he was pleasantly surprised, and when they didn't, it was "no big deal," because he knew the message was received.

Also, in the inception of meeting someone, the early stages of dating, you have to allow the other person to take their time, and figure out how to respond, and IF it's right for them to respond. That's why this is in the second chapter, for you. When you can be free like this, this is when you can get into the magic of the unexpected. Unexpected things will happen--they will get back to you when they get back to you.

Golden Nugget

I can tell you one thing, the more you enjoy this process, the faster it will go.

Why? Because when you aren't worrying, you are happy, and the time just evaporates. After all, time still does fly when you're having fun.

You should know, "They say the happiest people make the most romantic people, and they make the best lovers" (no, this isn't just me saying this).

The Online Dating Thing

What you should know if you are thinking about it, or doing it now.

I start this section with a warning: I'm not particularly a fan of online dating. I don't recommend it to my clients often, though I have in rare cases. For some of my clients, it has worked for them. I do know of a few couples here and there where they have met, dated, and married their future partner, after discovering them online. Most people have a perception like, 'It's hard to meet people, it's hard to find good people to date' especially in today's busy world, with our busy lives in our busy cities (which is why we see a lot of these sites popping up these days). Know that this is just a perception, an opinion, a view, and not necessarily the truth. A view can be changed, modified or transformed, like you saw in the previous section with my client and the boomerang. If you implement what I am talking about in these chapters, especially the *Golden Nuggets* you definitely will not need to 'resort to' online dating as some people do.

Why not do it? It lacks connection. It's hard to establish a connection with someone while you're looking at a computer screen, looking at someone's profile, trying to determine if they're a good fit for you. Isn't that why we go out to meet people the first place? To connect?

You might be disappointed, as I hear a lot of people these days are with online dating. Apparently, it isn't uncommon to agree to meet with someone whom you've scouted (or they've scouted you) online, and have the actual person in front of you be NOTHING LIKE the person you thought you were meeting online. Somehow, people are commonly 'bending the truth' about their online profiles. Whether it is their pictures, their personalities, or their likes and dislikes, something often isn't accurate.

These are things that can otherwise be prevented by meeting your mate in person, naturally, as you're out there living your life. This is what I find brings the most satisfaction, and connection from your mate and in your life overall.

Why do it? I have a client who is a very successful, busy lawyer who is very in demand in her field. She was looking online when we started working together. I recommended she shift from one online dating site to a different one. She started meeting more quality people, having more fun, doing more dating and encountering hardly any 'fake a-likes.'

Online dating can be good because you will be able to select from a lot of potential partners who meet your criteria for what you are looking for in a person. You also get to put yourself out there, and people can find you, which can be a lot of fun and excitement. This way, you get to sort through the people you feel are 'quality' and worth your time. Some sites even take the hassle out of searching and send you a list of people who meet the characteristics, or likes and dislikes of what you're looking for. Dating modernized!

Time to take a break – where are you now? Are you starting to see things developing? Are you starting to see this unfolding for you? Good! If not, give me a call at www.TheRelationshipMaster.com.

3
COURTSHIP

Back in the old days

A little history for us to consider

My father's side of the family is Italian. My nonno, (Italian Grandfather) Serafino was his name, courted my nonna (Italian Grandmother) Lucia by serenading her with a song at her window from below. This was in 1931, back in a little town called Patrica, in the province of Frozenone. This was commonplace back in those days. My nonno was a soldier, and he and his friends used to go to the windows of young pretty girls, and sing to them, to entice them to come out and say hello. When the ladies showed favour, they came out of their windows, and smiled, said hello, waved, and sometimes blew kisses. A brief conversation would take place, and ideally, some laughs were exchanged and the woman felt endeared. Eventually, the men might return to the same lady to sing a second song, or the woman may have come down to set a date, possibly a rendezvous at a nearby hill or café. If they had played their cards right, dating, and a relationship might ensue.

My mother's side of the family is English, from a town in England called Hinckley. And my grandfather Kenneth worked in a factory, which my grandma Irene's father owned. Not much is known about their history and courtship, which took place in the 1940's. However about a half a century before that, in major parts in England, the men usually sent a very fond and descriptive letter to a woman that they 'fancied.' If the female was interested, she would reciprocate by sending a reply with a handkerchief of hers. You may have seen it in old movies, where the woman sent her 'hanky' to her suitor with scent of perfume and/or a lipstick laden kiss. This is how the man knew she was interested, and his letter worked. They would then meet at a social setting in a public place, and it was mostly conversation from there.

In other parts of the world, it was done differently, but in a similar fashion. The background or culture of your ancestors may have had their own unique story. If you can see a pattern, the men did the courting of the women. Back then, and still today, the female is regarded as a beautiful flower, to be respected, treated eloquently and cared for. It is her choosing that determines if progress is made or not.

In olden days, people got married at age 15-19. If you were in your 20's, (at worse 30's) and you weren't married, you were hard pressed and considered unlucky and sometimes even shunned or looked down upon by your family and community. Why? In those days it was mostly about procreating and furthering the family lineage and name. It was however, about love *only in the beginning.* After that, once married, pregnant, or starting a family, it was a matter of staying together. Usually love came second after doing whatever you had to, to ensure the future of your family and livelihood for the kids as your parents and their parents had done for countless generations before them. But as we know nowadays, we are more in tune with our feelings and our other needs which come first. Our careers, our happiness, our romantic desires, being treated right, all of these are items that come into play. It is not just about having kids, surviving, and 'making it'. We pretty much have our survival handled in today's modern world. If we wanted, we could have food on the table, jobs, the bills paid, with relative ease. Also, not everyone wants to have kids in today's world as well. So things have definitely changed, and change is good. Change means options. Yet, it's good to know our history and where we come from.

Back When We Were Cavemen and Cavewomen

What were the roles, and why is it good to know?

Way back, when we were wearing leopard skins for clothes, and carrying large wooden clubs, (just like in the cartoons) men and women were essentially hunters and gatherers. Men were the hunters. They went out and killed animals for food for dinner and to feed the village, the family, and their wives. If the men didn't come back with dinner, the woman was not happy and things may have been rocky in the house that day. Women took care of the field, the crops, the family and the home. Men risked their lives by being potentially killed out there in the wild, by the elements or the very animals they were hunting. It seemed men were taking all the risk, for their safety and their lives. In those days, men possessed more strength and agility than women. This is likely why they went out and did the physical act of hunting. Why am I sharing this with you? Men like to feel rewarded, needed, and respected. You'll find that both sexes want to feel respected, making respect a universal necessity in any good relationship. Men are usually left brain oriented, which means we are go getters, act first, ask questions later, more impulsive types. If we didn't have men, it's possible we wouldn't have survived through those harsh times. Maybe we wouldn't have learned to fend for ourselves, to eat through the winter, to have pelts and fur to stay warm and progress throughout the stone age, iron age, and now the technological age.

In essence, women are nurturers and should be respected as such. They are mothers. They have feminine loving, warm energy. This is why you love your mother, and you fondly remember her homemade apple pie, when she used sing you to sleep, or kiss your 'boo boo' when you got hurt. For centuries, they were caretakers. They took care of us, and they still do. We are lucky to have them on this earth and in our lives, thank you moms! As men, we go through a lot, and aren't as emotionally aware as women. We hide so much and traditionally don't take things well when they don't go our way. This is why men on average are more stressed, live shorter lives, and typically have a short fuse, compared to women.

Women are calmer, more relaxed, and live longer. Wonder why? Men mostly don't know how to deal with emotions. Thankfully women have more emotional intelligence than men. That's why we go to mom, our sisters (I am lucky to have 2 sisters) and our girlfriends, or wives to feel grounded, centered and loved so often. They are where we go to feel comfort, relief, and nurtured when we need it. We can be pretty needy sometimes. Women help fill the emotional gap for men more often than not, which is why men seek out the wisdom of women when troubled. Women are mostly right brain oriented, which is a wiser, more thoughtful pattern and orientation.

In essence this still applies today. Women are still right brained predominantly, creative, loving, warm, and intuitive nurturers. Men are still straightforward, structured, rigorous, action oriented 'doers.' This knowledge can help you understand the opposite sex whether dating, or in a relationship. When you are wondering why your partner or potential partner does x, y, or z, (and it doesn't make sense to you) remember this section because it might help. These things are still deeply rooted in our DNA.

I am not making sexual/gender commentary on gender roles, or taking a pro male or female view. Please don't be alarmed, or feel oppressed. I am just stating what are historical facts and everyday observations of what I have seen. Nature has designed it this way and this is how we have evolved. You can do your own research and see this through if you disagree with it. In fact I recommend it.

The Dating Game as it is Played Today

Get ready to have fun! You are playing a game after all!

At this point in your journey, maybe it's all been all butterflies and roses for you. Or maybe it's been confronting as all heck, either way, it's fine. Has it been easy, if so why has it been easy? Is it because you are teachable? Open? If it's been hard, why has it been hard? What are you afraid of? What are your concerns?

The thing is ladies and gentlemen, **this is a game of cat and mouse, cops and robbers or hide and seek.**

Golden Nugget

It doesn't matter if you're male or female, everyone is playing this game, whether they know it or not.

Consciously or unconsciously this is how we approach and conduct ourselves when we are dating or pursuing, or being pursued by someone we are attracted to. It's like the game 'tag', there is a back and forth. I touch you, you're it. You touch me back, I'm it, and so on, and so on it repeats. The other person either responds or they don't.

The way I laid it out earlier isn't much different than how it is today, nor will it be different if you're picking this book up 50 years from now. The method may change a little, from a hand written letter with a stamp, to a text, a tweet or an email. The rules in the above sections, and the rules outlined ahead, are pretty much the same in the dating game, so do not fret. As long as you follow this guide, you will be fine. You are human, they are human. You have the same thoughts, problems, capabilities, opportunities and hindrances as everyone else in the world. Everyone in the world is dealing with or has had to deal with some form of what you are going through.

One of the only differences in today's game that's different from our past, is our modern day demand for perfection, to 'be perfect.' There is less tolerance for screwing up, more public scrutiny and fear of embarrassment/looking bad, especially with younger generations. What I mean is, if something happens that might be embarrassing, possibly committing a contemporary 'faux pas' there is a possibility that your partner may cross you out immediately without remorse. This is because of the pressure that exists today to 'look your best, and be your best all the time.' This has nothing to do with you and everything to do with them. (Note: If this is you, stop. You aren't perfect. No one is. Things happen, don't rule someone out because of something small and insignificant. You wouldn't want it to happen to you.)

When I was younger, I was kind of a funny guy, the class clown. I was a huge fan of Jim Carrey and everyone knew it. One day, the 'super hot popular girl' and I started 'going out'. It was two days in, and brand new. I was overly excited (she was the super hot popular girl after all) and from a distance after she got off the bus, and we said our goodbye's I sang out loud in front of a crowd of people, 'Good bye my loooooove!' In a achey, distorted, awkward voice on purpose! I was trying to be funny, acting out one of the beginning scenes from 'Dumb and Dumber.' The next day, she dumped me. She couldn't stand the embarrassment. I laugh about it to this day and feel no remorse or shame for the event.

I took that kind of girl out of my existence in dating. I didn't want to be with someone who couldn't take a joke. Not only that, but I didn't want to be with someone who was so concerned about looking good, that they weren't able to see the forest for the trees. It was her loss. Besides, events like this are actually a gift.

Golden Nugget

You get to create what you want from recognizing what it is that you don't want.

Courtship is all about playing the game. It's a process. And we'll discuss enjoying the process in the next chapter. For now, just focus on this being simple courtship, a back and forth, nothing personal towards you or against you. At this stage this is just a game.

The Rules of the Game

What are the rules and why play by them?

It's possible that by now, you're thinking this is a little unconventional. This isn't the normal way of doing things. If so, great! I'm glad! That means you might be seeing things differently by now, which is good! If you picked this book up, it's likely to create a different set of results in your life. This is really great, because

Golden Nugget

If you want different results in your life, you're going to have to do things differently.

However, for now, let's cover some basic rules of the game, and yes, like I said it is a game. Why do we need to know the rules now? Depending on the person you meet, you can navigate through any kind of person you meet. You don't have to be stopped by someone's particular disposition. You can be with them, and be with anyone if you want. You should know for starters, that some people love to play by the rules, and some people love to break the rules. Now the most basic rule is find someone, settle down, get married and have kids. That was the standard and while it still is in many cases, this may no longer be the case for many of you. This is not a problem, and more and more we're seeing multi dimensional relationships. I'll speak more about this in the next section.

For now, some of these are rules, some are just vital pieces of information you should know.

Do not share excessive, gory, unpleasant details about your past relationships. Your potential partner does not need to know all the nasty, terrible, evil that was cast upon you by your previous partner. This is unless you can be light and funny about it and it makes for good laughs. Make sure they laugh too, if they don't, stop immediately.

I don't care what you say, if they don't call, they aren't interested. Move on. A lot of people get caught up with, "How come, and why?" Or worse yet, "he/she will. I know they will," and they don't. They aren't. Stop kidding yourself. Move on.

Observe their behaviour early on, so you don't waste your time – are they overly critical? Are they an energy sucker? Do they leave you tired? Do they talk all the time? Do they have good friends? Are they consistently complaining? Are they respectful towards you? Are they fidgety and nervous?

Remember, it's a game. If you give too many signs that they've won you over, they will lose interest and the excitement will fade fast for them. They'll feel like they've won the game already, and they'll want to go play a different game.

You should compliment each other. If you don't, good luck getting attraction and excitement to build. Compliments are great signals to your partner that you're interested and becoming fond of them. We'll talk in a later chapter of the power of leaving crumbs like Hansel and Gretel.

Don't let yourself go too early. In other words, don't get too comfortable with the other person so much that you yourself start to slip in terms of hygiene, attitude, and manners. My brother-in-law waited 3 months until he let 'er rip inside the car with my sister in it. I believe his exact words were, "Okay, it's been 3 months. You're ready for this. I've been holding it since then."

Golden Nugget

Over half of singles know in the first 15 minutes if there is any chemistry on a first date. You should too. Trust your feelings.

The Rules of the Game that are Flexible

There are rules that you can bend, even break

The above is great and all. Remember rules are mostly just guidelines, which they are for the most part aren't they? There is another way, an exciting, creative, unconventional way, a way that really makes things interesting, if you're up for it.

You can create a mutual agreement with the other person as to just exactly how this will go. You can create anything if they're on the same page. **What on earth do you mean Michael?** Think of it like a real estate contract. If you've ever bought a house before, you know you can say things and put specific requests into the contract that are extra or additional. It's the normal business of real estate to put things in contracts like, 'at buyer's request, seller replaces doors' or 'purchase and takeover of property at buyers discretion, conditional upon financing' 'seller requests buyer moves in within one month of obtaining financing.' Well guess what? It doesn't matter if you are the buyer or the seller, you are a party in this contract. This is a relationship you are building. As in real estate, you're both moving, looking to gain something. You can negotiate terms and conditions in a relationship, so you can negotiate what you want into your relationship.

Why would I want to do this? In special circumstances mostly. For example, if your situation is unique, and sometimes it is at times in your life, you may feel pulled in different directions, or have conflicting priorities. Nowadays our lives aren't so static or one dimensional. As I mentioned earlier, it's a different world out there. It isn't so much about finding someone and settling down immediately in your 20's or teen years like my nonna and nonno. My nonno wanted my nonna, and my nonna, well she wanted to be a nun. I guess my nonno's charm was strong because they were married not long after the sweet serenading occurred. In 1999, for their 75th wedding anniversary, my sister filmed a mini documentary of the family history. On camera, my nonna confessed she wanted to be a nun, and was reluctant to join him in partnership and marriage. However, with the pressures of family, culture, and society and his sweet demeanor, she chose to set aside her dreams of devotion to God (and I'm grateful you did nonna, since I exist today because of you).

Our world today is less about compromise and more about having it all. This illustrates why my example above about contracts and terms and conditions is important, and may be growing in the coming years. Now I'm *not* talking about making a formalized contract for you and your partner, not at all.

Not too long ago, I met someone and we were starting to get to know each other and really enjoy each other's company. We hung out a few times innocently, but it wasn't long before things were really flying between us. We were flirting and eventually our feelings came out after a few phone calls and skype conversations, and we wanted to take things further. The connection was immediate and everything felt really great. However, we were both focusing on our business and careers at the time, and we didn't want to be sidetracked. The two of us were experiencing a lot of momentum, and had certain goals we wanted to achieve in the next 0-12 months. So! What to do? Well we wanted to take things further and see what we could really enjoy and experience together.

At the same time, we wanted to have the freedom to focus on our work, and making our goals a reality. We agreed to remain single and interested in each other. We agreed to remain uncommitted to each other, and keep the flame going. We knew we cared about each other and that our attraction was growing. We wanted to keep talking, and seeing each other on an infrequent basis, but frequent enough that we wouldn't lose sight of each other and our attraction for one another.

It might sound complicated but it really was quite simple! We used the super power of being unattached and still remained very attracted and interested in each other. This way we could have it all! We could focus on our work and keep the magic of the unexpected at play as well. What happened in turn was really special. We ended up supporting each other in our goals and dreams and used each other as a liftoff point whenever we needed a pick me up. We didn't make it official and that defies the normal rules, but let me tell you, we had one of the most supportive, loving, compassionate relationships I've ever seen.

Making Your Own Rules

You have an ace up your sleeve

If you haven't noticed by now, or gotten the feeling, let me tell you… **you are the X factor.** You really are the X factor in every situation. You can turn the tides to any situation to have whatever you want realized. I hope if anything, you are discovering a methodology to obtain your heart's desire. Isn't that why we subscribe to self-development courses, how-to websites and books? It is completely natural to want what we want and to have desires! Now, you might discard everything in this book and create your own method, and that's great! If that's the case, I want to hear all about it. Drop me a line, send me an email, I want to hear your method. This isn't a 'be all end all', it's just one method that's worked for me and a lot of others.

So please understand there is a variable to all of this, to this entire book. That variable is you. You are a powerhouse. You are capable of anything! You can create your own method, your own future regardless of this book. You can manifest anything you want, and any kind of partner or relationship you want too. I believe in you. If you believe in yourself, you can make anything happen.

Golden Nugget

The ones who believe they can achieve their goals and dreams are the ones who do.

So here's some data and research that shows you can make up your own rules, and a lot of people out there are doing that very thing. This might go against conventional wisdom or your everyday thoughts but here it is anyway.
The following if from a study conducted by Match.com in 2011 of 5000 of their members.

Myth: Women are needy and clingy in relationships.
Fact: Women need more independence in relationships than men do. In a relationship, women are more likely than men – across every age group – to want their own interests, have personal space, their own bank account, regular nights out with their girlfriends and vacations on their own.

Myth: Guys don't want to get married and have to be pushed into having kids.
Fact: Men are just as inclined to want to get married as women. In fact, 33% of men and 33% of women said they want to get married. Among singles without children under 18, more men (24%) than women (15%) say they want to have children.

Myth: Older people don't care about sex.
Fact: Older men and women are less likely to compromise on either love or sexual attractiveness in order to have a committed relationship. In addition, older singles find sex while in a committed relationship more satisfying than other age groups.

Myth: Single parents have no social life.
Fact: Not only do single parents go on more dates than singles without kids but more single parents are currently dating someone (21%) than those without kids (16%).

Myth: Young singles today are promiscuous.
Fact: More people in the 21-34 age group say they have never had sex. To be precise, 24% of men and 23% of women ages 21-34 indicated that they were virgins.

Myth: I love you implies a serious commitment.
Fact: 31% of singles believe that "I love you" means "I want you in my life" and 30% believe it means "I care about you." Only 14% think it means "I want to spend the rest of my life with you" and 19% that "I want to have a committed relationship with you."

Myth: Unemployed means unlucky in love.
Fact: 50% of singles would be open to dating someone unemployed if they found the person interesting.

Myth: Hook-ups never turn into relationships.
Fact: 36% of singles are open to a casual hook-up in the near future, and 54% of singles have had a one-night stand. 35% of singles have had a one-night stand that turned into a long term partnership.

It's a process, Trust it

How can I put my faith in a book?

If you are questioning me and my methods at this point, that's okay. I won't be offended. If you doubt this process, I completely understand. You may not agree 100% with what I am saying in this book and that is perfectly normal. The truth is you might have doubts. It's also possible that all of this resonates with you. What is important is that you reflect on the material and make your own decisions about it. Do remember though, the ideal person for you to listen to is someone who has what you want and has been where you are.

Whether you're following this process to the letter, or doing your own thing, either way, trust it. Trust this process. I read a great quote when I was doing research on the law of attraction. It said, "What you want, wants you." Repeat that to yourself five times, and see how that feels. Now think to yourself,

> *Golden Nugget*
>
> **"Who I want, wants me"**

and repeat it five times. How do you feel? Do you understand that people want to connect with you? Can you understand that they are out there and they are looking for you too? Keep this in mind.

Trust the process. Every breakdown leads to a breakthrough! There is light at the end of the tunnel. With every adversity, come the seeds of choice. The mountain is worth the climb.

With everything that you see, that you don't want, it is an opportunity for you to turn your back on it, and focus on what you do want. If all you're getting and seeing is people and circumstances you don't want, don't worry. It will come. It is just yin and yang, the dark and light, the good and bad. You can't have one without the other. If you're seeing no results, or meeting poor quality people (if practicing this for a few weeks or more) trust this process. It's important that you keep reading, and keep practicing what is in this book. Don't give up yet, we're just getting started.

You have been told this, 'Nothing worth having comes without some failure.' You have seen this in the greatest stories ever told. Why is it true? Because others have done it and are doing it. Everyone has overcome some hurdle, or adversity or struggle. So what is the reason behind you not being able to do it? Nothing. It's all possible. The universe is filled with infinite possibility. Science has proven that there are an infinite number of dimensions and possibilities at any point in time. Physics have proven that multiple realities exist right now. There are multiple 'you's' out there somewhere. There is a you that is married. There is a you that is happily, fulfilled with a family. There is a you that is content with yourself in your single life. There is a you that has the partner of your dreams. It's all there for you. It is only a matter of which one YOU choose.

Trust the process. You are attracting the partner you want.

During the Journey, expect road bumps

Steps along the way

You may meet some odd balls along the way. Pay them no mind and don't get hung up on what happens between you two. Remember this is a sorting process. You are picking through the lot of people you will meet. When I begin working with my clients, they usually go through this process nearly systematically. I don't tell them this at first, but eventually they get there almost without fail. They go from not meeting anyone to having an influx of people to choose from. When they apply what they know and do with what I have to add, they naturally attract a lot of potential partners, *like a magnet*. This is a process, they are usually sifting through the qualities and people they meet to get to the right partner. I have to keep reminding them, even when they doubt it, "You are getting to the right one." Sometimes they meet some off the beaten path types, and that's okay, because this is a process, and you have to go through the ones you don't want, the kind of people you don't want to attract, to get to the ones you do want. I must warn you, you will probably be weird-ed out by some people you attract. It is natural.

I had a friend whom I was helping out as she was starting to date again. She is a very attractive woman, she has plenty of great admirable qualities and she was just getting over a rough period in her life. Needless to say, she went through a few oddballs, including a guy who after two dates, invited her to his house. This is normal, not to worry, but what happened afterwards was not. He had a bachelor pad and the only place to sit in the entire place was his bed. Not cool, and all he had to drink was beer. Not cool. Needless to say she didn't stay. She even met a few other interesting candidates after that as well, but it wasn't long before she met the perfect guy. He was a good quality man who treated her well and knew how to treat a lady properly, with respect.

Sometimes you'll notice the weird things he or she does, and everyone does weird things. Don't judge them after the first or second one. IF it's a deal breaker, that's a different story. No one is perfect, everyone has quirks and odd habits or qualities here and there. Remember, exact perfection doesn't exist. If it did wouldn't we all be bored or boring ourselves?

With any project and undertaking that you take on, whether it be dating or a new career, or venture, there are bumps in the road. There are moments where you have doubts and have to regroup, gather up and come back together and give it another go. Steady on course. Stay committed. Trust the process, despite the bumps in the road. It will work out.

Remember this is about you enjoying the process. You need to have fun with it! Call your friends and tell them, 'You'll never guess what happened.'

Golden Nugget

Make light of it. Enjoy yourself in the process.

At the same time, tell your friends what you didn't like and what you did like about the person or the date. This will tell the universe, "These are the qualities I liked – and these are the qualities I didn't like." With that, the vibration you will be putting out will be like an order at a restaurant, "Yes I will have the grilled chicken breast but instead of the rice and potatoes I will have a salad and some veggies. Thank you." This is a vital step to attracting the kind of person you want, according to the law of attraction. Your homework is to practice this, and practice it all over your life, and see what happens. Watch the magic unfold but be careful, as doubt will sink a ship.

Good signs and bad signs

What are the indicators?

How do you know things are working out? How do you know this is a good possible person for you? Simple, you're having fun! You're enjoying yourself! If you are, then it's a great sign to keep going with it. It should be easy. It should feel a little effortless. You should feel good around them. You FEEL a connection. You get the sense that maybe there's something else going on between you besides just the communication. It should flow. Flow is so important. For those of you who are new at this, or not sure what it looks like I'll illustrate this for you. Most times though, it will become easily evident when you get yourself out of the way; When you get your head out of the way, when you stop thinking and shut off your thoughts, when you trust your gut, when you listen to your heart and body, instead of your head.

If you're looking for signs, here are a few-- a decent amount of phone calls, emails, or messages between each other. It should be easy, you should be interested in them, who they are, and where they come from, and where they are going. They should be interested in you too. They should be asking you a lot of questions. You agree on things. You have healthy discussions. You smile a lot. You laugh and they laugh with you. Also, as I said in the previous chapter, provide compliments. Giving and receiving compliments will also help you enjoy the process!

Some signs that indicate that this person may not be ideal for you include that you don't feel good! You didn't have fun. You didn't smile a lot. You aren't interested in them or who they are. You feel like they could be doing so much more, and aren't. You didn't walk away feeling stimulated or aroused, at least physically, emotionally, or intellectually. You didn't have any curiosity about who they are. They talked about themselves 100% of the time. You don't have the same interests, or thoughts, or feelings about things. Opposites do attract, and you need variety, but a baseline of similar interests is very healthy. Lastly, maybe they haven't called and it's been a week.

Since we're always communicating to the people around us, it will probably help you if I share how our communication is broken down and interpreted. 55% of your communication is being weighed mostly by your body language, 38% of your communication is received through your tone of voice, and 7% of your communication is received in your words. This is in front of a person of course. Another vital point is that the tone and body language are responded to first, long before your words are. So what does this mean? Well if you can remember the last time someone was mad at you and/or was yelling at you, you remember mostly the way they made you feel, and not so much the words. This is why we often draw a blank with the words people use, and we tend to put words in their mouth, but we always remember the emotion behind those words, because we're actually reading and remembering the body language and tone.

If you are feeling good about the interaction, it will naturally show in your tone and body language. People will be assessing your communication on these factors, which will lead people (and you) to naturally select who you want to continue with, without your understanding why. This is processed so fast by the brain, you might not even be aware of it. You might recall this when someone asks you, "What do you like about them? Why do you like that person?" The answer struggles to come to you, but if. I someone were to ask you, "How did you feel?" that answer usually isn't a problem.

What vibes are you putting out?

What are the messages you are sending?

In the first chapter I talked about who you are being and what you are emitting. This, on a deeper, scientific level is a function of your vibration, or the vibration you are emitting. Your way of being and your vibration are the same thing. Since your way of being is like a laser beam, the way you are being is the laser beam you are emitting. Take dishonesty for example. People can sense if you are lying, or being deceptive. Something happens when you lie to them, or when you are lied to. Whether you know it or not, your brain (think of it as feelers or antennae) picks up on the signals. How? You know how it feels to be lied to, and you know what it feels like to lie, because we've all done it or experienced it before. In the first chapter when I was talking about lying, it likely resonated with you. Your vibration is picked up by the other person's brain, since they have the same 'feeling antennae' as you do.

Do you remember that song by 'Marky Mark and the Funky Bunch,' "Good vibrations?" For those of you who don't know, yes that was Mark Wahlberg. The song was about putting out 'good vibrations' and how good vibrations feel, and are received. Now this was in the early 1990's but this was a common saying then, and it still is.

You've probably said it before, "I don't like the vibes he's putting out" or, "I didn't get good vibes from that woman." You may have said to your friends, "That new guy so and so is dating? I didn't get good vibes." Sometimes you can't explain it either. You might have thought, "I don't know I just didn't like the way he made me feel." In those cases, you may not have made sense of it yet, but your gut and your brain have already interpreted the signals/vibrations and have told you how you aren't a match for them. That's why there is no connection present. In fact, what is present is a disconnection!

It is important to know what vibes you are putting out. How you may ask? Through awareness. Awareness = the ability to know, and be conscious of something. By being aware of who you are being, or what vibes you are putting out, you have the advantage of knowing what the other person is receiving. What you are sending is being received. Take the example of having good intentions, or being generous. These ways of being are felt and understood intuitively by others. Sometimes however, people will mistake your kindness, love and generosity, for a sham, and that's not your fault, so long as you are genuine. What is coming up is their previous experiences is something that is incomplete from their past. My advice is to ignore them and move on, or if you really care about the person, put in the effort and clarify your true intentions and use that magical power of being unattached to the result.

How to avoid screwing it up

We have self-sabotaging natures

Well, you might not know it, but you do sabotage yourself. Yes you do. In fact, we all do. It is common. This IS human nature. What? You don't agree? If that were the case, wouldn't we all have the things we want? Would we have the things we want in a much easier fashion? Would every project flow seamlessly without interruption? Would we all be able to focus fully and see all projects through to the end? How many relationships or perfectly good partners have you sabotaged?

We might not realize we do it but self sabotaging is a part of each of us, and there are lots of reasons why we do this. I won't go into them, but I wanted to share mine with you. You see for a long time I was afraid of my own capability. All of my life I dreamed I would do great things and be a leader for people, who accomplished great things and helped others accomplish great things in their own lives. I saw this vision my whole life, and as I grew older and took on more and more in my life, sometimes that ability scared me. I sometimes saw the raw power that I had to cause change in the world, and at a certain point, that ability scared me. It scared me to the point of taking no action. Why? I was scared of the responsibility that would come along with this capability, terrified actually. Sometimes I might be presented with a great idea or amazing opportunity or connection and I often didn't feel I was ready for it, so I would let it die, or leave it alone.

Sometimes I would throw a spoke in the wheel of a project, as I feared the responsibility that came with power, or success, or acclaim. I also feared who I would have to hold myself up to be, if I wasn't ready. I'd have conversations going on in my own head saying, 'You can't do this yet. You need to learn 'x' first or accomplish 'y' first, then you can get there." I'd hear the voice in my head say, "You don't deserve success yet, you have to earn your way, and prove yourself first." Sometimes it was so bad the voice in my head would say something like,

"Stop, don't do that! Who do you think you are?" Ouch! I am happy to say this book is a step over that self-sabotaging nature.

You might screw up a relationship or two, with a partner or potential partner and you may not know why. In fact, you may have done this already and as you're reading this you may acknowledge that you've done this in the past. If you are beating yourself up and condemning what you've done, stop beating yourself up, it happens! We do it all the time. It might make you upset to realize this, but don't worry. Again it is important to be aware of your own conversations of, "Can I do this? Am I ready? Is it worth it?"

Golden Nugget

All that boils down to is what you're committed to. Why do you want a partner, why do you want to date or why did you pick up this book in the first place?

Go to your notes from the first chapter about why you're doing this, and become present to those reasons again. Everyone needs a reminder.

Exercise: I recommend taking a short personality assessment at www.positiveintelligence.com – Take "The Saboteur" Assessment. It is a way to discover how much of your brain is geared towards sabotage and how much of your brain is geared towards success. It is measured as a percentage so it's a very valuable assessment. It will give you tools to use to bring your brain into a higher success focus. It is completely free and takes two minutes. Do it now.

If you fall off the bike... and you might

Get back up and try again

Don't give up. If you've fallen off now, or you fall off in the next month, keep going. If you get excited about someone you meet, and it doesn't work out, don't be concerned. I know this might sound easier than it is, but a lot of it is about letting go and listening to the magic of the unexpected. As I said before, this is a process, there is a method to the madness. You will find him/ her. He/she is out there. This might be a three month, or a six month process. Sometimes I work with a client from three months to nine months, to get them where they want to be. On average, usually it is a 6 month process.

Now, this is a time to look at and refine what you are doing. Take a look at your thoughts and actions and see if there is something you can do differently. If you aren't sure what I mean, ask a previous partner and write down and remember what he or she says if he or she is willing to have this kind of conversation with you – that's why it's important to never burn your bridges and end your relationships on good terms.

Take out your pad, here are some questions you can ask:
What could I have done better as a partner?
What could I have done differently, that would have made things easier?
What were some of the things I did that annoyed you?
How could I have communicated better with you?
Where could I improve the most?
What would you recommend I do differently, to appeal to someone I'm looking to date? (For example, it could be anything from wardrobe, mannerisms, etc.)

And now, you have an opportunity next time that behaviour comes up, to do something differently. Never mind the thought of, 'they should love me for who I am.' They will. But you have to meet them first. And this is why you picked up the book in the first place.

This is one of the best parts of the process. Thomas Edison, when making the light bulb said, It took him 10,000 versions to get the right bulb. When asked how come he failed 9999 times, he said, "I didn't fail. I found 9999 times it wouldn't work." This is the same as with you, you can improve on your ways of being, and improve your chances of attracting the right partner for you.

Golden Nugget

You are either at the effect or something or causing something. And you should be causing something.

This is all about you being a better driver of that bicycle we learned to ride through trial and error all those years ago.

As I said earlier, this is a process, and you need to trust the process. Soon you will discover, it is not about trusting the process so much as it is about you trusting yourself.

Should I stay or should I go?

How do I know if I need to move on?

This book does not advocate that the first person you meet is the right one. Also this book does not advocate that you stay with someone you are not happy with. You wouldn't keep using a perfume or cologne you didn't like, and you don't keep a pair of shoes or jeans you don't like, and you might not keep living in a neighbourhood you don't like.
Why stay with someone who doesn't fulfill you, respect you, take care of you, or love you. Everyone needs love, we can't live without it. It is an essential need. That's one of the reasons you love your family and friends so much. It's because they provide you with love when you need it and we all need love. So how do you know if you should stay with someone or leave them?

How you know is that **you know.** You will know. If you don't know, it's because you haven't been listening to yourself. If you are listening to yourself and have doubts, fears, and concerns, then you know. You will know because you will hear yourself. You will listen if you feel uneasy or unhappy or unsure around them. Now be careful.... this may take some time to develop, because as I said earlier, *it is all up to you*. It is up to you to be happy with the one you're with. You are the common denominator.

With one client I worked with, her breakthrough and hurdle to overcome was being a demand for what she wanted. She went through all these guys who she thought were nice, okay, decent, and sort of attractive. The problem was that she was unsatisfied with those guys, but she wasn't aware that she was unsatisfied. She wasn't present to the fact that she was just going along with whatever came along. She wasn't finding the right partner for her because she was taking whatever was coming. She needed to start being a demand for the kind of man she wanted to be with--the kind of man that was A Quality!

She had to stop putting up with all the B and C quality guys that were coming her way. Once she started to be a demand for the kind of quality man she wanted to be with, she left all the not so great guys behind. What a relief that was for her. What a time saver that was for her,and what fun she started to have. She actually started to enjoy herself more, once she cut herself loose from the guys who were sub-par for this amazing woman.

The Little Things

Why are they so darn important?

You want to pay attention to the little things. Why? Because they add up.

Golden Nugget

The little things will determine the sum of the parts of your partner.

Plain and simple, when you think of a jug or a bottle of water, you see it as a whole, as one body of water. What you don't know is that water is made up of droplet after droplet after droplet of water. Think of a dripping tap or a leak in your house. If that leak drips long enough, you've got a puddle, and pretty soon, a bucket. 1) Pay attention to the little things, 2) Keep a small mental note of the little things that you like which this person does, and 3) Try not to nitpick, this isn't a detective list of clues, it's just something to notice.

It works the same with your current or previous partner! Do they say thank you, do they bring you flowers? Do they encourage you? Do they love your family? Does your family love them? Do you like the same things? Can he kiss you the way you want him to? Does she mind when you hang out with the guys? Did he open the door for you? Did she nag you about the things you aren't doing and 'should do'?

One thing I hear a lot of these days is, he/she looks good on paper, but something isn't right. Follow your gut, it is likely correct, and good for you for following your intuition. You see, intuition plays a large part in this process.

Golden Nugget

Finding the right partner is about having a "knowing feeling", that this person is right for you, which must stand the test of time.

It is about trusting your feelings. Love, connection, and partnership is a feeling you have. You know when you should proceed further. You feel it or you don't! The reason it doesn't make sense, if the person's resume is good, for you to be together, is because your feelings matter. People these days know their survival is handled, so we're more into creating our lives the way we actually want to live them, and it all adds up through the little things.

Add to your previous list of your partner's characteristics, the little things they do that you liked most.

4
ENJOYING THE PROCESS

What do you mean enjoy the process?

Easier said than...

Okay, this is where we're going to get really down and dirty! You've already done a lot of work! Yes you have, and I applaud you for it. You should pat yourself on the back right now, and your head, and your heart! Now it's time to enjoy the process! This is all about having fun at this point. If you aren't having fun then why are you doing it? I know you have your reasons. Now it's time for you to remember and consciously apply 'having fun' to your life and into this process of finding your next partner.

Remember it's a game, as stated in the previous chapter. Sometimes it's a game of cat and mouse. It's a game of chase more often than not. Ultimately, it's a game, and games are supposed to be fun! Think of all the games you played as a kid! Tag, hide n seek, cops and robbers, house, or red rover. You played them all because they were fun! Well your soul knows that this game is going to be fun too. There are many souls that your soul could connect with, so it's a fun game to discover and play at the same time.

If you view dating or finding a partner as 'tough, a struggle, or challenge', then this chapter is especially for you. If going on a date strikes you as an agonizing, nerve wracking experience, then you probably forgot how to have fun. Somewhere along the way, you got really heavy about the whole thing, really in your head about this endeavor. It probably became very significant for you as well, and you abandoned it as a fun activity/event.

Remember, there is no difference between you and the people out there on the street, or in their offices or cars. We're all the same--we're human beings. There's no reason you can't have the partner you desire. There's just no reason. It's just a matter of time now, so you might as well enjoy it, since it is all coming together.

By now, maybe you might see everything coming together. Remember in another chapter I said happier people make the best lovers? As well, happy people want to be with happy people. Do you want to be with a happy person? Do you want to be happy yourself? Good. This chapter is super important and it is imperative to have that happen. Can you see why? If you are happy and having fun, your relationship will flow. If you are happy, you can find happiness, you will vibrate happiness, and that is magnetic. Also, if you're happy you will not be consumed by the pressures that you put on yourself to be a certain way, to act a certain way or fit a mold of your partner. This will lead you to naturally BE the superpower of being unattached.

What having fun looks like?

You get to define it

I was on a date once that I didn't know I was on. Wait, what? I had met a great girl at a Christmas party and then a few months later we decided to connect and see what would come out of it. It felt mostly social, and possibly business, so I didn't think it was a date. We were in the same circles, and connected to the same people, we seemed to be committed to the same things so we thought we would get together to see where this would take us. She picked a place for coffee in the evening, which was a place I had never been before. I was helping my parents move to their new condo during the day, so I didn't think much of it, so I dressed in super casual, comfortable clothes.

When I got to the coffee shop, I was surprised and a little nervous. It was a very upscale coffee shop! The girls in there were wearing heels and business dress. The guys were in long sleeve shirts. "What the heck?" I thought. Uh oh... and felt out of place. I was in comfortable unfashionable hiking shoes, blue jeans, and a zeppelin t-shirt and black zip up sweater. "Oh crap!" I thought again as I ordered a coffee about 10 minutes early. I could feel some of the other people's eyes on me, and didn't like the feeling. I felt uncomfortable. Then I stopped myself... wait a second. This isn't a date, as far as I know. I didn't know. I did think, she is a pretty girl, last time I saw her, I remember she took good care of herself. She'll probably be looking good. Then I realized I was totally caught up in my thoughts, which were frantic! This wasn't fun. Then I remembered, hey I can choose how I want to be. I can choose to be self-conscious. Or I can choose to let go of my worries and have fun. I chose right then and there how that meeting would go. There was no point in me worrying, since this wasn't necessarily a date. Even if this was a date, what would I want? I would want to enjoy it. I would want to have fun! So I set that as my intention for the evening… and I laughed at myself and the concerns I had made up in my head for nothing.

Three hours later I had had a great time with Tiffany. We had a lot of laughs, a lot of great conversations, and a lot of fun! We connected on multiple topics, and many interests that we mutually shared. At the end of the evening, I still didn't know if it was a date or not. We hugged goodnight and I thought I'd like to see her again, and I did. The thing I want to share with you is that I allowed myself to be in the experience of my nervousness, and my concerns. Then I left them with the cashier. I experienced the concerns and let them go. I took on being present. If I was present, then I could contribute to her and she could contribute to me. If we had opportunities to work together or refer others, then I would surely miss that if I wasn't being present. I took on having fun! In the creation of my intentions, I was fully able to do that. Would you believe both of my intentions were successful? She gave me an opportunity to be featured on TV, and we had a great time!

I want you to discover for yourself, "If I was having fun, what would I be doing? What would it look like? How would I feel? What would I think, feel or say?" Take out that old pad of paper, and answer these questions. Let them be a guide so that you can come back to them whenever you need to remember and be guided.

This is a journey, so strap yourself in!

Why would I need to buckle up?

I want you to get ready, and strap yourself in, ESPECIALLY if you've had a tough go of it in the past. Prepare yourself for fun, but prepare yourself nonetheless. For some of you this may be a rollercoaster ride, as I said, especially if you've had a tough go in the past.

If you've had a tough go at relationships in the past, then you might have to do some work to overcome that past. If that's the case, buckle up. Don't worry. Smile for the camera. You can do this! You will do this! If you want it bad enough, it shall be. Repeat this phrase when times get tough or if you're ever in doubt, "If it is to be, then it is up to me."

I say be prepared, because you never know what you will encounter. I don't know who you will come into contact with. I don't know what type of men or women you will meet. I don't know if you will meet creeps, perverts, oddballs, or crazy people. I use those terms loosely, since they are all labels and based on your own personal perceptions. The truth is, you will attract and encounter a myriad of people in this process. You will get to a point where you will meet a whole bunch of people. Sometimes my clients go from being single, to having to choose from a boatload of people who are interested in them in the midst of this process. This is the work of the universe, which gives you a lot of candidates to choose from and then you get to make your selection, to refine the options. But we'll get to that later.

Again, this could be a rollercoaster ride. You will meet different people. Remember this is a fun ride. That's why you got on in the first place. I hope one of your reasons for being on this journey was to experience fun with someone and share parts of your life with them, to have happy, fun filled experiences with them. The ride might get a little bumpy before then.

Dropping Hints and Leaving Crumbs

Remember Hansel and Gretel?

Do you remember the story of Hansel and Gretel? The brother and sister who went into the woods and found the house full of candy? Before they went into the forest, they left crumbs and bits of cookies and bread so that they could be found and find their way back if they needed.

Well you are going to do the same! You're going to have fun with it! It will be exciting as you start to meet people you are interested in. Since this is a game, you will want this ace in your sleeve for when you're out there playing. This will be exciting for you as you leave the crumbs, and exciting for others to follow and pick up the pieces.

Be careful not to be manipulative. Some people manipulate others and those that do the manipulating enjoy it and revel in the knowing that they are causing confusion for others. You mustn't do this. Part of my vision for writing this book is to bring people together, to bring people to a greater place of self-love and love for others. Manipulation is not in the plan.

I'm talking about dropping clues, leaving hints, maybe a little playful teasing. Leaving cute messages, being playful, giving compliments, giving a little gift, and spreading and sharing your thoughts, appreciation, or compliments for the person you are interested in. Something I do is 'use it sparingly' - spreading it out, so to speak. If I notice several things I like in someone, some behaviours, or quirks they have, some small things that they do… I will make a mental note of them. I will remember them. Instead of showering them in the beginning with love and compliments, I will share one or two with them at a time, spreading them out over our time together. This is a fun way for me to keep the excitement and interest between us. It's great to get to see their reactions when they arrive at the newest crumb they found. You could compare this to playing poker. You don't show your best hand first. You don't want to give away your best cards either. If you did, your partner might think, 'Well, I've already won this game. I know what cards they play. There's no fun here.' Then they will move on.

Remember that this is a game and a process. Relationships and the game are supposed to be interesting, the opposite of boring. This is just a matter of enjoying the process, and keeping things interesting.

I recommend, if you have things you like about this person, keep some things close to your chest and save them for later. This way it's not used up all at once. That's not to say that you won't find more things that you like about them.

Golden Nugget

Keep the good things you love, and spread them out over time.

Have and look for lots of good things to share and talk about... it will lengthen and make the process more enjoyable for you and the other person. Everyone loves compliments, gifts, and thoughtful messages. I'm not talking about holding back and withdrawing. I am talking about making a point to give little crumbs and bits of a big cookie. You are one big cookie, who has lots of crumbs to share.

Playing the field

Just how many fish are in the sea?

It's not important to know how many fish are in the sea, but there are plenty. You just need to know they are there. That's why you've heard that saying so many times. It applies to your situation if you're feeling low, recently dumped or starting over. This applies to both men and women.

That's why you have to play the field. Place a lot of bets, start a lot of conversations, take a bunch of actions. You place bets, yes... but not too many bets. You don't want to get caught, especially if you're playing the field, or connecting with fish in the same pond. However, you can place bets in different lakes or networks. There nothing to be ashamed of here, since you are not hurting anyone. You don't have any commitments, you are a free agent, so to speak (I know, lots of lingo here). The only thing you have to do here is make it known that you are dating with your new fishies.

If you aren't sure where to look in these lakes, ponds, rivers, no problem. You might want to think of people you may never have considered. For example, people who are older or younger than you are. Other examples may include people at your work, your co-workers, your co-workers friends if you go out together or are social like that. Aside from that, you might be thinking, "How on earth do I talk to my co workers about this?" Simple, you just tell them you are looking to be in a relationship, and you might be open to blind dates or introductions. How about schools or community centers? Maybe the gym? The main thing

Golden Nugget

You have to GET OUT MORE. YOU AREN'T GOING TO MEET THEM SITTING AT HOME.

Connections happen in person. Things will happen, you will meet people outside of your radar screen that you can't see right now. But they are out there. You just have to get out there to find them. Remember, who you want, wants you. They are out there looking for you too, and at the moment, you just can't see each other on your radar screen.

Your Parents: Your First Example

What your mama' told you, or your dad

Near the end of high school I dated someone special. We met at drama club rehearsals (take notice: having fun!) We had a few friends in common but never knew each other or talked. We started to get to know each other and it wasn't long before I was crushing on her. In the play we were a couple, which was fun in its own right. To make a long story short, we dated for a few months. I liked her. We had a lot of fun together, inside and outside of the drama club. I took a different approach to getting to know her- laughing wildly, being silly, outlandish and really out there with my humour. It worked. We clicked on a lot of things, and she had a silly side too which brought mine out even more. However, we only dated for two months. I was pretty heart broken. Two months was way too short to get to know this amazing fun loving creature that I had just started to really fall for. It didn't quite make sense in my book. Everything was going well, why the split?

It made sense when I looked deeper at Amanda. She was resigned, disenchanted and pretty much disconnected to love- real love anyway. When we were together, we had conversations about love, me as a hopeless romantic, fully believing and present to the power of love and all its lovely wonders. She was in disbelief, disenfranchised, indifferent and overall distant when it came to truly loving or knowing love itself. Why? What happened to cause her beliefs this way? It was her parents. I had gone over to Amanda's family home for several lunches and dinners over the few months we were dating and several months thereafter when we decided to be friends. Her parents were not in love. It was painfully obvious. Her parents were passive aggressive, visibly disconnected, and emotionally distant. However they were committed to staying together, for their children. In their classical traditional culture, it was unruly, and truly unholy to separate, even if you no longer knew love with your partner. They had three kids, one of them was fairly young, and separation was not an option. Amanda's experience that she was constantly subjected to, constantly witness to, was an example of this as what love looked like. In her eyes, only through what she had seen, through no fault of her own, this is what the future held. This is what the promise of love was. It was undeniable. I remember even in high school she said, with a smirk and enough surety to kill a cat, "Love isn't real. It's only temporary. We all end up wanting to kill each other."

Well I had seen the difference. I completely believed in the fullness of love, the reward of love, the possibilities of love, the intangibleness of love. My parents? My parents were my guide, my baseline for what love should be. My parents are still together after 40 years, happily in love. My parents although they bicker like every couple does, still love each other very much (thank you mom and dad I am so grateful). Lou and Freda touch each other from time to time on the shoulder, on the arm, and on the hand. Lou does not talk over Freda incessantly in conversation. Lou valued Freda's opinions. Freda pinches Lou's bum here and there in the kitchen as he walks by sometimes. Freda cooks all of Lou's meals. Freda doesn't mind when Lou interrupts her while she is reading her book five times in one hour. Freda books vacations for she and Lou, and although Lou resists right up to the airport, once they get to the beach Lou says, "You know, I'm so glad we did this. I needed this. Thank you." Lou buys Freda flowers and smiles through his teeth when he gives them to her, instead of looking at the floor or looking away. Freda buys tickets to plays and theatre for herself and Lou and picks out Lou's clothes to wear that evening. Lou says, "After all these years, you still dress me well!" One time, when money was tight, Lou bought Freda a compass for her birthday, and in a little note he wrote, "So no matter where we are, you can find your way back to me."

I am happy to share right now that as of this moment Amanda is in a long term committed relationship with someone she cares about very much. I have a hunch that they will get married. I could be wrong, but I was friends with Amanda for about 10 years, and very good friends after we broke up. I've seen the people she's dated and her attitude towards them. I believe this one will work out naturally.

Why am I brining this up? Because it is an important part of the puzzle. You must look into your parents, if nothing else at least to begin to inquire. Why? They may be running your relationships. In the background, you may not be aware of it. Again, this is quite normal. Subconsciously, what Amanda had witnessed in her home for many years was just on repeat. Part of her may have even been acting in a form of rebellion, as punishment to her parents since their traditional values and verbal requests made her aware that marriage and grandchildren is something they want. Yes she is Italian.

The absolute truth is that the future is open. It is unpredictable. The absolute truth is that anything is possible. History is written, yes, but your future is unknown.

Golden Nugget

You get to create your future.

You have the power to say how it goes. We are creators by nature. We are the only species on this planet with an ability to create in this manner. We are so lucky. No matter what, you have full control of your thoughts, attitudes, actions and behaviours.

Take out that pad of paper and take some deep breaths. Ask these questions: *What did my parents teach me? What did I learn from them? What did they show me? How did they treat each other? How did they show me that love should be?*

Your parents are your first example of love, yes. But they definitely don't have to be your last. Ask yourself one more simple question, "Does what my parents showed me serve me now?" If yes, great. Keep it. If not, create it newly. In fact, do this regardless so that you may create your future right now.

Take out that pad and ask a new set of questions after you've answered those above. Whatever you do, have fun with it! Ask yourself, "*Who am I 20 years from now? Who am I in love with? Why am I in love with them? How do we talk to each other? What do we talk about? What are the little things we do to express our love for each other?"*

Have fun – Really – Have fun

You can do that! It'll be the best thing you ever did!

This could be a total blast! If you want it to be... Remember chapter 1? You can be anything you want to be, at any moment in time. Who says you can't have fun all the time?

In the previous section, with Amanda, when she broke up with me I actually had a really clear feeling that said, 'this isn't over'. I was able to get over the break up quickly because I just had a feeling I could not deny… a feeling we would be together again someday. We definitely ended too early and it felt cut short. We stayed friends for 8 years and were very, very close, in a purely friendly way. We still had the silliness about us, and we did a LOT of fun things together. We created plenty of fun amazing memories we had together. We were always laughing, coming up with crazy stories, games, and trouble for us to get into. We were at times best friends and a big part of each other's lives. Funny how that happens… I always had feelings for her that never went away fully.

It was like a good book that you started and if you didn't finish it, you might always have wondered how it ended or what else happened to the characters, sometimes in the back of your mind. At some point eight years into our friendship, everything shifted. I started to notice the signs of attraction, true attraction from her. It went on slightly, slowly for a few months from October to December. I took notice and was curious about it--nothing but curious (remember the magic of the unexpected and the power of being unattached). Then on Christmas Eve we exchanged gifts. The gifts she bought me were very thoughtful, overly well thought out in a way that I wasn't used to from her. On Christmas Eve that year, everything changed. The air felt different. I could have sworn the heat went up in my apartment, though I didn't touch the dial. When friends were nearby we couldn't take our eyes off each other. My fingertips sizzled. My limbs went numb. I got a glimpse from her eyes. We locked eyes again and again and I channeled a message through my eyes and said, 'Are you thinking what I'm thinking?' And she gave me one slight nod that said it all. That one nod told me yes. We dropped everything and headed for the other room and kissed one of the most passionate, deeply moving, pent up energy releasing intimate kisses I've ever experienced. Wow.

We were together for 2 years. At first she was still hesitant, and I could feel the past of her parents still with us in the form of a wall in our relationship. I knew it would all work out and at one point I told her at some point she would have to let me into her heart. I knew that once she did, there would be a huge, amazing love waiting for her like she had never known before. We did a lot of work together, and had the help of some very powerful self-development courses and it took time but it happened. We were very much in love. Eventually she was able to be more emotionally available and invested in the relationship, even more so than I was. She wanted to move in together and really commit to each other. We did that, and although we didn't stay together long past the 2 year mark, it was such a beautiful, deeply loving, growing, incredible relationship!

What a wild ride! What a rollercoaster! The same goes for you in this process. It can be terrifying and EXHILARATING! Even the terrifying parts can be exciting and fun! After all, it only takes a second to change your mind, about something.

What would life be like, if you had fun every day? What would you do? How would you feel? Take a gander… and take out that notebook. Ask yourself:
What would life or the world look like if we were having fun all the time? Imagine another planet… where fun was an important a part of your day, just like eating? On this planet, 'Fund em' people woke up in the morning having fun, and went to bed having fun every day. If your life looked like this now, what would you be doing? Who would you be meeting? What kinds of things might come out of your super fun filled life?

Curiosity

The Game Changer

If you notice, I'm including a lot of things which hopefully by now for you are 'game changers.' That is my intention with this book anyway. That's why you picked up this book, no? To change the game you are playing? Since this is a game, ("the game of life") it can go so many different ways! It has so many different beginnings, middles, and endings- it is designed to be fun. One way to ensure it stays fun is to be curious about how it will play out. Since there can be so many possibilities as to how your life unfolds, bringing curiosity to it will surely keep you guessing, and definitely keep it interesting.

Here is an interesting quote on curiosity:
"It implies an approach that can shatter the taken-for-granted-ness of our

everyday reality. Wonder is the unwilled willingness to meet what is utterly strange in what is most familiar. It is the willingness to step back and let things speak to us, a passive receptivity to let the things of the world present themselves in their own terms. When we are struck with wonder, our minds are suddenly cleared of the clutter of every day concerns that otherwise constantly occupy us."

Read this twice if it hits you like a, "What the heck, and huh?" Understand that it is very wise to have your life be simpler and to bring more of a 'flow' to your life.

A simple way to approach this is to create more, "I wonder what if…" moments in your life. When faced with what seems like a problem or wall of a situation, bring curiosity to it. Think to yourself, "I wonder what will happen?"
I wonder what could happen. How would look it look if it did happen, or if it did not happen. What would I do instead? What might it lead to?

Take a look into your past: What partners failed? What dates didn't go well? How could they have gone?

What about in the present: What might happen if this person and I got together? What might happen if we dated or dated again? What might happen if we did this or that?

Take your time and let things speak to you. Let things happen to you. Allow yourself to be struck by ideas as they develop.

Are you kidding me?

Leave the disbelief at the door

This chapter is still about enjoying the process. At some point during the process, you might be surprised by who you meet and what happens. Oh the things people will do!

Here's some fun examples of things that have happened to friends and clients of mine:

Selina
Went on a blind date several years ago after her friend insisted his friend really wanted to meet her. She said no many times but finally was worn down and agreed. While eating lunch she tried to keep conversation alive. However they had nothing in common. Finally he finished eating before she did and she made a joke about him possibly ordering something else. His response was, "I will just stare at you while you eat" and he proceeded to actually watch her while she ate. Needless to say she couldn't eat another bite. Date Over. Her first and last blind date.
Pamela
Once spent close to an hour of dinner conversation talking about how much she loves and is proud of her eight nieces and nephews and how children have impacted her life. She explained how she sees herself working with children and empowering children and the guy told her how much it 'cost' him to have an 18 year old son. He actually kept receipts and had an exact total. This was a buzz kill for sure. Then when she told him they didn't need to see one another again and wished him well in life he said he liked her so much he would consider having more children even though they are expensive.
Diane
Once had a date get totally and completely drunk on a first meeting. He was barely coherent by the time she high-tailed it out of there. They weren't at a club but at a restaurant. Diane also had a guy ask her out on a date and then during the date, it was apparent he wasn't interested in her, but just wanted 'access' to her best friend/roommate. He wanted to find out about what she liked/didn't like, etc. Not cool.

Hank
Hank went on a date with a girl to an amusement park. They approached one rollercoaster which was a wild one. It had curves, loops, and went backwards and forwards. While approaching it and looking up at the track, admiring its design, Hank's date fainted right there on the spot. Hank was a good guy, took care of her, called security and went in the ambulance to the hospital and fed her electrolytes.

These are real stories and things like this might happen to you. In fact, you can count on some off the wall things happening, so be prepared.
The point here is not to get hysterical about them. I'll elaborate more on this in the next section. For now, whenever you have those moments I highly recommend you just laugh. Really, just laugh it off.

One of my favourite movies, "Michael" (about the angel) with John Travolta had a great line: "You've got to learn to laugh. It's the only way to true love." This is a great point. You could say that laughing could bring you closer to the one(s) you love. When you think about true love, you could think of how true love has laughter in it! Wouldn't it? Well then yes, you'd have to learn to laugh to find TRUE love.

Strangling Yourself

We get so caught up in our own stuff

We really do! These days we become so concerned with every little thing that happens around us. Whatever happened to that saying, "the world doesn't revolve around you?" Even though we become all consumed with every minute detail in our lives, we really do operate like we are the drama centers of the universe, and that is crazy! Everyone knows the universe revolves around the kids on Jersey Shore (okay low blow). Although what frequently happens in our relationships, or at the start of the relationship anyway, is that we tend to panic and fret before it really gets under way. If you can remember, you probably sound similar to the people on that show when you are whining, moaning, and groaning around the circumstances of your life/partner. Well I'd like you to take a moment and see just how nuts that is. Picture how much more peace and stability you'd have in your life if you could let go of strangling yourself in those moments. Just breathe naturally. Breathing sounds so simple, but it is an important action to take when we feel things aren't going our way.

You might be thinking, I breathe all the time! Well sure we all breathe, but we don't do it intentionally. Intentional breathing is something different. This is when you stop everything you are doing, you can be sitting or standing, keep your eyes open or closed, and you take deep, slow breaths. 3-5 are ideal.

Golden Nugget

Focusing on nothing but your breath is a powerful way to slow your world down, and gain a handle on a situation.

It's a great way to prevent yourself from getting stressed and overwhelmed with emotions, and thoughts that run through our overactive brains. With this, you can calmly gather the facts about what is really happening around you, instead of what you think is happening, or what you think they are thinking, doing, saying, or feeling.

If you have panic attacks, stop and breathe. If you stress out, stop and breathe. If you worry and fret and struggle, stop and breathe. I don't mind saying this again. This is a process. What prevents us from enjoying this process is our emotional state and thoughts that get in the way. Some of you have been struggling with this for years and a lot of it is based on your thoughts and emotions. Some of you have been wanting (or secretly wanting) the right partner for five, ten years or more. I hope you pick up this book if you've been struggling with this for more than 10 years. If you know someone who has been struggling for that long, please give them a copy of this book as soon as possible.

I'm not a health guru or a health practitioner, but I know a thing or two about health and how to be healthy. I also know that being healthy is attractive! You want to be attractive don't you? Of course, there's nothing wrong with feeling good in your own skin. There is especially nothing wrong with looking it too. If you are strangling yourself, mentally or emotionally, often times you end up strangling your partner as well, and that won't go very well.

Make Tweaks Along the Way

I get to make adjustments? YAY!

That's right - You *get to make adjustments*. It's an opportunity. Things might not go smoothly, or perfectly for all of you. You may need to make adjustments along the way. This is why some people choose to work with me. You might not do everything naturally, we aren't robots after all.

What do you need to adjust? I don't know since I can't see you, or hear how you are going about things. Ideally, you may have seen the adjustments you need to make already through reading this book. If that's the case, then great! If you have received some inklings of what you could take on or do differently, then go with it. Our intuition is usually right, if only we can trust it. As I said before, trust your gut and your feelings.

There is no, 'be all end all' fix. It is different for everyone. For some of you, you may need to be more forward, courageous, or brave (remember, you can be anything you want.) What are the actions that go along with that? Make a note for yourself so as to remember and recall it often. Some of you may need to take a step back... relax, unwind, lower your guard. Your walls may need to come down. You may have to let people in. Some of you may need to stop yourself from thinking, 'it'll never work' or 'I've tried everything already. It's just not happening.' You might have to shift a combination of your thoughts, your way of being, and your actions. They will all have to come together full circle, in time. Not to worry, when you start with the 'being-ness', the thoughts, and actions will come. As the saying goes, 'Be, Do, Have.'

Remember to still have fun with it! This isn't your work life, this is not your career or family life. This is your love life. It is supposed to be fun. You don't want it to become a chore, so make some simple, small, fun adjustments.

What you put in, you will get out

How much are you investing?

Like anything in life, what work you put in, will determine the kind of result you get. You might want to think of finding a great partner as if you were investing money. The more you put into the investment, the greater the potential for reward. The more risk you take, the greater the potential return.

You can put in a little, practice a little, and this will move forward a little. Over time, this will progress somewhat. It's also possible that you will make a small change and see huge results! Sometimes that is the case with people. It can be surprising. The one little thing someone wasn't doing or could have been doing differently makes all the difference in finding that person they've been waiting for. Sometimes they're right under your nose, lying in wait for you to come around.

However, most of the time, there is some more work involved. Don't worry, you are doing part of the work by reading this book. The other work you are doing is the exercises-the times where I give you a moment to visualize something, or the notes I ask you to make in your book.

Golden Nugget

Getting out of your comfort zone is required.

That is the work you must do. Remember, how much you invest means how much of a greater return you will likely receive. The other work you need to be doing is actively putting this to use in your life. In your day to day life, what will give you the most benefit is to remember these conversations we're having and notice how they play out in your life. Notice them in the people you meet and the way you feel and think about them.

You made an investment by buying this book. That was the first step. It was a big step, good for you! Check in with yourself on your participation level. How much are you putting in? Now go full steam ahead. No fear in this area is necessary. There are so many people out there who are well qualified partners for you. It won't matter if one or two relationships don't go the way you want them to. Think about this in terms of the previous section too. An adjustment you could make is to simply start to apply these things in your everyday life. Watch what happens!

Taking it easy

What do you do to unwind?

If the last section made you tense or antsy this section is for you. If you had thoughts like, "What do you mean go full steam ahead? I can't do that!" This section is especially for you. In general, quieting your mind and relaxing yourself will aid you in many ways. You might find shutting off your mind to be a good idea. Our mind tends to get in the way of our momentum or our path. You have doubts, fears, concerns and they are not in short supply. This especially happens when you try to figure out when someone is right for you or if they like you as much as you like them. There are many ways to relax and unwind, but you must have some. Take a moment and write down your methods of relaxation. For me, it's meditating, reading a book, going for a run or walk, talking it out with a friend, or watching a good movie. Meditation is very good for you. You probably know this already, and if not there any many blogs, studies, articles, and websites that will talk to the benefits of meditation. The main one is it relaxes your body and quiets your mind. Many people view it as 'weird' or difficult, like some arduous process to understand. But it really is simple. Sitting in silence for 10 minutes is a great place to start. You don't have to say, "omm" or touch your fingers together. I will leave you to have your own discoveries with this.

One of my favourite things to do to quiet the questions and concerns is to talk to a trusted friend. Now, if you ask your friends, I am sure some of them will tell you that occasionally, you drive them crazy, especially if you call the same one or two and complain. What works really well for me (and for them) is that I go to different people. Also, I only speak to people who will understand, be compassionate, and understanding and always offer advice that is constructive. I don't recommend calling anyone that will tell you to simply, "Get over it" or "Go find another one." That isn't helpful. We need a little bit more than simply that. I also speak to people who have some education or distinctions in a form of self-development, teaching, healing etc. Talking things through is a really great way to relax yourself and let your concerns go. It's all too easy for us to let our mind run with all kinds of assumptions and conclusions that aren't necessarily real about the people we meet, such as, "He doesn't like me," and, "She isn't going to call" are things we easily make up without even trying.

You have to have an outlet to outflow the 'stuff' that gets in your mind and heart. You will drive yourself crazy if you don't, so you must allow yourself to truly relax, with whatever methods those are for you. (Make your notes now if you haven't already.)

The thing about relaxing and being 'at ease' is that you will have less tension in your body. You will have more clarity in your mind, and less clutter in your heart which will make you all around more attractive and sexy to others. How? Well, you can see it on someone's face when they are distracted. You can feel it in their presence when they are confused. You can see it when they are agitated and jittery. What does the opposite look like? It looks like someone who is clear, healthy, free of worry and concern, someone who knows what they want and goes after it is attractive. Think of it as a strong magnet.
The other reason why you need to relax and integrate patience is that sometimes it's a "slow burn" as one of my clients put it. He eventually discovered that it is about building relationships, trust, experiences, and being comfortable with other people, so it may take time. He said, "There is no ticking clock. But don't think it can't happen, because it can." He states he had to "back myself off the ledge sometimes" meaning he had to calm his nerves, relax, and integrate

patience before racing to conclusions and assumptions. *If you are a woman and are in your late 30's or early 40's and concerned about your 'ticking clock' – I understand. Please email me right away.*

Golden Nugget

Remember, the more you enjoy the process itself, the faster and easier it will go.

There is a great quote from a wonderful book I love called, "Ask and It Is Given." I want to share with you.

"It is easier for most of you to clear your minds, having no thought, than it is for you to think pure, positive thoughts. For when you quiet your mind, you offer no thought; and when you do so, you offer no resistance; and when you have activated no resistant thought, the vibration of your being is high and fast and pure."

Definite Trouble

Avoid This Sticky Situation

You could get to a point... where you are so good at this, you have mastered the process. You have mastered being a point of attraction for love, where you attract people non-stop. Wouldn't that be a problem we'd all like to have? This is a great space to be in! Celebrate it!!! When you were younger, were you mocked? Made fun of? Were you called a number of names by others? A lot of us were. Wouldn't you like to show them? Yes! There is nothing wrong with that! It's very redeeming isn't it? Would you rather have several partners to choose from, than none? I thought so. You worked this hard to get here. So enjoy it!

Now, having too many partners can be a problem, believe it or not. Some simple things that could happen are that you could lead yourself to be confused and lose sight of your ultimate goal, which is to find *a partner.* I do recommend having fun and enjoying this stage, if you get there (it takes time and practice). But don't forget the other person. You want to be careful not to lead people on. You still have to be good to people see? You might have to manage yourselves. If you attract several partners and are dating a few of them, pretty soon you'll want to start to cut out the ones you don't want to be with. They call it 'trimming the fat.' Don't overfill your plate. Don't settle. Don't get caught up with those who are not worth your time, you don't want to be consumed by them. It can take a lot of energy to manage all the conversations, meet ups, emotional interest and progress you make.

This is the refinement part of the process, and it's important to keep refining. Keep letting go of the ones that don't work out for you, those who aren't a good fit for you. If you have a feeling, (remember your intuition) in most cases it will be true and you've got to follow your gut.

The danger in getting into this situation and staying there for longer than necessary is if you don't, your situation may stay the same, or you'll have a new problem called, 'I'm having so much fun I don't want to stop.' There is a way to be responsible about this if that's what you're choosing, so as not to offend anyone. How do you do this? You be honest and authentic with them. Hide nothing. Be open about where you are right now and what you want at this point in your life.

Maybe you need a time to have some fun and play the field. Some people do need to spend some time there. Don't make yourself wrong or feel ashamed about this. Feel no guilt. Be there. Choose to be there. If you've never had success with dating, and now you are, I recommend you let this ride for a while. As I mentioned, have fun with it. You want to get comfortable in this environment, in these new clothes so to speak if you've never been here before. Do these clothes feel good? Do they fit? Good. Enjoy them.

Learning How to Reel Them in and Revel

How can I be the ultimate magnet?

You are in the sweet spot when you are in a state of caring, but not caring that much. Remember the superpower of being unattached! Remember this is about being unattached whether it works out or not, knowing that you will be fine regardless - is the ultimate place you want to be. If in the previous section when I was saying, 'don't overwhelm yourself with too many partners" you thought, "Ummm that's exactly what I want." Then okay. No problem, enjoy! But if you picked up this book to find the right partner, then pick up the book when you are ready to come back to this part. Or pick up the book once you've had your fun. Some people have never been in that super magnetic space here and have always wanted to be there. I say enjoy it. Come back later, whenever you are ready.

How to be a super magnet involves owning who you are. That's right, owning who you are. This is confidence, but it is more than that. It involves walking into a room and if someone walks up to you immediately and has a problem with you, you just smile, totally unaffected and say "that's nice." There's no better feeling, than knowing you are untouchable, unshakable. Knowing you can do these things is part of the super magnet. Knowing who you are is a big part of it, and that is super attractive. People naturally want to know themselves. Everyone wants confidence. It is attractive. You can take this into other areas of your life if you like--business, leadership, career, etc. Its no coincidence why people in the business world who are confident succeed the most.

I was dancing with a female friend of mine one time, Danielle. We were at a bar, and the place was really moving, it was a really good time! Let me tell you, she was on fire! She was dancing like there was no one in the room, which is the only way to do it (the experts will tell you). She was having a blast, and you could tell no matter where you were in the room. It was evident in the way she moved, her facial expressions, her presence, it oozed out of her. I was amazed! Everyone in the bar was noticing her! She might not have been the most attractive girl in the bar, *and that's the thing,*

Golden Nugget

When you tap into that space, it doesn't matter if you're the most physically attractive person in the room or not, you will get noticed.

That is when you become the most attractive person in the room. You know deep down, looks are only part of being attractive. Well, we were dancing together, because we hadn't seen each other in a long time. She had had several drinks, and wasn't even dancing in a super sexy fashion. Mostly, just as I said, we were having a good time. Slowly I noticed multiple guys nearby, checking her out. Then I noticed they were standing close to us. Then they got closer. They were watching her more and more. I told her these guys are into you! They were smiling! Thankfully, they weren't the creepy type, they were just admiring her, her energy, and the vibe she was giving off which was contagious. I backed away slowly and told them to come and talk to her and they did! She was in the sweet spot. She couldn't care less if those guys approached her. She was just having fun. That caused the magnetic pull to be even stronger.

You can be this way out there in the world, every day without having to be at a bar or on a dance floor. This is what I teach my clients. It becomes a selection process for them from all of the partners available in the universe. This is where you get to choose, like at a restaurant. You sit down at table, look at the menu and make your choice. Does person #1 have what I want? Does person #1 make me feel good? Do I like person #1 or #2 more? In the end, you listen to yourself. In the end you listen to your heart. I can't tell you who is best for you. Only you will know, and only you can make that choice.

Typically after about four to eight weeks of working together my clients begin to experience this phenomenon. Some clients however have more to uncover and let go of before we get there to this near perfect magnetic state.

AND THIS IS SUCH A FUN state to be in! I mentioned in the introduction that when you are excited by your love life, you tend to share it with everyone. Women notice when other women are 'glowing' and they instinctively ask 'who is he?'

It's in these moments you feel you have nothing in your way. Everyday feels like Saturday. You feel as though you could have a terrible day where your boss drops five new assignments on your head, and you wouldn't mind (that much) and for some of you that has happened before when you're in love. Don't things just roll off your back?

Here is the key to this entire book:

Here is a secret I will share with you that I have learned. Getting what you want is the most fun you can have in life. Why do we do the things we do? We are looking for happiness. We are emotional beings. We are always looking for our next achievement, our next success, which brings us what? Happiness. Isn't everything we do in the name of happiness? Of feeling good? Yes, it is. Why do you go to the movies? Why do you go to parties? Why do you go to the gym? Why do you travel? Why do you go to the amusement park? To have fun, to feel joy… to feel good. It is your birthright. If at any point you aren't having fun, remember, "Why else am I doing this?"

5
THE OTHER PERSON

Getting to know them

Who is this really about?

Don't get me wrong, this book all about you, however this chapter is not. This chapter is all about them. We should spend a little time on them, no? They are the one you are seeking after all. Whoever they are, they are out there. And finding them is the reason you picked up this book.

The previous chapters were about you, and the build up to the person you are seeking. If we were to stretch this book out over a few months (usually how much time I need with a client) then you would go through this process at the same pace as you are reading the activities that are happening around you. However, you might read this book in a few days, or a few weeks. You take the time you need to get the full value out of the exercises and information in this book. You can go back and reread sections that are relevant to the situation you find yourself in to get coaching and tips on the best way forward.

In this chapter we will discover everything we can about them. We will identify all the things we need to know, in the early stages anyway – it changes further down the road. In the chapter on values and commitment, I will give you all kinds of insights that you need to ensure you are working towards the right person. Remember the filtration process, the distilling methods we talked about earlier? Keep this in mind throughout this chapter, since you will be selecting the best person or persons for you, to advance to the next stages.

When my clients start the dating process after they've done some internal work themselves, they often have to choose wisely whom to move forward with. As we have mentioned, this is fun and also necessary for things to advance. Consider it a tournament, like in sports where only the best move is forward and further away from the rest. Your time is valuable, your love is precious, your energy is yours, and it's your choice who you want to spend it with. So this chapter will all be about getting to know that other person, what is great about them, what makes them who they are, and what are they committed to..

With these questions you will be getting to the essence of them. You will be going deeper into who they are, which is a very good thing. Since most of us wear masks or put up a 'front' to look good (the majority of the world is trying to 'look good' every second of our lives, the sooner we can all admit it and let go of that need, the better we'll all be). First impressions are great, and looking good feels good, of course.

Golden Nugget

However, there are deeper levels to our humanity, to our being, that is who we are at our core. We have to be careful to see more than just meets the eye.

Your questions will give you sneak peeks into who that person is, at their core. This is so you know who you are really dealing with, and who you will really end up with, should you enter a relationship with them.

We've all had experiences where we began dating someone, and then a few months later we're wondering, "Who is this person? Is this really the person that I fell in love with?" All of our work here is to completely avoid that ever happening.

Being Interested

Why do I need to be interested?

If you're thinking, "Hey this is about the other person, why do I need to be interested? Aren't they supposed to be interested me?" The answer is no. Flat out, no. You have to BE interested, before you can be interesting. There is a saying that goes, "If you're bored it's because you are boring." That's pretty darn accurate. You can always find something to do, something to occupy your time and energy. There is no reason for you to be bored for longer than you choose to. So I say, "If you aren't interested, it's because you aren't being interested." "Interested' is a way of being. You can be anything, at any moment you want, remember? So let us explore being interested. For the purposes of this inquiry, I don't mean interested in someone, as in the romantic sense. Not yet. What I mean is reflected well in the definition:

Interested: adjective
Having an interest in something; concerned
Having the attention or curiosity engaged
Characterized by a feeling of interest

I share this with you first, because everything else we do inside this chapter will be around this. Be curious and interested in who they are. Not only is it the key to finding out more about person but by being inquisitive, people will feel good, they will feel special. People love to feel good and feel admired. When people like to talk about themselves, this is a natural occurrence. Let's face it, we are happy to talk about ourselves and we love to have the spotlight on us. This is a key to get better related with someone you already know you like, to have them feel good, and you want them to feel good! If they feel good then they'll remember they felt good with you and that will be one thing to lead them to want to see you again. This isn't about playing games, or playing. I am just explaining what works and what has been going on in your life already, and showing it to you.

But what does it look like to be interested? To be engaged? You know what it looks like. Think about it now in your mind. See it for yourself. What did you come up with? Take out that ol' pad, dust it off, and write out what it looks like to you to be interested. What are the bodily actions? What are the movements? How does it look to you? Go ahead.

Good, now your job is to play the part, and play it for real! Not for jokes, not for nothing, but because it will serve you in two ways. You want to see them doing it, when you're talking to them, and when you want to display interest in them.

Again, you are likely doing this already, you just aren't aware of it. I'm bringing it to your awareness so you can use it any way you wish.

Lastly, and this is very important, when you are interested in them, you will learn all the things you need to make a good decision about where and whether to move forward with that person. Then it is a matter of looking at what you want, looking at your needs/wants, your deal breakers, and how you feel about them. Trust yourself. Do they match up? Remember in the other chapter……

How to have a date be great

Dates are like an interview. But more fun

Going on dates is such a great thing! They are like a job interview, but way more fun! You get to meet a potentially attractive person, spend time getting to know them, have a great time doing a variety of things, sometimes there's food involved, sometimes games, you can expect to be intrigued, and maybe even fascinated. You'll find likes and dislikes, similarities and differences, and maybe even get some action!

Notice my context about this? This is my opinion, my perspective, but also my context, and you have one too, about everything in life. We all do, its human nature to make assessments, judgments and evaluations. We do this to form our context. It is the way we see the world, or the area we are looking at. Your context is very powerful! It is very important to know what your context is, it is a way of living life. Remember the glass half full, half empty? Well that is a context through which we view life. It is how you see things. How you believe, and feel about them. So notice my context for dating above. What is your context? Take a moment to reflect and take notes. As yourself how you feel about dating? What do you like/dislike?

If you need to, create a new context so that you can feel excited and empowered about the dates you go on. You'll want to do this since you walk into the date with that context subconsciously before the date event starts. So you might want to bring one in that makes you feel good. Go ahead...

A date is the time to be your best. As we discussed in the first chapter, the best is all about being yourself. **On your dates, you don't have to be anything but authentic.**

Golden Nugget

Be yourself so that you aren't lying to yourself or your date.

Be yourself so that you don't feel the need or pressure to be anything else now or in the future. Be yourself so that you have nothing to hide. Be yourself so that you can feel good about yourself. Be yourself so that you can love yourself. Be yourself so that you honour yourself.

There are basic rules for everyone when on a date. And they are mostly guidelines since, as I will cover very shortly, the rules can be bent.
1) Don't come across as desperate or needy – be unattached
2) Don't be too pushy or aggressive – no demanding or overly suggestive remarks
3) Open up and talk about things you might normally hesitate to talk about – Not the sexual partners you've had, but sex is okay.
4) Give a few small physical cues here and there to your partner – gentle, arm, hand touch when appropriate.
5) Leave something to the imagination – don't give it all away.
6) Go with the flow – be easy going and don't have an agenda.

I was going on a few dates with a girl named Jasmine, except I wasn't sure if they were dates. I know this might sound funny but we met at a Christmas party and had good conversation, found each other on Facebook but didn't talk for a few months. In February we connected and arranged to meet up in March. But it felt more of a networking connection than a date. My mind wanted to confirm what it was but I instantly threw that concern out. We went out for a coffee, and it was a great time! We laughed a lot and connected on a plethora of mutual interests and topics. We hugged at the end and I said to myself, 'What a great fun time!' (Notice I was unattached to the outcome.)

The next morning she texted me and connected me to a TV appearance opportunity. I went for it and was immediately looking forward to finding out if I would be on the show. I called Jasmine back and thanked her for the connection and offering me the chance. I also thought in common courtesy, I would thank her via taking her out to her favourite restaurant – any of her choice – if I would in fact be invited on the show. We laughed and agreed. Well, I got word I'd be on the show! Thankful and excited about seeing what conversation we would come up with this time, we made plans. We had our dinner together, and had another great date. But was it a date? The same thing occurred; great conversation, plenty of laughs, and obvious electricity. *(Key signs to a great date and potential partner!)* And yet I didn't know if it was a date?

We stayed in contact and had a few great phone calls over the span of a few weeks. I internally battled with, 'Is this a date? Is she into me? Am I into her?' Well it was obvious I was, since I was having these conversations with myself (that's one way to know). But I wanted her to know. I wanted to make it formal at this point.

I was clearing my thoughts with a friend and said, "I now wanted to ask her on an 'official' date." My friend then urged me to take action and make it an official date by Thursday. I agreed. It was Tuesday. She called a few hours after my conversation with my friend and said she was under doctor's orders to refrain from any overly exciting/stressful physical activity for a few months. I made a joke, *"So I guess you're not allowed to have sex then eh?"* We both had a great laugh! I then followed up with, "Are you allowed to go on a date?" (Pretty clever I know.) We laughed again and made plans. The universe works in mysterious ways.

What's even more interesting is prior to the day we were going to go out, we decided to go somewhere like a park (in Toronto, Canada where I live, people like to get out as much as possible, since our summers are so short). Throughout the day of the date I was thinking, 'It's already been 2 dates – I'd like to just stay in a quiet place, where the house is empty and cozy and get to know each other in a quieter setting.' A few hours later she texted me saying, "Well Michael, its official. We will not be engaging in any outdoor activities. It's freezing outside! I'm just going to be real with you. I kind of wish we were further along this dating thing so we could just curl up on my couch and drink hot beverages." Again, the universe works in mysterious ways. Take a look at the law of attraction at work here people. She read my mind! Or did she? Look at what my thought was earlier. Look at what I was vibrating! Fun! I was thinking the same and was blown away by the synchronicity, always a good sign of a great fitting partner for you.

If you're wondering what we did, yes we did just that and had a great time. We made a deeper connection and I discovered things about her that I really liked that I just might not have had the chance to any other day/date. I was truly enthralled by who she is after that moment. Her honesty and authenticity gave me a true demonstration of who she is and who she can be. Instantly after that message, my interest and curiosity in her grew five-fold.

Different questions, to bring you to the same result

Why are questions so important?

Knowing what questions to ask the people you meet is key. Below is a list you might want to write down in your notebook. (Include later) Now I'm not suggesting you pull out your notebook on the date, and start to ask these questions, of course not! But write them down so you can look at them from time to time - we study for tests because we want to do well on the test. We prepare and spend time on outfits, hair and looking good for a date, because we want to feel good, make a good impression, and impress them. *Well there's one important piece that is so pivotal for the dates you go on, and yet we don't prepare for it.*

Golden Nugget

CONVERSATION.

Great conversation happens through a flow. That flow is enhanced and greatly benefitted by asking questions. Most importantly, a great question asked at the right time can make all the difference in a date.

Questions create openings, exciting discussions, fun, laughter, and all around good feelings. What do you ask about? Talk about each other than the news, television, the drama in the world, the everyday blah's ... Talking about those things are fine in an early state, however, if the conversation gears more towards the two of you as individuals, there will be a greater connection - which obviously demonstrates romantic interest in each other. If this is going to work, there has to be interest. Interest creates intrigue, intrigue creates fascination, fascination creates depth, depth creates connection, connection creates love, love creates commitment.

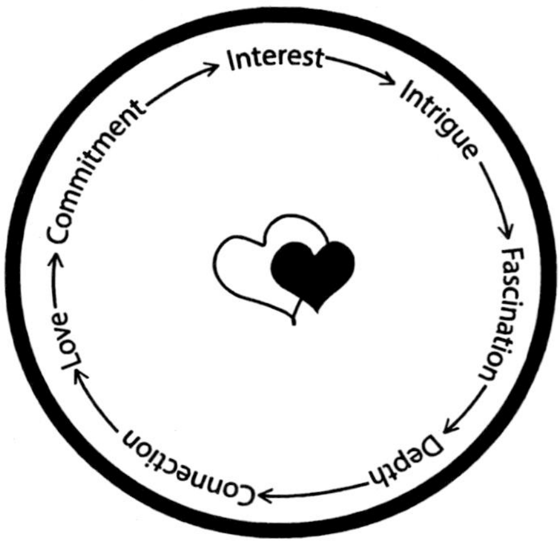

Commitment is a longer term concept. However, commitment also creates a relationship. We'll talk about commitment later.

Questions create flow in a conversation that take on a life of their own, in a sense. Once you practice this you will become more adept at it. Remember, questions create openings. Questions will have you stop talking (which is very important) and start listening (which is extremely important!). We are humans, and humans don't know what we don't know, which is why we like to learn and know more. You want to know more about this person. You want to find out more, as much as you can, without pressuring or interrogating. This might take some time to develop for some of you and that's okay. The point is to ask them questions here and there, sparingly. Not all at once. Otherwise you will scare them away and ruin your chances of developing a relationship with them. Oh, and if all else fails and they notice or get weird, ask, "Wow you sure are asking a lot of questions." Be authentic, laugh it off, and blame it on me. Tell them 'I'm reading this book and this guy says to ask these questions.'

Here's a list of great questions you can ask your potential partner. These can be a little bit intimidating if you aren't secure/comfortable with asking them, the same as if they aren't secure or comfortable with answering them. Don't let this or that bother you. These are deeper questions because you are trying to get deeper, and that is the whole point.

What are your commitments? (Ought to be interpreted as what are you involved in, what do you do these days? It has them examine their lives and truly look, if they haven't.)
What are you committed to? (What matters to you, what do you put your focus on. It could be 'loving others, loving myself, my family, my kids, my career.')
What goals are you working towards?
What do you love to do?
Who is your daddy and what does he do? (Okay just kidding, I threw that in for fun)
What makes you tick? What gets on your nerves?
What do you look for in a partner?
What do you want out of life? (Don't ask where do you see yourself in five

years, it might come across a job interview, unless you make a joke about job interviews, then it's fine.)

Here is a basic list for those of you who have not dated in some time or are rusty. Subjects that are a basic- family, travel destinations, favourite places to go in the city. Favourite books and movies are a fun and obvious conversation starter.

Treat everyone with Respect

What did your mother tell you?

All of my relationships have ended with integrity. This is not an easy thing to accomplish, and it takes work, but I have done it. Over my life, the odd one has been filled with drama and I have learned how to manage myself, the emotions and the conversations that come up inside of them. But after this drama, I have always worked to ensure things end peacefully, with both sides complete and content with the separation. I respect all of my partners and everyone I have dated. It has brought me much peace in my life, success and love. Some of my previous partners have gone on to be great friends. Sometimes we fall out of touch over time, sometimes all I get is a text message on my birthday. I respect each of them for how they have contributed to my life, what we experienced together, and where they are now. I declare that all of this has happened because I am mature and I respected them then and to this day. An aspect of how a relationship ends is a demonstration of maturity.

Why is respect important? Simply put, we are all equal. There is no one who is better or worse than you. We are all the same. You've heard this before and this is nothing new. Yet I share this with you because we all need reminders every once in a while. This is not just a reminder, but a recommendation for you to immediately incorporate notion into your life. You attitude will come across during your dates and your partner will understand who you are in this area whether you share it or not. It will come across in your communication and way of being.

Overall this is how they will remember you. This is how they will reflect on you in the future. You never know what will happen in the future, since your future is still unwritten. Anything can happen. Chances are, you've probably had an experience in your life when someone from your past has come back into your present. You can count on this in your relationships. They will come back in some way or another, as a friend, a lover, a fling, a date, gathering, or connection. You never know. Remember my story of Karla and Katherine. With one of them, I've gone on to receive recommendations and opportunities from them both.

Respect them before, during and after. Speak only well of them. I know this is hard, but do your best. If you have to say negative things to someone, the best thing to do is to say them only to a friend that you trust, and never, never say negative things in writing. Don't trash talk. Don't gossip. If you are, stop it now.

In a course I took not that long ago, gossip was defined as 'damaging the listening of another' meaning, how someone perceives or listens to the other person. Say nothing that might damage the way that person listens to or perceives them.

This is wise. You never know how or when it will come back to you. But it will in some way.

When I was just a wee lad in Grade 5 I was in love with a girl named Lisa. She was super cute, pure hearted, confident and delicate like a flower. We were BF/GF back then until Grade 6. We saw each other from time to time and it was exciting every time we met over that summer. I remember being very excited to see her on the first day of school in Grade 6. I vividly recall what she was wearing: Black t shirt and blue overalls with shorts. I know we were both excited when we caught first glance of each other and for a few moments after, the smiles never left our faces. That first day of school was a great one. Then by the second day we did the usual, "Hey how was your summer?" with our friends and shortly after my best friend at the time, Grant came to me and said, "I just talked to Lisa and she said if you don't take her out soon she's going to dump you." I was shocked! I really cared about her, more than other girls and could not believe she would say that. I was hurt, and bewildered. I reacted strongly thinking, 'if she feels that way then why be together?' And as a naïve young boy, I said to myself, 'It's better if I dump her than she dumps me.' I told my friend to go and tell her it's over (remember the early days when you communicated with your girl/boyfriend through friends?).

Turns out my friend was a liar and made it all up. Ouch. In hindsight, breaking up with her probably crushed her. We weren't close and didn't talk much throughout school. But for many years throughout the rest of elementary school and high school, we stayed friends and had the same circles of friends. I still thought about her and cared about her in a deeply hidden and introspective way. I always wondered what would have happened. For years throughout high school, I experienced a lot of grief and regret around her and what happened. She grew into a young woman, and became very sexy.
Well time teaches you things, and time does heal all wounds. But sometimes they leave a scar, and I definitely had a scar, but at some point I stood inside of the fact that we would get to be together and we would share a relationship together again.

In my early 20's we found each other again. I have no doubt in my mind that I fully attracted that with the law of attraction, which wasn't even common knowledge from "The Secret" yet. But I had let go first. Each time our paths crossed in our teen years and early 20's I had to deal with her becoming prettier and prettier each year. I had to let go, and do my best to be what I was learning was the power of being unattached. There was always something between us, this link. That smile. That cute, cute smile. It never went away. All the while I saw that generous and beautiful heart.

We finally got together and reconnected. She called me up way out of the blue, and we went on a few dates and started going steady. It was beyond an exquisite experience. Imagine 12 years of build up in imagining, fantasizing and pondering what it might be like to be with this person again, to be with someone you've secretly loved for 12 years. Growing in every way possible as a human, as a teenager, into your 20's, knowing love, knowing sex, wanting and wondering what they are up to, what they are doing and who they are now.

It felt like coming home in ways that words can't describe. The intimacy we shared those first few times was, well..... wow. I appreciated every ounce of her body and touch. However, after two months it became obvious that we were different people now than 12 years ago and different from each other, too different. It became obvious we had to go our separate ways... she chose to do it by not returning my calls at first. This was very crushing after a while. I was so emotionally hurt that I felt ill. It was a Friday when I got the picture, and she finally called me and told me that evening. I was sick on Saturday. I went to work and felt like garbage. People asked if I had the flu or the stomach bug. It affected me that much. But it made me stronger. Every relationship always does.

Honoring them

What is honour really?

That is why you need to honour the people you are with. The point of telling you that whole story is at the end of everything, I honoured her. I honoured our time together and I honoured our experience. I understood that I really needed to experience that whole thing. That experience was something I so deeply wanted to have. I could be nothing but grateful and appreciative of it finally taking place. Maybe she needed it too. Maybe it was 'supposed to' happen that way. Maybe she needed to have the satisfaction of leaving me, I don't know (although I don't think so since she didn't do it rudely or abruptly like I did to her). I had to honour her for that as well. She could have left me any way she wanted. If you think about it, she had every right to denounce me publicly, or leave me with more questions than answers. Right after we broke up, she went back to her ex-boyfriend, and then was married to him a few years later. I respect that decision.

Like everyone in your life, they are there for a reason. They serve a purpose. They come into your life at this moment to teach you something, to bring you something. They do something for you in your life. You must understand, everyone comes into your life for a reason and you may not always know that reason right away. Since life is a journey, it might as well be an adventure. On any adventure, you have people that offer you different things and teach you different lessons.

If you look in on your life you will see the people who are in it and what they do for you. Make a list right now, of the major people in your life, and what each of them gives you. List family, good friends, co-workers, those that you have ongoing relationships with and what they give you. Then list previous and current lovers and what you gained from each of them (the last three to five is a good place to start). This isn't about material gains by the way. This is about feelings, thoughts, cognitions and beliefs. Some things you might have received from them are knowing you am sexy, knowing peace, learning how to adapt, learning how to persevere, or the value of communication, the importance of good intentions, maybe even how to dress well.

This will help you honour them.

Always honour yourself

You're # 1

Honouring yourself means living your truth, being who you are. It also means living your life with integrity, doing what you say you will do, and cleaning up any messes when you don't. Honouring yourself means loving yourself, for who you are AND who you aren't. It means giving up trying to be perfect for someone else, for the person you like, even the person you are married to.

Honouring yourself is trusting you gut and intuition and acting on it. Honouring yourself means staying true to your values. Staying true to what you know is right, internally. It also means never going against those values, not for anything, or anyone no matter how much you like them, no matter how much you want them to like you. This means, don't do something you know you shouldn't do.

You might be saying, "Well gee, that is obvious." But it isn't actually. We do make mistakes. We do things we know we should not do. Some of us do it all the time.

That can lead to a life of misery, unhappiness, and confusion.
It's a bold statement to say "never betray your values." We are human, and part of being human means making mistakes. Mistakes are inevitable and no matter how hard we try, they are unavoidable, since we aren't perfect. Not a single one of us (remember)? But you can repair the damage if you do. Restore your integrity with yourself. Restore your integrity, your word, your bond, with others.

Golden Nugget

Restore your love for yourself.

Restore your self-respect. Forgive yourself. That's all there is to do.

This is another hidden key to being attractive. If you are in love with yourself, not in a selfish way, but in a integrated way, others will be attracted to you. Why? Because this is something every being wants. Deep down, there is a desire to be whole and complete. So when one being meets or sees a being who is, there is a natural pull to want that being in its life. Integrity = being whole and complete. A construction beam is in full integrity when it is whole, complete, unobstructed, and without dents. The same goes for the hull of a ship. Another way of saying this is 'needing no repair.' The other person wants to be with someone who is in no need of repair. The drama queens, the people with "issues" as you might call them, are people that you naturally stay away from.

Exercise: List here where you haven't forgiven yourself for something you did or didn't do, where you are still incomplete. Become present to it. How do you know what it is? Because it comes up for you and you feel it. Forgive yourself and you will have the peace to move forward and be a happier person and better partner.

But what about me?

The more it isn't about you, the better

Most of my own personal success in finding a great partner came because I forgot about me. I wasn't interested in me. I didn't pay attention to me. I paid attention the other person. I sort of disappeared. I had no concerns about my own satisfaction. I was satisfied just being with another person and learning about them, and later on, learning to love them. I can tell you that this makes the other person feel wonderful. Since mostly we are so caught up in our own lives and our own needs which we are looking to have satisfied, it went a long way for my partners to feel so paid attention to.

It's like when your boss or a co-worker or someone random in your life, out of the blue appreciates you. They thank you genuinely, they give you a large amount of recognition and love. Sometimes you become blown away, and react as if, "Wow really?" You are amazed. You are happy. You feel good. You are thankful. Sometimes you're so taken aback you hang out with your mouth open and forget to say thank you. If you haven't experienced that before, I hope you do. If you haven't, do it for someone else. Wouldn't you like to give another person that feeling? Do it. That's your homework. It may take a little practice, but you have to let go of your concerns and needs. Trust that your needs will be taken care of by assisting others.

How do you do this? Give up your needs, if just for five minutes or two hours. Not permanently, since it's important to take care of yourself. But really let go and disappear yourself in the span of spending time with the other person. Bring the curiosity we talked about earlier. Bring a sense of wonder to your new date. Again, you don't know what you don't know. So let it go. You will be taken care of. If you think about it, this is a marvelous idea and phenomenon for your life. Take care of others and your will be taken care of. Simple and easy, I know.

But it's just something you're just going to have to trust me on. By showing interest in them, they will show interest in you. You will care for them, and they will care for you. You will care for each other and grow together. That will come in time.

Other people's energy

How do you read someone else's energy?

As I mentioned earlier, everything is energy. However, men and women both have their own unique energy as well. They are separate, and yet part of a whole. It is like the brain. The brain is made of two halves, left and right. The left brain operates in logic and pragmatic thinking. The right brain is creative, and expressive. Both are part of the whole. It is good to understand this, since this is who we are and how we operate as human beings. In a good relationship, each partner understands the balance of energy and dynamics and plays off one another. Healthy couples HAVE POLARITY. Polarity is a good thing. A good couple has balance. It is neither better nor worse. Both people are equal, and you should know that both energies are very strong when coupled together!

Males are typically left brained and have a lot of male energy, naturally. Females typically have a lot of female energy, naturally. You'd be surprised to know however that these days, 90% of the population of our world is left brained thinkers, which means we have an abundance of masculine energy in today's world.

Male energy = direct, logical, focused, determined, linear, analytical. When this is taken to the extreme, a person is closed off, has a limited view, and is usually constricted/narrow. Female energy = creative, artistic, and moves in curves. It's about expression, it is unpredictable and random. It views life in possibilities. If this energy is overdone, it can be out of control, jumbled, and is common to mood swings, and disorganization. Remember, both are parts of the whole. In summary, male energy looks at the parts, and female energy looks at the whole. Both are necessary in human beings, and one could not live without the other, like Yin & Yang. There is a brilliant web series on Youtube you can find called "Spirit Science" of which I am a huge fan, which discusses this in depth.

You can read people's energy, and what kind of energy they more or less possess, just by talking to them. Knowing what you know now after reading this, you can recall the people in your life of whom you have had relationships with. Ask yourself, did they have a high amount of male energy? Were they too rigid for you? Did they have an abundance of female energy? Did their 'wishy washy' behaviour get on your nerves? How about yourself? Give yourself a breakdown, a percentage, out of 100%. How much male energy do you have? How much female energy? Both sexes have some of both. Also, men can have a feminine essence and females can have a masculine essence. Males should not be afraid of admitting they have feminine energy (take metrosexuals for example) and female's should not hesitate to admit they have Male energy. No one is ever 100% and 0%.

Golden Nugget

Every emotion, every feeling has energy. Energy has mass.

Remember as I said earlier, we are emotional beings. We give off energy and emotion. By reading other peoples energy, you can understand where your potential partner is at. You will sense how your partner is feeling, and what they might be thinking. By reading/feeling their energy and understanding their body language, you can get a really good sense of whether or not they are interested in you, intrigued by you, repulsed by you and/or falling in love with you. With this understanding, you could adjust your behaviour accordingly. This will allow you to gain mastery and practice in finding the right person for you. You won't have to waste your time and energy, and you'll be able to get closer and closer to finding a great match for yourself.

If this sounds wild and 'woo woo' to you, don't worry. Have you ever felt like, "I knew that was going to happen!" or "I knew you would say that!" Yes, well, it's not just coincidence. Just keep this in mind when you are on your dates, and when developing a relationship with someone.

Acknowledgement

Something so simple and easy to do

Okay back to them. Do you like someone? Want them to like you? Want to make a great impression? If they are a real catch, you might have some competition. Regardless of who they are, you might have competition. It's a big world out there and if you're dating, there's a good chance they are too. Here's one way to stand out. Acknowledge them. What? That's right. Acknowledge them. You can do this a variety of ways. It's a simple compliment yes, but it's also much more than that. You are discovering something special about them, something special that they might have done differently. You go deeper. This is important, since this goes below just the surface level. What I'm talking about is many levels deeper than your average compliment. This makes a huge impact on the person you are giving the compliment to. Why? Because you aren't acknowledging something outside of them, like their car, apartment or their clothes.

Here's a couple of examples: "I finally quit my job and decided to change careers." Your response could sound something like, "Wow, that's incredible! That must have taken a lot of courage." Or, "I can't imagine how many people stay in the same career their whole lives or stay in jobs just because of habit or being scared to do something else. You must be a very strong person." What might the other person think? What would you think if you were on the receiving end of this? "Wow. Yeah. You're right. Thank you. I never saw it like that before." Or "No one's ever pointed that out to me."

On the other side, here is an example of acknowledgement going too far, (which might leave the other person a little freaked out and concerned: "I finally quit my job and decided to change careers." You respond, "Wow. You are amazing! You are just so amazing! I can't believe how amazing you are! Who does that? You must be a brave soul." What would they think? "Umm... yeah. I guess so. I don't know about brave but, yeah..." See the difference?

It might seem small but this is powerful stuff! You are acknowledging who they are, and better yet, who they have chosen to be. This impacts them internally, on a deep level more than any surface kind of compliment like, "you look nice." This type of compliment is still important, we all like to look good, and put time and effort into looking good, so don't stop doing that. But to do something different, and occur to your potential partner as different, this is a great place to do it. There is one condition to this. In order for this to land properly, you must be genuine in your giving of this compliment. It must come from your truth. My example is just one kind of compliment you could offer someone. If you are really interested in taking this on and making a good impression on your partner, then it's got to be genuine. It doesn't matter if it doesn't come out sounding 100% right. What will come across is your emotion and your authenticity. This is especially true if it is something that you can tell might be a difficult situation for them. It will come across 1000x more to touch them in their core. Why? Because there is enough distrust, hesitancy and negativity out there in the world. You as their partner are someone who can be a shining light for them. That is what a partner is supposed to do. So whether they know it or not, you are showing them who you will be. You are already telling yourself who you can be for them. All you need to do is practice it and you will lead yourself to a deeper loving relationship in your future.

Acknowledgement is a funny thing. It isn't so much for the person receiving it, as it is for the person giving it. The person giving the acknowledgement is wanting to express their fondness for the other person and their realization of something important, which is why it must be heard. Hearing and receiving acknowledgement is another thing. It usually says something about a person's degree of self-worth if they can accept it or not. You are expressing yourself in that moment, and that expression should never be suppressed. This is a beautiful thing and nothing to shy away from. Acknowledgement is a form of love, a form of affection, and a sign of attraction. It feels great to receive it and if it doesn't at first, it will with practice.

Let me share something here with you. I acknowledge you, the reader. You whom I do not yet know. I acknowledge you formally here and now. Every single one of you. For picking up this book. For reading it. For coming this far. For reading this through and through and getting here. Why? Because I know it may have taken something for you to buy this. Maybe it cost you a little more than you were willing to pay. Maybe you weren't sure about its effectiveness. Maybe you doubted it and bought it anyway. Maybe you trusted your gut which told you to buy it. Maybe you really had doubts that it would work, and you bought it and read this far. Maybe you felt you had a million other things you should do or focus on, and you didn't do that. You picked it up anyway. Maybe you wanted to do something about your dating life, maybe you didn't believe you could have a great partner, or a great relationship, but you decided against listening to that everyday normal doubting voice in your head. Really, I acknowledge you, for coming this far! Many people might have passed by the website, advertisement, book shelf, where this book was. Although not everyone needed it, some of they may have. But they didn't take this book. You did. So this is for you: for being open and being committed to your life. For being committed to your future partner, your future relationship, your own future, which you may have declared, "this will be different from my past." For some of you, confronting this information is not easy. For some of you, going this far may have confronted parts of you that you never had to confront before. So officially, I am giving you love.

This will come back to you in kind. Stay committed, stay with the process, it works, I know. It has worked for me and many others. In closing this section, you can acknowledge anyone for anything. It's like a saying I heard a while ago: "Instead of fighting for dirt, find and share the gold."

This will take practice. So take a moment and think a little deeper about the people in your life currently. Think about the things they do, and why they do them. Think about what they might be going through. Think about their thought process and the things that they have come up against or might have to come up against to do the things they do. Think about the internal struggle and internal thoughts and feelings they might come up against inside their world. Your job is to practice it a few times this week. You can acknowledge family, friends, parents, anyone. Just be sure and go deep. People are usually starved for acknowledgement their whole lives. Imagine what it will feel like when you are the one to give it to them.

Rejection and Failure

What to do when it doesn't work out?

Human nature is afraid of failure and rejection is no different. Many people are terrified of rejection. That is completely understandable. We put ourselves out there and risk what feels like everything, and if it doesn't work out, we feel shunned. We feel ousted, and we feel like failures. It takes a lot of courage for some of us and to have the answer 'no' in front of our faces is a lot to bear. A lot of us decide, "It's better to avoid trying then face getting rejected."

Well guess what? That's pretty ridiculous when you think about it. That's a pretty great way to let life pass you by isn't it?
The reality is, rejection is an everyday part of life. Everyone on earth experiences it in one shape or another. It happens now and then, and trying to avoid it will limit your possibilities and opportunities in life, not improve it. Besides, it hurts more to sit on the fence, than to get off and make a choice and deal with the consequences.

When you think about it, all that rejection is, is a let down of your expectations. You expected it to work out and it didn't. You expected and wanted them to say yes, and now you feel bad. It's perfectly normal to feel bad. Feeling bad is healthy every now and again, it helps you feel good when you do feel good and appreciate it when things work out even more. Don't dwell on feeling bad. Get over it, it happened, move on.

This is more than just, 'don't take it personally' although that is simple and it helps. How do you really handle rejection? There are many ways, and here's the first:

Handling rejection is actually super simple. Ready? **It's not about you.** It's not personal, because it's not about you. Their decision has nothing to do with you. Every decision people make is usually made based on their past. This is about their brain patterns. The latest neuroscience has showed us that we mostly live on a repetitive set of brain patterns. Our decision and even emotions are running through a familiar repetitive set of brain patterns that occur again and again and again and again. These patterns have run their course so many times, that they are ingrained and we simply repeat the past a majority of the time. Even when we think we are thinking, it is usually those brain patterns running again and again. When a choice, or decision is made at an early age, we often stick to that and repeat those same conversations. So their rejection is not about you. It's usually about something that happened in their past that the brain is trying to relive. Phew, that's a relief. It may take some time to actually live this way, and incorporate this into your knowingness, but it is true and a very powerful tool to help you to let go of rejection. Just remember, it's not about you!

Hug it out – "When someone touches us, our anterior cingulate cortex—the region of the brain that registers both physical and emotional pain—releases opioids, the body's most potent painkillers," says Naomi I. Eisenberger, a UCLA doctoral student. This is a simple way to relieve the stress and anxiety that comes with rejection.

In reality, rejection doesn't define anything. The Beatles were rejected by a company called Della Recording, which no longer exists. They publicly announced, "We don't like their sound. Besides, guitar music is on the way out." Claudia Schiffer, one of the most world renowned and attractive women of the 90's, was not very popular in high school and was utterly convinced she was not attractive. Beethoven's music teacher said he was 'hopeless at composing.' George Lucas and his 'Star Wars' movie was rejected time and time again by movie studios. Rejection doesn't mean anything, it dictates nothing about who you are, and your life. Ultimately, that choice is up to you.

Failure is sometimes a symptom of having high expectations. You might need to lower them. Now I didn't say to lower your standards. It's just something to look at if you find that you are left feeling disappointed a lot. Lower your standards/ expectations. If something didn't happen the way you wanted it to, or in the timeframe you wanted, give it more time. Give yourself a break.
Avoid living in the hope that they will 'come around' or 'change their mind.' I want

you to promise me you will never believe this. This is a pipedream and a true waste of your time and energy. You think they will come around? Nope, that's it. They aren't coming back and they aren't worth the wait. The wait could be forever. And forever is a long time to waste your energy and emotion, when you could be with someone else or many other someone else's in that same amount of time that you are waiting. The sooner you move on, the better, but you have to actually move on, not just pretend to and brush it off like it was nothing. If they meant something to you, you have to acknowledge that first. Then let go (if you need to, go back to the "letting go of the past – completing your previous relationships" exercise from the 1st chapter).

Understand that everyone who comes across your path provides a learning experience. Everyone has a lesson for you to learn in life. You may have understood this before, if have haven't, think about it. Everyone provides you with something. You have to understand they came and went for a reason. You attracted them into your life so they were brought to you for something. Even if you don't see it, all of your partners are getting you closer to your goal, your ideal partner. They are all part of a process, helping you get closer and closer to the right partner for you. I have taken this view my whole life, and it has served me in respecting, and appreciating every person in my life. I treat them with gratitude and look forward to the next person in my life, and look for the gold in the people I'm always with. This helps me stay present with the people I'm with.

Getting off of Single Island

Make the JUMP!

It might be time for you to get off of single island at this point. For some of you, you will be ready now. Some of you have been ready for some time. And a few of you will need to wait until the end of the book. Either way, no matter where you are, you have to understand that this is a process, and in this process, anything can happen. This is about being involved, being a part of something. Getting out of your comfort zone, and stepping into the unknown. This is about getting off the island of being single and alone.

You must believe that anything is possible. You must believe that it is possible for you to be in a relationship. Not just any kind of relationship, but the relationship you want. FYI – here are some things you need to know:

It might not happen on the first try, the first date, or the first relationship. You might meet someone and think they are it, and they might be. On the other hand, it might not last long. You will have to understand that they have come along as a pit stop. They may be there to potentially teach you something, to give you a little boost in the relationship world. Maybe it's to grant you encouragement to move on to the next one. However, if you get caught up in it, and it isn't right, then you might stay stuck. Stuck is not where you want to be.

There is a random effect. There at things at play here that you do not - we do not understand. For example, although it may seem unrelated, did you know that there are many documented cases in the medical world, of people who have schizophrenia where one personality has cancer. It is tested and verified through medical analysis. Yet when the same physical person, becomes the other person, or other personality, upon testing for cancer, no cancer is present. This person is cancer free. We are talking about the same body, but this person registers no trace of any cancer whatsoever. How can that be possible? The same human being, with the same body and blood, when changing personalities, has a total difference in the state of health and disease within the same individual.
Anything is possible. Things will happen that you might not necessarily understand. People will come into your life, and you will wonder where they came from and that is a good thing. You will have all kinds of new occurrences and probably people from your past will come back into your life too.
Getting out there is so important. You have to get out of your shell, and get out there in the world. You've got to take on exposing yourself, and sharing yourself. I recommend saying yes as I mentioned before. Say yes to new invitations and events that you might not normally venture out on.

At this point, everything is simple. If you've been implementing what I've been teaching and been focusing on in this area of your life, you will see results. After this chapter, the hard part is basically over. For many of you, the hardest part is finding someone, or meeting people. If you've been doing the work that I've requested then Activity = Productivity = Results.

Whatever you put your attention on, you will see results. "Thoughts become things." "You will get whatever you think about, most of the time."

From a law of attraction perspective, as you have been reading this book, you have been vibrating this material. As you are reading it, you are incorporating it into your mind and your being. You have begun vibrating this desire you have to find a great partner. You have been reading the how, and the how is great to know since we are so logical. However, you don't need to worry about the how. You have been sending out the requests in the universe. If you haven't been reading this book all in one sitting, then you will have been sending out the frequency and vibration and the request has been sent over time which is a wonderful thing! The request and frequency you are sending out will be picked up by others who are looking for the same thing. Remember, everything is energy. So, as far as I am concerned, it's only a matter of time for you.

But you will have to make the jump! You will have to make it happen, to get off single island. You will have to make a choice that you might not normally make, and you will be glad for it. Sometimes it will show up when you least expect it, so you should be ready. If you want things to be different in your life, you will have to do things differently.

Here's the last tip on the other person for this chapter, and then I'll tell you a fun little story. When dating - ask yourself - do I want to see this person one more time? If yes, proceed. If no, then say no thank you. Give any constructive feedback where you can. If you are three dates in ask yourself the question - do I want this person around me?

Example: I was on a date, and after the date we went to my place to have a little wine and tea. It was only our third date so I didn't have too many expectations about what would happen, except I knew I wanted to finally kiss on this date. I realized when I went to look for the wine, and I bought it a few days earlier, I left it in the fridge. As we sat down at the kitchen table, I got two glasses and pulled the bottle out of the fridge, still sealed, and near ice cold. I poured us two glasses and then looked at the bottle. As she was talking I scanned the bottle and HOPED TO GOD it said, 'serve chilled' - it didn't. I felt a tinge of nerves and instantly broadcasted what was going on in my mind. We laughed and laughed. We made several good jokes for a good few minutes about it. "Even if it did say serve chilled," she said "this is much more than chilled!" I laughed and thought to myself she is handling this well! I knew I was too, but the point was it was date #3. And going over to someone's house for the first time can be a big step. I love how she handled the situation. Not only did she laugh at my joke, but she made her own jokes too! Which I really liked! Notice this is much different than if she would have made a stale face, a disappointed face, or if she would have criticized the wine or the taste. Worse yet, she could have just as easily said, 'silly boy, or you goof' etc. and she did none of that. Shortly after that, I knew I wanted to proceed and jump when ready. I asked myself the question, 'Do I want this person around me?' And my answer was yes. We had a great date and a great night – lots of laughs after that. When I look back at how she handled that situation, I saw that if she can be this way around this simple kind of thing, it's a great indicator of how she'll be around other similar situations. This example told me a lot about her. She likes to have fun, she likes to laugh, she can be easy going, she doesn't ridicule or become confrontational, and she maybe can enjoy herself in almost any given situation. That's the kind of person I want to be around.

6
VALUES AND COMMITMENT

What is a value?

Your Values = Your Life

This chapter, like all others, is extremely important. In this chapter, we will go deep into what makes a person the right person for you and it is all about values. You can understand someone pretty easily by looking at their values. You don't always take someone at face value when you meet them. And that's because like they say, 'Actions speak louder than words.' Before we go on, let's look at the definition of a value so that we know what we're talking about.

Value, *noun.*
1. Relative worth, merit, or importance. The value of a queen in the game of chess.
2. Liking or affection. Favourable regard.
3. Sociology. The ideals, customs, institutions, etc. of a society toward which the people of the group have an affective regard.

Ones values are of the utmost importance in relationships. They determine what you will disagree or agree on. Now of course, you aren't looking for a clone here, but

Golden Nugget

You want to have values that resonate with the person you will ultimately spend a lot of time with.

Why? This is what matters to them. What matters to you. What you live by. What you are all about. To have this kind of dialogue with someone requires maturity. This is an advanced topic I assure you, and one that the majority of the population rarely discusses. This is where you want to be though. It cuts to the chase. It gets to the point. It doesn't beat around the bush. Don't overlook values. It is completely aligned with who you are.

When I meet someone, after one or two dates or conversations, I usually get right into it. Sometimes I don't even have to bring it up, it just comes out. I met someone and within minutes of our first conversation I was completely impressed by her and blown away by her values. She didn't say, "Michael these are my values." She said she hosted an annual event all across the world, which incorporated a very popular dance, broadcasted across 30 countries and raised $250,000 for charity. What did I say after that? "Wow!" I was stunned by this human being before me. I had to get to know her more! Why? I could tell her values are creativity, self-expression, making a difference, and huge actions that lead to huge results! WOW! I had to get to know her better. I was completely enthralled with the person standing before me. My attraction and intrigue was piqued, and I moved beyond what I normally do and insisted we chat over the next few days.

Values are exactly correlated to your actions. There is no lying about them. If you value getting things done, you will value being productive or accomplishments. Conversely, you won't be found procrastinating, or delaying your actions and putting off your to do list. If your values are kindness and generosity, you would be found easily giving away your time, your energy, your love and compassion to others. You wouldn't be seen complaining about your time, the people in your life, the activities you do with others, or how much you are taken advantage of. It's that simple.

Now if you catch someone doing something that isn't in line with their values, you might instantly want to criticize, chastise and point it out to them. You don't get to do that. They are human. You are too. Everyone makes mistakes. You might find that in this book I contradict myself, but if you were the one saying "A-ha! You weren't compassionate!" or "See – I told you, you weren't a good person." Well your values would seem highly judgmental, unreasonable, and quick to react.

Values are actions are lived. They are visible and that includes you too.

So next time you meet someone great, or if you've met someone great already, go back to your wish list from chapter 2. Does it match? Where does it match? Are those still your values? Be amazed! This might be a good time to go back and choose. Is this one really important to me? Does it work for or against me?

Why are they important?

If you look at how you live…

Remember what I said in the first chapter about vibrations. Remember what I said at the beginning of this chapter regarding 'resonating values?' Well resonating values means that they as a person are aligned with you and what you are vibrating! Since you are always vibrating (and you are) and so are they, if your values resonate, you will vibrate well together. Which means it will be a fit! A good match!

The sooner you can get to know their values, the better. But remember to avoid interrogating them. Right about now you're probably wondering, "How the heck do you have a conversation about values?" You start it. You ask. You listen for it. There is a chapter coming up about communication, which is mostly about listening. If you can master some of the things I share in this chapter, you will be able to hear people's values, just by listening to them, and paying attention.

Remember values refers to what one cares for. This is all you have to pay attention to. I was on a date once where we were driving to our destination on our second date. We talked about family (a great early conversation to have). I remember I got right into it and I held nothing back. I shared about my struggles in dealing with a certain family member. I shared that I loved this person, and we would always be family, and at the same time, I decided to distance myself until they got the help they needed. It was automatically normal for me to be straightforward and honest about the situation. I was just being myself.

Later on in the date, she commented on how courageous it was of me to share myself so openly like that, with no hesitations. Like I said, for me it was nothing. For her it was me being open and authentic, which is what I value, and I consider it in line with my values. It was easy. When she asked me about it, I said, "This is who I am. If you're not interested, or if it's too much for you, I understand. Then we can part ways and prevent ourselves from wasting each other's time." This might sound rash or harsh, but I was just being honest. I prefer it this way. That way, there's no guessing whether we should spend additional time together or not. This way, we know early on, and we don't have to go deeper, and then discover later on that we aren't a good fit.

I'm happy to say, she didn't bail out after that date, or the next one, or the next one. That for me is a great thing since I liked her! If she can be with it, and doesn't run away or get all weird, then it's how I know they're the kind of person I might really want to be with.

Better yet, after I shared all that with her, we had deep, meaningful conversations and a very pleasant time together! We fostered our connection which grew stronger after that moment in the car and the conversation thereafter. **So what does that tell you?** That's where the meat is (avocado if you're a vegetarian). **It's in the values.**

You could say that one's values are the software running on a person and the person is the hardware. What do I mean? Pretend you're looking at your computer screen. You're using windows the whole time you're using your PC. But you don't feel like you're *USING* windows, or that you're *LOOKING* at windows. But, there you are, 100% of the time looking at windows running on your screen while you do everything you do on your computer.

What is important to you in a relationship?

A simple question…

While it is a simple question, it is subjective - values differ from one person to another. The point is to find a match to yours since your relationship will be about your combined values and that is what your life is already about. If you want children, they will receive and live in these values as well. It will happen by osmosis. I'm going to make some suggestions later on but you don't have to agree 100% or go with my suggestions. They are just suggestions. In the end, you have to listen to yourself, not other people. So we're going to say this one more time...

Golden Nugget

In the end you have to listen to yourself.

Answer the question, "What is important to me in a relationship?" You probably have the answer to this already which is great, but before we go ahead, take a look at it again. You must really get this correct for yourself. When I work with people, this is something we often come back to. Is it great communication? Or touching and physical contact such as cuddling? Is it frequent displays of affection? Is it creativity, or spontaneity? Is it honesty? Is it exploring, travelling, going out a lot, or staying in and being comfortable?

It is essential to get this straight and go deep. You can lie or fib, but ultimately you can't lie to yourself. What am I talking about? In your body, you have cells. There are trillions and trillions of individual cells that make up your body and what you are. These cells have individual consciousness. These cells all respond to you and your thoughts and emotions. Remember that you are in control. You are in the driver's seat of your life. Each cell in your body has individual awareness and individual consciousness. Each one is alive. They are a part of you and they are you. This might seem odd but they are also unique to themselves. They know you and they know when you are lying to yourself. For those of you who think you have tried everything, and that nothing works, this might be why. You just might be lying to yourself.

Values and Decisions

How do I know I'm choosing the right ones?

If your relationship is going to work, if it's going to be great, you must never settle in your values. For some of the people I work with, the key for them is to raise the bar. They need to raise the bar regarding the kind of person they feel they deserve to be with. You might want to hold yourself to a higher standard. Sometimes people just date whomever comes into their life and I mean anyone.

This might be the case for some of you. Never settle for less than anything amazing. When it comes to love, you must never settle. Never! Not if you're looking to be happy and in a real, long term loving relationship. If you were to settle, you'd be dooming yourself and potentially dooming your relationship. You can bet that you will have poor experiences, a feeling of emptiness and also ask yourself, "Is this the right person?" for as long as you are together.

Now, how do you know you are or aren't settling? It comes down to trusting your gut, your intuition. Everyone has it-the the inner voice that tells you what is right and what is wrong; that internal sensation that moves in your belly; the one that guides you into your decisions. It is that sense that something is 'knocking on your door' when an inclination to take action occurs. You might want to consider trusting that feeling and listening to it 100% of the time. I know it sounds crazy, but yes I said 100% of the time.

Even if you make mistakes – even if it doesn't work out in the end, don't beat yourself up. Try not to obsess over the thought that, "I thought it would work out! But I thought he/she was the one!" It is not something to be upset about. Why?

Golden Nugget

You did what you thought was best for you in the moment.

And in that case, you **DID DO** the right thing. You have to understand that it was right. It was supposed to happen. How do you know? Because it happened!

You did what you thought was best for you at the time, which means it **was best for you at the time.** So if it didn't go the way you wanted it to... what can you learn from it? What lesson did you need to learn from that experience, or from that person? Since you attracted and manifested that experience into your life,

(remember you are always vibrating, and always attracting everything into your life with your thoughts and vibrations) what did you need to learn from it?

Family Values

Your own values or your families?

They say 'you are a byproduct of your environment.' That includes your family and your parents. There is another saying, 'guilty by association.' Remember these?

Your parents are important in this inquiry. Remember what I said earlier in the book about parents being the first relationship example? They really are and you need to face that, instead of avoiding it. Why? Well, your parents are your primary example of a relationship in your life. You observe what you observe. What happens in front of you, happens in front of you. Just understand that it has an effect on you. Everything you witness, see and hear, leaves an imprint on you at a young age. Whether you agree or not is irrelevant. It might sound harsh, but again it's the truth.

My parents have been together for 48 years of marriage at the time of this writing. They are both in their 70's. I am so proud of them, and very happy they are still together for many reasons. What you need to know is that my parents always had a healthy relationship. I can still remember at a young age, my dad stealing a kiss or two in the kitchen every now and again. My mom got flowers on special occasions and more. Also, my mother put plenty of time and thought into planning trips together. My mom also helps my dad drive these past seven years or so as dad isn't as quick as he used to be. I always saw them talking things out, when there was a problem or a disagreement.

It was very positive for me growing up around that kind of love. That kind of environment and energy is very healthy for a child. I am sure it's a big part of the reason why I can do what I do, helping people today. I am not a parenting expert but I once read a quote that said, "The best thing parents can do for their kids, is to make it obvious they love each other very much."

In this section, I want you to reflect on your parent's values, and the environment you grew up in. Was affection obvious? Did good communication reign? Were they involved in each other's lives? Did they have fun around you? Did they yell at each other in your presence often? Did they talk in derogative ways to each other? Were they quick to anger?

Take some notes in your notebook.

I really want you to consider this carefully, especially if you want to have kids in your future or have kids already. Good parenting is so essential in a child's development.

After you have examined your home life growing up, you get to choose if you want to keep those values, engage in those behaviours, or change them and pick new ones. This is a creative process as I mentioned, and you are creative beings. Additionally, it's good to see and notice in case some of those behaviours come creeping up again in your next relationship.

Remember what I said earlier about you listening to yourself in the end. You really do get to choose.

The Measuring Stick

Consciously, or unconsciously, they are doing it too

As if you were two sports teams, sizing each other up, you and your new partner will be looking for similar values. It is a normal thing. While it might be an unconscious process, and it might take a few months to truly determine if you are a match. You are both on the lookout for any signs.

It is said that as human beings our brains are programmed to 'find the wrong in things.' I don't want to freak you out with this, however it is true for the vast majority of people. You know this yourself, as we often default to looking for 'what's wrong.' Some undeniable examples include, "What's wrong with me? What's wrong with my work? What's wrong with my relationship? What's wrong with my partner? Here's what's wrong with the world today. Here's what's wrong with my boss and so on.

We'll come back to this in another chapter. For now just consider that old saying, 'actions speak louder than words' and know that your actions and words ought to be a match. Now that's obvious but in the case of your values and theirs, if you say you value X and do Y instead, then it obviously isn't a match. This will raise some pretty big flags for you if you notice this about your partner or vice versa. Sometimes it will be completely unnoticeable for a time as well, it is something you must pay attention to.

If you say you value health, but never exercise, then are you sure you are committed to health? If you say you value health but eat big meals at 10 pm five times a week, then it's not a true value is it? If you say you are committed to loving your partner but don't show much affection, is it a match? Maybe, if you're okay with not having an expressive kind of relationship, then sure. But maybe not, and then they're/you're going to want out.

This is a good opportunity for you to consider who you were being at the time with regard to your values and your behavior to understand a reason why any past relationships didn't work out.

Good signs of Male values

Masculine energy represented as values

Okay, I know I'm going a little taboo with this list. This isn't a be all and end all list. I'm not a scientist, or a politician, and I'm not advocating for one gender's supremacy or rights over the other. I'm just stating what I've seen and what works in my experience. Ultimately male and female energy is healthiest when balanced inside the individual. No one is 100% masculine or 100% feminine. Everyone has some of each inside of them, and there is no right answer. Think of the Yin Yang symbol, it is 2 parts that make up the whole.
When I was writing this book, someone recommended I have a book for men and a book for women. I chose to keep everything together, so that both genders can understand each other's point of view, and then understand themselves better as well.

Regardless, here are some things to consider.

Take a look at his living space. Yes I know you do this already. How does he keep his things? How does he keep his space? His car? Yes I am cringing a little as I write this. His family? His friends? Can you bear how he eats? Do you respect what he does for work? Does he respect what he does for work?

For men, a big part of expressing who they are is done through work, business, volunteering, their impact in the community and a good sense of accomplishment. It is about giving back and creating or producing values for the world. Masculine energy is about getting things done, being organized, following through, and knowing what directions to take (there's that stopping for directions thing again).

What matters is his mission, his purpose. He must be driven by it. He must have clarity around it. His relationship should actually come second to his mission. I know this may sound backwards but to quote David Deida's book, *The Way of the Superior Man*, *"If a man prioritizes his relationship over his highest purpose, he weakens himself, disserves the universe, and cheats his woman of an authentic man who can offer her full, undivided presence."* To truly understand the masculine man and masculine energy, I highly recommend this book.

He needs to have good friends. You are the culmination of your five closest friends after all. But do not try and change his friends or change him. Do not try and control him. This is in the best interest of both of you. If he doesn't do certain things that you would like him to do, like come to the door when he picks you up, or offer to pick you up in the first place, Then please just tell him. Men don't always have the answers, but men do have a commitment to make their woman happy.

I think of myself as a pretty considerate and generous guy, but I wasn't opening the car door for a girl I was dating a few years back. It just wasn't on my mind. She told me she would really appreciate it if I did, and I went, "Oh, okay!" I was genuinely happy to! I really was, since I enjoyed the idea of making her happier and ensuring we have a better time together. Since then, I often open the doors for my dates! It just wasn't something I was conscious of at the time.

Guys, if you're reading this, don't worry about getting all the dirt out. It won't matter. Women won't be overly concerned in this area. Not if they're the kind of woman you really want to be with. They will understand.

Guys, if you're lucky, you were raised with sisters or women in your life at the very least. Why? Because it goes a long way when interacting with women. If your sisters had a hand in raising you (like mine did, thankfully) then they will teach you how to have some style, how to be considerate, and how to be thoughtful to a woman, because some men just aren't. If you weren't, ask your female friends for advice.

Women, a lot of men feel you may be being too hard on them. They call it nagging, complaining, distracting, etc. They may not know how to handle it or this way of being. How do you know if you are being too hard or being unsupportive of your partner? You need to ask. "Do you feel supported by me? How can I best support you?" At first he might be thrown off but if you ask the question and promise it to be free of repercussions, you will get a straight answer.

Good signs of a woman's values

Feminine energy represented as values

Golden Nugget

Remember, good couples have polarity.

Both the male and female have masculine and feminine energy but in the right places.

My friend once described it well. He said, "Think about it like tango. One person is leading and the other person is being led. The one being led is the expression of the one that is leading." With the male and female energy and values, this is a great example. It is about a having a match. You have to complement each other.

Feminine energy is a good example of the person being led in Tango. She compliments the man by allowing him to take the lead. She grants him permission to lead, and in response she is the beautiful accentuation in the pair. She is what everyone is looking at. She is graceful, sexy, and alluring. She captures everyone's attention. She is the one they watch. And yet it is he who is leading her through the dance. She truly complements him and as a result, they achieve a magnificent performance together.

Consider this in a great relationship. She knows how to laugh at his jokes. She completes him. She supports him in his goals. She makes him feel good. She smiles a lot. She gives him confidence when he is in doubt. She encourages him to act if he is hesitating.

When men are helping other men consider a good woman, they say 'Look at her mother, that's how she will look and act at her age.' Don't be discouraged. This is of course just a generalization and not necessarily the truth. For example, one of the most wonderful women I ever dated, Jennifer, had a mother who was an ex-addict. Jennifer was not an addict and had no intentions of becoming one of course. She was however, an indescribable person of authenticity, softness, grace, peace, and love. How lucky I was to be with her. It was not my choice to end that relationship. She had been in two long-term relationships, one after the other, one for seven years and one for four years, consecutively. After we had dated, she decided she needed her freedom. I couldn't fault her for that. It made complete sense to me, so I was not upset. The only regret I had at the end of that relationship was that I did not give 100% of myself to her in the short time we had together.

Jennifer challenged me. She pushed me. She caused me to grow. She touched my weak spots and illuminated the dusty cobwebs I didn't know I had. Men, woman can do that. If you are the right man, the right woman will not stop testing you. It is their nature. Women will not stop in this regard so do not expect them to. Women, thank you for what you do, we need you.

There is a great scene in the third 'Matrix' movie that illustrates this simply. Neo understands that the purpose of the Male Father-type character 'The Architect,' is to 'balance the equation.' While the purpose of the Female Mother-Type character 'The Oracle' is to 'unbalance the equation.'

You could say the male provides structure and execution while the female character provides creativity and mystery.

Values: An exchange, like trading cards

Swap 'em, if you got 'em

To me, relationships are the greatest place to grow and learn as human beings. They are the greatest place to learn about yourself, people and the world. One way this is done is through the exchange of values that you and your partner have.

Plain and simple, if your partner has cooties, they might get on you. In fact, they will get on you. You will connect, swap and trade values. Just like playing cards. This is one of the ways you will learn and grow.

If it doesn't work out, and you don't last with the person you're currently or recently dating, sometimes you can chalk it up to values. You were not a match. Your values didn't align and that's okay. That's grown up talk for 'it didn't work out.'

Consider that adults don't always talk like adults. In fact, sometimes we're trapped in a childlike language called, "I don't wanna" or, "You can't make me" and he/she didn't do what I wanted. Because of this, sometimes break ups end in drama, foul language, or gossip towards each other. I can honestly say, I haven't had a relationship end in that way since I was 18 years old. I'm proud of that, and it's because I look for the deeper meaning, the deeper truth why things didn't work out. In addition to that,

Golden Nugget

I honour every person I come into contact with.

Sometimes when you are reacting in a childlike manner it is actually your inability to describe what is happening, or what is actually having you (or them) make the decision to split, in articulate language. This takes work. We'll be covering break ups in another chapter.

At this point, you might be dating other people. You might be dating new kinds of people you've never dated before. If you've been reading this book, and doing the exercises and spreading them out over time, then you should be breaking new ground in your ability to find a great partner, and keep a great relationship. If not, reach out to me. If so, great job!

Regardless, there comes a point in the process where you have to identify to yourself and to the world that the current people you are unsatisfied with, are not the kind of person you want to be with. This is likely because they don't have what you want, sure. It is also the case that their values don't resonate with yours.

Golden Nugget

There will come a time when you have to turn your back on what you don't want, and focus on what you do want.

There is a difference here. It is subtle, but it is important.

I want you to consider something- the value of INTEGRITY as a universal value that you now look for, whether it be in man, woman, or someone who is transgender. This is one of the greatest golden rules for this book. Integrity is about your life working, your relationships working. It is being reliable, something that you can be counted on for. When you make a commitment, you can be expected to honour it, and when you make a decision you will follow through with it. This is a concept that our society is beginning to require more and more- the need for integrity as a requirement for workability (the ability to make things work).

What in your world doesn't work? What in your life doesn't work? What about your relationships don't work? How can you make it work? What do you need to put in or change so that integrity (that is workability) is present?

This leads us to our next section on Commitment. Integrity is required to be in a conversation for commitment.

The C Word

Why do we fear commitment?

I know a woman who married a man in her early 30's. She had a picture of herself by the time she hit her 30's and it went something like this: Married, happy, starting a family, with an established career. Well, she had the career but no marriage and no kids. She was in a long term relationship with a great guy for seven years. But after seven years, he wasn't getting serious, so they broke up. She started dating again. She met some guys, and after a while, found one who really piqued her interest. They started dating. Her parents didn't feel great about this guy and they made her aware of it. Something didn't sit right (remember what I said earlier about your parents and their intuition). But she went ahead and dated him anyway. You could say she was blinded by her desire for kids and for everything to work out. So they kept dating and she became pregnant. Right after this, after dating for eight months, they figured getting married was a good idea. To make a long story short, they were married and then she had the baby, and that's when things got interesting. They started fighting a lot. He wasn't around much of the time. After about six months of being a part of raising their son, he started acting somewhat shifty and odd (his behaviour was already odd, which is what triggered her parents intuition in the first place). It wasn't long before arguments became screaming matches and he would walk away. He moved out, skipped out on contributing to payments and fatherly duties and more. Shortly after that, he left the country.

She found out somewhere in the midst of all that, that he had two sons with another woman. Today, he has another child with another woman in another part of the world. This man has no integrity. He is incredibly insecure. Raising a family, and being a responsible human being, is a concept that he cannot run away fast enough from. His behaviour shows this. He lacks integrity, and is the opposite of being whole and complete. The interesting thing is that I saw this man several times, and he was always twitching all over his body. Do you remember the first chapter? The section on truth? He is a great example of the lies he kept to himself, manifesting through the body.

Integrity is wholeness and completeness of self. This is what I want to you to be. Whole and complete, just the way you are. This means having nothing outstanding, nothing hiding, having no personal, karmic, or soulful debts. This means being able to keep a clear head, free of lies and untruths. It is a process, but it is essential to having a great relationship. I tell you this because I want this for you. I want you to experience freedom. This is what integrity brings. This is what a pure commitment brings.

What was that man's reason that he acted with no integrity? I don't know. It could be that he grew up without a father. It could be that his parents were divorced and separated. It could be that he didn't know how to be honest with himself or his partners. Either way, he had no integrity and was burdened by his inauthenticity.

What did he fear? Responsibility. It's one of the things we all fear. It is a deep basic human fear (try to look at this objectively, from an integrity perspective, which is completely different from a right and wrong, or morality perspective).

Commitment, a curse

Something to feel burdened by

Many of us are afraid of being challenged or called out on our behaviour. Mostly, we are afraid of 'being wrong.' We associate being wrong with being bad. Being bad is bad and being wrong is the worst. Most of us are so committed to being right. What a disease of the mind, body and soul this is. Would you like to suffocate your relationships, not only in romance but at work and in your family? Then all you have to do is maintain a commitment to being right!

Golden Nugget

Some of us hold on so tightly to being right, it's all in the name of avoiding looking bad.

This is not what you want your life to be committed to, is it?

We get so confronted when others hold us to account for what we do or fail to do. We are so afraid of failure. We do anything and everything to avoid it. This is one of the biggest reasons why commitment occurs to some of us as a threat. Commitment can seem like a threat of attack or a burden to bear for some. A lot of people don't want to be responsible for what is on the line if we fail. This includes if we break our commitment. I understand this to be the case with some people I work with. It can take a lot of time and energy to be willing to be responsible should it not work out.

Here's the opportunity! Like anything, it's all about perspective. You can be bound and weighed down by your commitments. You can be burdened by them, and that would be all too normal,or you can be that they are a part of you, like your heart, or your kidneys. You commitment and your values can be something to live by; something for you to base your decisions on; something to be guided by. Your commitments are like a roadmap if you will. If you have a commitment and a set of clearly defined values, then you can use them to aid you in your journey.

It can be as simple as asking yourself the question, "Does this fit with my values? Is this in line with my commitments?"

Ask yourself right now, what are my commitments in life? Is it family, career, fitness, healthy eating/living, meditation, spirituality? What is it?

Look at your last three major decisions. Were they the right ones? Were they made based on your commitments or values, or were they based on your whims and wants.

Take a look at your last relationship and determine where it went off. If you know the answer to this already, then great. If you can look at it on a larger, more mature scale in terms of your commitments, this will serve you better.

Commitment, a gift

Something to be empowered by

Your commitments are not something for you to get right 100% of the time. You won't always get it right. They are something you will struggle with. They

are something you will tussle with. And guess what? Your commitment in your relationship is no different. You will be tested.

If you ask any couple that has been married for a lifetime or longer, they will all tell you the same thing. "It's not always easy. It takes work." You could say that human beings are inconsistent. We definitely make mistakes, of course. And we certainly don't make the right choice every time.

Golden Nugget

That's why your commitment is something to honour.

It will be impossible to keep your word 100% of the time, but you can honour your word 100% of the time. This means to honour the agreement and commitment you have made with your partner. If you say you will always love them, always treat them with respect, kindness, appreciation and so on, you can always honour that commitment. How? By taking responsibility for your mistakes and failures and admitting when you have broken your word and your commitment. This will have your partner still feel honoured, and keep your commitments true.

Notice that this is different than blame and failure. This takes away the heaviness of what failure usually brings.

With this, your commitment can become something you are known for. It creates something you can actually be acknowledged and recognized for. In time, you will be able to look back on your commitments and admire them. You will be able to admire yourself for sticking with them. You will know yourself as someone that doesn't wash out, flake out or drift, when the going got tough, is worth more than I can put into words. Your partner will love you for it.

On a side note, I asked a couple recently, what had them commit to each other despite their difficulties. They have many difficulties by most standards including financial, and a mental health condition in one of the partners. When I asked why, the response was, "When you find someone whose personality and values match yours like we did… we want to do everything we can to hold on to it."

This is the brilliance of commitment and choice. You have the freedom to choose any person, and any commitment you like.

Unequivocal Equality

You must be equal partners

You can't skip this section. One woman I was working with had an easy problem to solve with a current relationship she was in. She was in her late 40's and was in a relationship with a man for about half a year and she was somewhat happy in that relationship. She had her own TV show and radio show and was committed to helping women build their careers and build success for themselves through marketing and the media. She liked this guy a lot. How could she not? He was a doctor, he was handsome, he was very successful and he treated her to luxurious dinners and outings. This made her happy. However, whenever she had some success and a breakthrough in her career or one of her client's careers, she would be ecstatic. In those moments, her partner would mock her. He would make jokes about her line of work and take the case that her work wasn't important on a grand scale.

Now you might be thinking, "What an asshole!" Indeed. It was obvious to me that this man didn't respect what she did, and in part, he did not respect her. Nor did he respect her mission. So I asked her, do you love what you do? She went on for five full minutes about how this was her life's work, her passion, her purpose, what she lived for! So I asked, then how can you be with this man who laughs, and scoffs at the very thing which you live for? "Oh… well. I'm not sure. I have to think about that." I said, "Okay, great! Think about it, and let me know what you decide." A few weeks later she told me she had landed two really big interviews with big name celebrities and he poked at her again when he found out. She had heard the last of it and told him, "It's obvious to me that you don't appreciate or support me and my efforts! I want and need a partner who does, as this is a big part of my life and who I am. So I'm not the woman for you." And she walked out on him on the spot.

As I said earlier, you must never settle. You must never cave under pressure or under what others say to you. You must always be true to yourself and what matters to you. *To have a great relationship, one that will really work, you must be supportive of each other.*

Golden Nugget

At the very minimum you must see each other as equals.

There must be a commitment to equality. No one is above the other person.

Even better still, if a horse pulls weight, that horse can pull 1000 lbs. When another horse is attached to the weight being pulled, they won't pull twice as much, (2000 lbs.) They will actually pull 4000 pounds, which is 4x as much as one. Couples are like that too. A couple that works together can be powerful forces to be reckoned with (which is why you see so many power couples out there in the business, media and political arenas). When people are committed to the same goals, they combine to make a powerful team. If you are committed to separate goals that is okay. You don't have to have the same goals. As long as you are respectful and supportive of each other's ambitions and goals, more can be achieved!

Alignment is wonderful

And it's not a guarantee

You want to make sure your values align with the person you are with. This is how to achieve harmony, and ensure a great relationship, obviously. However, this isn't a foolproof indicator of the one, but it is an ideal indication, especially in the first three to six months. This is where you should really begin to understand the person. This is where you will really get a sense if it will work out or not.

This is a way to deeply connect with someone, a way to really understand someone based on their values. Remember, it still might not work out. There is no guarantee for this.

Golden Nugget

This is a process after all, and you still have to trust the process.

Just because your values align, doesn't mean everything will be sunshine and roses. Many other aspects of the relationship dynamic are still at play here.

What it does mean is that **you are getting closer to the 'right partner' - The right partner for you.** This is as simple as continually defining what you want. Eventually, you get to the right place when you are clear within your own personal being of what your values are and resonance of the other person's values with your own.

Should you compromise? In the beginning, sure. But what I want you to know is by the time you get to the person you ultimately want to be with, you won't have to compromise.

So compromise sure, until it starts to erode who you are. Until it starts to change you in a way that you don't want to be changed. Until the feeling in your gut and heart says, 'this isn't what you want. This isn't who you are.'

One of the toughest lessons I had to learn in my younger years was that it's okay for certain relationships to fall apart. In this case, for me it was friendships. I held on to a certain group of friends for years, even though I knew it didn't make sense for me to be friends with them. My interests were different than theirs. I wanted to spend my time doing different things. I wanted to have different kinds of conversations. I wanted to take new actions, and go different places. And they didn't. It took me a long time to learn that we had grown different from each other. That we could no longer relate in many areas. But I was too busy trying to be a nice guy. I was too occupied with fears of what would happen if we separated, who would I talk to, and what would I become.   And finally I had enough of these conversations in my head and I said, 'It's time to jump off the ledge and find out!' And I did. And it's a darn good thing I did, because I probably wouldn't be here if I stuck around there.

One of the people I look up to in this world is the founder of Mindvalley, Vishen Lakhiani. In one of his sessions where he was speaking to a group of us at Awesomeness Fest, he said, "You might be trying to fit everyone through a door with you, while you're trying to fit in it. Picture all of these people trying to fit through the doorway at the same time. But not everyone can come with you through that doorway." This is what I was trying to do. Lesson learned, it isn't possible.

Is there a match?

Ladies and Gentlemen, do we have a winner?

How can you tell if you found a match with your partner's values? You will see them. You will hear them. You will feel them. You will begin to develop a spider sense. Your intuition will guide you very well here.

Now there is a difference between your intuition and the judgments you have. Your intuition is the part of you that is in your body. It is in your gut and in your heart. What about the head? It gets translated through your head to your mind

and mouth. Remember, as I said, your intuition is all in the body. Why? The body is a sensing and feeling centre. It is where something called knowingness resides.

As you go through this process of dating and finding a great partner, you will get better and better at understanding that feeling, and recognizing that knowingness. And then there will come a time when you will have to make a choice-a choice to CHOOSE this person as your partner; free from reasons. Simply making a choice as a choice, because everything tells you this choice is right.

Another tool you can use, which might sound crazy and yet, is incredibly effective is interviewing each other. I know it sounds wild, but this is something a previous partner and I discovered, which was a hugely effective tool for us to use every six months to take an inside look into our relationship and what was working, what wasn't working, and what we could do better. I know it sounds scary but, after it was over, we both felt great about it and we were totally empowered to make our relationship even better each time!

This is something you will want to consider doing at the later stages in your relationship, or if you're in one now and you've picked up this book again, because you've read it before or when you were single. You want to do this when you are comfortable enough in the relationship. When you've known each other for more than a few months I would recommend it. You can also do this when the fun and love is wearing thin in the relationship as well. This well help you get to the source of the dissipation of love.

Use this self assessment tool to see where you are in your communication skills and what you need to improve on.

The 7 Degrees of Communication Self-Assessment

On a scale of 1 (low) - 10 (high), rate yourself according to how true the following statements are when you apply each statement's significance to your current Communication Habits.

Circle the number that represents where you best fit on the scale.

Connection
I naturally and easily connect with almost everybody. I have genuine interest in other people and I find the good in them. I love meeting new people as well as deepening my relationships.

1 2 3 4 5 6 7 8 9 10

Engagement
I help others feel safe by conveying my kindness and competence. I stimulate engaging conversations by focusing on supporting their interests and managing their concerns.

1 2 3 4 5 6 7 8 9 10

Gaining Understanding
I listen intently when others speak with me. I ask many open-ended and clarifying questions and confirm my full and accurate understanding of their thoughts, feelings and perspectives.

1 2 3 4 5 6 7 8 9 10

Giving Understanding
I communicate honestly, openly, respectfully and directly, acknowledging the other persons' interest and current awareness level. I then confirm their understanding of the information.

1 2 3 4 5 6 7 8 9 10

Achieve Mutual Understanding
I enjoy understanding and responding fully to people's questions, concerns and combating interest. I work with them, through collaborative dialogue, to uncover, or create the best possible solution in our mutual best interest.

1 2 3 4 5 6 7 8 9 10

Getting Mutual Commitments
I am comfortable working with others to make commitments based on our conversations. I'm comfortable making, and encouraging other to make informed decisions.

1 2 3 4 5 6 7 8 9 10

Follow Up
I consistently fulfill all commitments I make to others and I respectfully encourage others to keep the commitments they have made with me. By doing this, I habitually strengthen and deepen my relationships with others.

1 2 3 4 5 6 7 8 9 10

For now, we have to get to our next chapter, a chapter I am very excited about: Sex and Intimacy!

7
SEX AND INTIMACY

Intimacy 101

That which you've been waiting for

It's funny. I wonder how many readers will jump to this chapter first. When I was writing this book, several people I spoke to said they would jump to this chapter right away. What is that about? What the fascination with sex? Why is it that we are so curious to seek out sexual information and stimulation? Maybe I should have asked.

Anyway, here is the chapter you've been waiting for - imagine this. You're at work and it's a special evening for you and your partner tonight, and you both know it. However, in the morning when you leave for work, you don't say anything. You just wink, but it's a special wink to your partner. You leave the house, excited, a little warmer, a little happier, with a little extra spring in your step. Throughout your day at work, you're working, you're busy, you're at the office and you're talking to people.... but every once in a while, you remember, tonight is a special night. You have nothing to do, nothing to worry about. The rest of the week isn't even a concern, why? Because tonight is when you get to spend a little extra time together in a very special way in a way you don't spend with anyone else. You know what I mean. So you smile a little more. You give extra change for tip at lunch. You buy coffee for the person behind you in the drive through. You have this smirk on your face throughout the day. Maybe you even feel a little warmth in your belly, a little fire if you will, which when leaving the office for the day, quickly ignites inside you throughout your body.

What is this I am talking about? This is something special. This is the anticipation of intimacy and great sex with someone you love. This is the excitement and the bliss of having a great sex life with your partner. It doesn't matter if you are just dating, married, or in a relationship. When you have this special connection with someone it is thrilling. It is beyond exciting! It makes the relationship more exciting, more fulfilling, and more healthy, believe it or not! It is a basic requirement of a relationship. Anyone who says otherwise is either in denial or is resigned about their sex life. If you don't have this, you don't have much. I say this not to insult you but to awaken you. To what? To the obvious truth.

Golden Nugget

Plain and simple: Sex is one of the best and most fruitful ways to connect and express love for your partner.

Better still, it's actually a way to open yourself up and learn more about your humanity and yourself as a spiritual being. Once again we are spiritual beings having a human experience. If you are missing sex in your life and your relationship, you are missing out. It's huge. If you don't have good sex in your relationship, it has a high probability to fizzle out.

Sex and intimacy are a healthy part of any relationship. It's not just something you do in the beginning. It's something you should be doing all the time. And there are different levels of sex and intimacy, which is about different levels of connection and pleasure, desire and depth. Any level is good. The point is to have some level of it. But for now, no need to worry. We'll explore more in the coming pages.

Intimacy 102

It isn't just about sex

For those of you who are triggered by this chapter and confronted by it, I completely understand. Sex can be nerve wracking and even scary! Intimacy can be upsetting and startling to some. Especially for those of you who have been sexually abused or traumatized, which unfortunately is a large part of the population, approximately 25%. You are not alone. This is not okay. This is totally unacceptable in our "educated" world today. However, sadly, it still occurs. I won't get into this topic much as this is not my area of expertise. However, I would like you to know there are many resources and many support systems out there where you can have assistance and transform this area if you wish. And I hope you do. There are a great many reasons why.

For example, the right partner/lover can connect you to your soul on a deeper level, more than you ever imagined. Sex and intimacy can make you question life-question the very fiber of your being. It can take you to places of deep ecstasy and pleasure. It can take you outside of yourself. Actually, it is perfectly normal to have an out of body experience while having sex. You can achieve very high states of being and awareness through sex. But we'll get to that later. I just want you to look at things newly for now.

Having sex only once in a while with your partner is not enough. Especially if there is a deep connection, real attraction, and if you really love the person you can have it with. Not having sex is a rip-off in life.

I would like you to read this chapter as if it was the first time reading about sex. Forget everything you know if you are unsatisfied with your sex life. You cannot base your opinion about having a sex life if you have had unpleasant sex in the past. It is not permanent. It is a constantly evolving part of life.

Golden Nugget

Sex should be a constantly evolving part of your relationship and your life.

Why? Because it never has to stay the same. Just as you change, your sexual desires and abilities will change.

Sex is an intimate connection. Great sex is highly intimate. It takes longer than one experience to make a real decision about it. Think about this as more than just sex. It is intimacy. Moments of intimacy are some of the most unique and fascinating moments I have had in life. Intimacy has been described as many things. One great explanation is, *"The exploration of the tiny space between two human beings, and the sparks and emotions that fly inside of that tiny space. That which can seem so insignificant and yet so precious, so massive and so universal, so delicate and so juicy; all in its finite nothingness. Something that can make you seem so purposefully connected, you question whether there is any actual separation at all."*

Intimacy is not just in the bedroom. It's all over your life. It's anywhere and everywhere. Intimacy is all about being present. The focus lies on being present. It is not watching an experience through a lens. It is that you are the lens. You are intimately connected to everything in front of, and all around you.

To have progress in this area, that is to expand it and better it, you must be willing. Everything starts with willingness. So what do you want? Take a moment and do some work. Make some notes (I never said this was going to be easy, but I did say this would be fun. So have fun with this). What is sex to you? What do you want out of sex? What is intimacy to you? Why would it be important? Let me give you a head start. It is a place to go, to let go, to surrender, to obey your emotions, and your body; to be on an adventure with your partner, to be in the fullest experience of love and connection. To know what it means to be alive.

It takes trust

Without trust, intimacy is a lie.

A big part of intimacy and sexual satisfaction is Trust. I want you to consider that trust is the only thing between you and ultimate connection as well as indefinable pleasure. Trusting yourself and trusting your partner.

Trust is an interesting thing. It can take time to truly develop in people. Trust is a two way street of course. But let's consider something shall we? Usually it's looked at as something external. Well what if trust was something completely internal. What if it had nothing to do with another person? What if trust was all about you? What if trust was something you completely brought from inside yourself? If it was, then other people would be irrelevant. Trust then, you could say is a willingness to put yourself out there- to take a risk, and still be able to take the consequences that come with it. What we're talking about here is Surrendering and no matter what happens, accepting the responsibility, which includes **your responsibility to heal yourself, owning the wounds and celebrating the satisfactions that comes with it and forgiving yourself for whatever occurs.**

It involves nurturing and caring for yourself. It is quite the feeling, it is magical, actually. Have you ever had 100% trust in someone? Have you put all your fears away and locked them in the closet, or opened up your willingness to be naked with another human being? This is what it means to trust, to be intimate to the deepest depths with another human being. Do you know what that's like?

Would you like to?

It takes trusting yourself

You are the common denominator

If you are sexually unsatisfied, lonely, or have no idea of the concepts of intimacy of which I speak, you need to accept that you are the common denominator in your life**. It is all up to you and it has always been up to you.** Don't you view the world through your eyes? Don't you touch people with your hands? You don't touch anyone with someone else's hands. And you don't see anything through another person's eyes. What is it you don't understand? What is it about yourself and your sexuality that you are hiding away from? What is it you won't face?

You want to confront these questions, if you want your life and your sex life to expand. Without your sexuality, life can be boring. Life can be mundane. Sex is an access to a greater experience of life. Sexual energy is creative energy. It is hot, it is passionate. It is the spice of life. Sexual desire is within all of us. It is part of us from our childhood. It is creative energy- the energy and ability to create. Create what? Create life!

What else can sex do?

Sex is more than just sex

Sex also has the power to heal, and as I mentioned, it can open doors. But you have to trust yourself to get there. You have to allow sex and intimacy with a partner to work its magic on you- to heal your heart, to cleanse your wounds, to open your mind and body. As a result, your spirit will open too! There can be great healing by opening yourself to love and allowing the nurturing of another person's sexual energy to penetrate you. It should start with someone you trust, and in the same manner, a person whom you can trust will hold you, nurture you and take care of you. Men ought to be aware of the healing power of a woman's love. And women could be open to the healing power of a man's love too.

Also, you must be aware of sexuality as a distraction. There are those who use sex as a distraction, to take you away from your power, (like the man who abandoned his family in Chapter 6) to take you away from your focus on what you need to be doing in life, and in your relationship. Sometimes sex is used to distract you from your problems, to distract you from things you want to put off. You may throw yourself at your partner to experience relief and comfort. While this is satisfying, it will not last forever.

See you aren't having sex all the time, and it's not possible to have sex 100% of the time, but you will be together 100% of the time, in an emotional and spiritual connection, through a bond of spoken agreement. If other integral parts of your relationship are not working, it won't work overall. You might get to a point where you can't even look at your partner there is so much that isn't working and is lacking integrity. So sex will not be possible either. Remember integrity is wholeness and completeness of self. So to abandon yourself into just sex would be a definite disservice to yourself, and to your lover.

You see, great sex won't be possible, unless your relationship is working and healthy. Allow me to briefly insert that you may want to reread Chapter 1 again at this moment, specifically the parts on loving yourself, being yourself and your future and past.

In another way, sex can be a way out- A way to escape, to leave behind the confusion and frustration of your life. This can be used to reconnect to your partner and what matters to you, and that is perfectly okay. There are movies that show this pretty well. Sometimes a character that is shut off, mentally or emotionally, chooses to surrender and let go and throw themselves into sex and intimacy. Those moments become the only moments where they can really escape and be themselves. This is somewhat sad, since there is an element of pretending or "mask-wearing" if you will. To be one person in one area of life, and to be another person in another area, would cause separation. And separation prevents wholeness. Do you want to be the same person throughout your life? Can you see the benefit of being consistent?

What do you want?

Become in tune with your desires, your deeper desires. What is it that you want to experience?

This is very important. Pull out that notebook again. Think about this and then write it down.

Would you like to experience surrendering to the wholeness of your being? Would you like to experience a divine connection with the universe or god? Would you like to experience your partner's strength, love, and vulnerability? Do you want to show your partner what it means to really be loved? Do you want to experience that for yourself? Would you like to let go of all the control you have been holding on to? To experience your first sigh, your first deep breath, at the release of all concern? Do you want to feel loved? Like you are the only one who matters?

Is it pleasure you are after? Would you like your eyes to roll back into your head with ecstasy? Do you want to scream in delight? Would you like to make your partner scream your name in celebration? Would you like to have an out of body experience? Are you looking for a way to melt all of your walls and surrender yourself to love?

You must know what you want.

You wouldn't believe how many times someone I've met has told me, "Wow, it is so refreshing to know a man who knows his heart, who knows how he feels, and knows what his heart wants!" And other times they are amazed at how I can "speak from my heart and have it be authentic." I appreciate these comments because I am not playing any cards or any games. I am not faking anything. It is the real me. I am in tune with my desires, and that allows me to have incredible connections with others and have very fulfilling sexual experiences.

Knowing what you want is a very rewarding way of living life. How come? Because the secret to a good life is feeling good. We all want to feel good. And you feel good when you feel good. And you feel good when you get what you want. This may sound redundant but you need to know what you want, before you can go out and get it.

This exploration into sex and intimacy can give you that. Take a moment and think about what you want. Share it with your partner. Share it with a friend. Just share it with someone. Make a note to have a conversation with someone. Bonus points if you share it with someone you are dating. Don't be afraid to honour your desires.

What does your partner want?

You have needs and they have needs. You both should get what you want.

This section is super short. We are not mind readers. You know what assuming does. So don't do it. There's only one way to find out. You'll have to ask them.

When I met Jessica Louise, my partner, we met at a tradeshow while I was promoting one of my previous books. I was speaking to some women and when I finished talking to them, I turned around and there was Jessica. And I just went, "Wow." In my head of course. I did pause to let the moment sink in, then I said "Hi" and shook her hand. Then I said "Michael" smiling through my teeth. To which she said "Jessica." And the rest was history.

Just kidding.

We connected in that moment and there was obvious chemistry and sparks between us. We chatted a bit, but I was in a relationship at the time and so was she. We exchanged business cards and she'd seen me in a online business group we were a part of, but didn't think anything of it. Six months later and I'm at my friends birthday party and she was there to our mutual delight and surprise. The same connection and sparks were there as when we first met. (She has great energy, a great smile and knows how to communicate well.) But she was struggling with her relationship which was on the fritz as was mine. She asked me for some advice and I gave it to her impartially as an advisor.

She said the guy she was with wasn't giving "it up." (Wasn't having sex with her.) She went on to say that she 'has needs' and her 'needs weren't being met.' I completely understood.

Although I was surprised to hear this, because she is a beautiful and sexy woman, I made no judgments. I advised her as if she was a client on what to do and that included maintaining her wants and being focused on that.

We stayed in touch briefly, chatting over Facebook and had some laughs. She was adamant about what she wanted and told me all about the things she wants in a partner. My relationship was then over for a few weeks now and I enjoyed reading about what this woman who had so much to offer wanted in a partner.

She went on to be very, very specific about the kind of man she likes and wants to be with. She was very vulnerable with me and really let me into her world.

And I was taken back. Such courage! Such vulnerability! I was attracted to this woman emotionally and physically. She had a great personality already and so I said to myself, "We would be a good fit."

I knew what she wanted because she told me. And I listened.

I suggested we meet for tea downtown as I may know a man who meets your qualifications. (I really did.)

We met for tea, as she was up for the conversation and networking, and we chatted. About 1.5 hours into the evening she started wondering "Where is this guy?" So I just took a breath and said, "Well, it's me."

I suggested we help service each other's needs because "I have needs and you have needs. And I wonder what would happen if we put our 'needs' together in a room." It was great. "We both just got out of a relationship and I don't think it's a good idea to jump right back into something, so we can keep this strictly physical for now."

We laughed, we giggled, I explained myself and we had a good time. She said she was flattered and would need a day or two to think about it. We connected back to the moments at the tradeshow and our friends birthday party about how we were mutually attracted to each other.

She came back two days later with "Yes. Let's do it." I had a feeling she would. I was very happy. She was very happy.

For many months, we took care of each others needs sexually and enjoyed every minute with a very high degree of satisfaction. The sex that we were having was truly out of this world. We'd both been pretty sexual throughout our lives and had a lot of great experiences and great partners.

But this was different.

We were in tune with each other. We were on the same exact page sexually. We had great communication. We trusted each other and we surrendered to the passion, heat and fire of our sexuality.

It was so good I joked about how people are not normally having this kind of sex and that it was so good, we should teach people how to do it.

Four months later and we created “The Sensational Sex Seminar”. We became closer and closer as time went on and we knew there were feelings that were starting to develop. When I noticed it wasn’t just me that was feeling the increase in eye contact during sex and the overall connection, I asked her out on a date.

Even after we started dating, I took the time to get to know what she wanted. We both admitted to having a high sex drive. (Which we knew already from having such incredible sex together.) But when we went on our first ‘real dates’ I asked her how often she felt it was important to have sex. She told me her wants and it matched what I wanted.

We tell the full story as to how we came together and how we came to have Sensational Sex to the fullest at The Sensational Sex Seminar. You can find out more about one of our events and how to increase your sexual satisfaction, by going to http://www.TheSensationalSexSeminar.com

We’ll even teach you the “Four Levels of Sexual Satisfaction” and how to get there with your partner.

Attraction and sexual satisfaction

What is at play in sexual satisfaction?

Esther Perel has a great TED talk which I recommend watching. She said in her research she found that “people were most frequently attracted to their partners when they were in full confidence, on stage, watching them at work.” This involved seeing them in their element, doing their thing, radiating their natural self in their purpose. She said while they were looking at their person, from a comfortable distance, what is normally so well known, has once again become so elusive, and so mysterious. People she worked with said, *"I look at them and get a shift in perception, which is living in the mystery that lies right next to me. There is no neediness in desire."*

She also found that caretaking is a powerful anti-aphrodisiac. Meaning, having to be a caretaker for another person removes the attraction that is normally at play. Needing them is a turn off, it reduces the erotic charge. Also, when a couple is laughing together, or when surprised and when there is novelty, attraction builds.

This makes sense, wouldn't you agree? What matters is newness, excitement, intrigue, and creativity. Put yourself in these situations, create these situations and see what happens to your sexual attraction and desire. Watch your partner. Observe. Play games together. Do new things every so often. Laugh, and have fun. These are the creative energies that are at work.

Hopefully you can see now that sex can be a place to play. It is an obvious place to have fun. It contains childlike behaviours. Remember, I said sex is our birthright.

Esther also said something very key: "When you're vigilant, worried, anxious, and insecure (I will also add in some cases, righteous)... you can't lift your head to take off in space in playful, imaginative, ways."

For Example: With one woman I dated for a few years, we worked on our sex life constantly. At least I wanted us to. You see before dating her, I'd had great sex many times, with great partners. I knew what great sex was (and if you know what great sex is, you know what I mean). I knew what it required. I knew what it took on both parts. I knew what kind of place you had to be in mentally and emotionally, how it felt, how it looked, yes even how it sounded (stay on track people). I'm obviously all for great sex and deep intimacy and as such, I'm comfortable with my sexual side. She was not so much. It took work, and it took time. And that's okay. I really cared about her, so I was patient. But I would be lying to you if I told you that it wasn't frustrating me from time to time. I was very communicative and wanted to make things work. I asked a lot of questions, and I tried to help her in any way that I could. I was there for her and we explored a lot of different areas. However, I was younger as well, so my understanding and abilities were limited.

Sex or (love making) for me, is an obvious way to show how much I care about a person. **It is the ultimate physical expression of an emotional connection.** However, her mind was literally always in the way of an essentially emotional and physical connection. I could see and feel that she was not present with me. She was for lack of a better word, 'in her head.' But you know what? **Sex is not in the head. It is in the body!** You have to be in tune with your body for great sex to be great. You have to **tune yourself out** of **your mind, to tune into your body and allow great sex to come naturally.** Thankfully, she eventually learned to be in her body after she had some epiphanies and realizations about what was holding her back. Once she became present, her enjoyment of sex and intimacy multiplied as did mine!

You must do your own searching and looking if you are having the same situations occur. In the process of writing this book, I have become trained and certified in Hypnosis and Time Line Therapy. Both of these tools are a very powerful access to release negative emotions, limiting decisions and any blocks that are holding you back in any area of life. It is a very effective way to release anger, sadness, fear, hurt and guilt. Check out my website at www.TheRelationshipMaster.com for more information.

If you can be there physically without being present mentally or emotionally, you might "get off" for sure. But if you can bring yourself there mentally and physically, AND be emotionally present, then you will be able to connect, feel, and act in ways you never thought possible. This will open you up to divine connection, incredible bliss, and ecstasy. You and your partner will immediately feel the difference. Both of you will receive more and more pleasure.

Ultimate Connection

There is an ultimate connection waiting for you

Have you ever stared deeply into someone's eyes and told them with an invisible message that you wanted to melt in their presence? Have you ever felt someone sending you this message with their eyes? Have you ever felt such intense emotion and connection, with the very simple act of 'being' with someone? Have you sensed their energy as it connects with yours simply by sitting in front of one another?

I have, and my partners have too. It is a beautiful and magical thing. You may read this and think, 'this isn't possible,' but I assure you it is. As I said in the first chapter, anything is possible, and everything is energy. There is a way to feel the energy around you. During intimacy, there is a gift, an undeniable ultimate connection that is available to you and your partner. It is unlike anything in the world. It is one of the most unique and tantalizing ways to experience energy and love that I have ever felt.

How do you achieve this connection? Firstly, by letting down your walls. What walls? You hear people talk about 'barriers' right? That's because they do exist. You can read them off of people. Some people are more 'standoffish' than others. Some people are more 'withdrawn' or 'secluded' as you yourself may have described. The walls they put up are real, and they are in their mind and heart. Those walls are blocks that they have consciously or unconsciously put up to prevent people from getting too close to them. True intimacy is somewhat of a foreign concept to these people. Unfortunately they are blocking an essential access to connection and love.

You do not want these walls. You do not need these walls, not if you are interested in experiencing the ultimate connection that is available between yourself and another human being. They do more harm than good. You see the walls are not real. They are not necessary. They are in your mind. The walls are a figment of your imagination and yet you've had them for so long they seem real. If you are lucky, patient, and comfortable enough, you may have had the unique experience of disarming another human being's walls. Wow. What a gift that is. You have the ability to show them a new world. This world can be a breath of fresh air for many. **Someone who has walls up is fighting a war within themselves.**

They are in a state of duality. One side is fighting to keep the walls up, to win, to be right, and to hold on to the hurt, so as to prevent something from happening again. And the other side is the natural expression of love and peace within the self that is naturally there. This is how you come into the world-with everything being well, knowing no hurt, fear or guilt, feeling no need to protect one's self, being an abundant source of joy and love to everyone around you.

Unfortunately, most people in our western world are in the first state most of the time. When the walls come down, your rightful pleasure can come in (remember that birthright of pleasure which I spoke of earlier). Everyone deserves pleasure. Everyone can experience this ultimate connection. It is my intention through this book that you unlock the ability to experience it for yourself and with your partner.

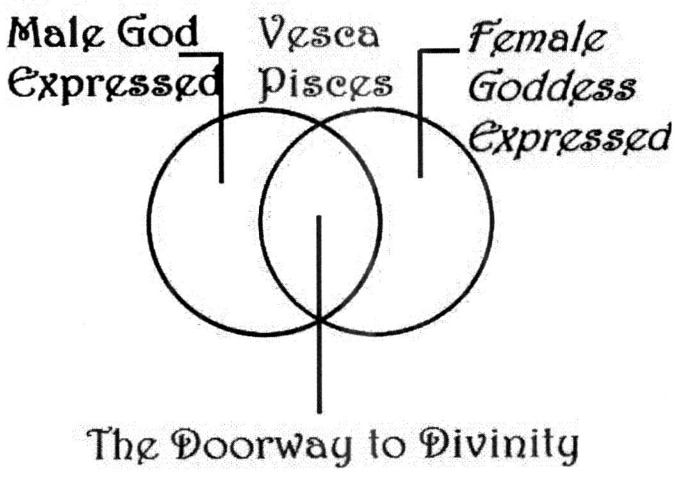

Another access to get to a place of intimacy is to stop thinking something is wrong. These days the human brain is constantly searching to fix something. It is automatically assuming there is something to fix.

Golden Nugget

In Intimacy, there is nothing to fix.

If this is you, then at some point, you will have to shut your mind off and learn how to just '**be'** together.

Deep, ultimate, powerful connection requires letting go of fear. Fear is in the way of vulnerable, perfect intimacy. Again, remember, intimacy is a way to deeply connect on a profound and magical level. What does it mean to connect, to experience oneness, to have no separation? Fear is separation, and it is a lie. There is no separation between us. We are all one. You and your partner are one. Human beings are one, part of one soul, one planet, one entity. It doesn't matter if you believe it or not. The world is coming to understand this more and more every day. One day in the future this will be common knowledge. It will be as common as potatoes. If you think about planet earth from a distance and zoom in to see the activity of those on the planet, you would see we're all the same. We're all moving in the same way thinking and acting in the same way, heading towards the same goals, having the same features, the same needs and the same wants. It would be hard to pick anyone out from the crowd, since we're all moving so similarly.

We're all the same, just a little different.

Exercise:
Find someone you feel comfortable with i.e., a friend, a lover, a new date, an ex, a flame, etc. Do this exercise as soon as possible. With your clothes on, stare at each other. Yes, I know, it sounds silly. But stare into each other's eyes. You can do this anytime. You can be sitting on a couch, sitting on the bed, or standing in

the living room. I want you to really look into each other's eyes and experience the other person. Don't talk. Just experience the other person in this vivid moment. Then experience your togetherness. Experience your similarities. Allow the layers to peel back and reveal themselves. Allow yourself to be vulnerable and just gaze into the other person's eyes. Don't worry about smiling laughing or blinking, it will happen. And that's okay. Just be with it. Persist and continue to look into each other's eyes until something starts to happen. You'll know when it will happen. And when you are ready, you will melt into each other. This is a beautiful thing. And you must try it to know what I mean. Have no intention. Have no goal. No purpose. Just connect. It could take 5-20 minutes. If you haven't felt it, you aren't doing it for long enough. You must resist looking away, and laughing although that may happen at first, just keep with it. If you cry, that is a beautiful thing too. That is your humanity coming out. What you are touching is each other, on a level that is so different from mere physical contact. If you are lucky, you can experience an incredible state of wonder by simply doing this exercise. You might become excited or turned on. That's fine. If you are comfortable with intimacy, you may even experience a sensation of being connected to the universe through this person's eyes. This resembles complete bliss. It is possible.

Keeping the Fire Burning

How much heat do you want?

Once you are in a relationship, you are sharing a large part of your life with the other person. Fact! You should experience everything there is to experience with this person (which will happen anyway if you are really connected). Therefore, you should be able to ask for what you want, right? You should be able to be straight about your desires, should you not? Of course you should! And what is the access to having what you want in life? Drum roll.... asking for it!!! But how many of us do that? How many of us are more concerned about upsetting the other person, than asking for what we want? How many of us tiptoe around our truest desires, and most authentic wants? Too many of us!

I too was guilty of this for a very long time. I realized that I was feeling stifled my the relationship, and I wasn't getting what I wanted. Initially I started blaming my partner (in my head of course). I resented her for being unable to read my mind. Then I realized just how crazy this was! It was at this time that I started seeing she had no idea of what I wanted to do and experience, why? Because I wasn't communicating with her! (more on this in the next chapter, which is a must read).

There is so much you can do together in sex and intimacy. You have to understand, even if it doesn't seem like it, there is a whole world to explore in your physical, emotional, and spiritual connection with each other. Again, you will be spending so much time together, so why not fill it with exciting explorations of each other's body, heart, and soul.

If this strikes you as odd, and you feel like I'm speaking a foreign language to you, I understand. If you can't see past the same 5 positions with your partner, I completely understand. I will offer these suggestions to help you explore and increase the fire or keep it going in your relationship. For example:
Music – Music adds a whole other dimension to love making. Like dancing, the music can dictate your mood, your flow, your movement and overall experience. It is the same case with sex. Music is a wonderful way, and one of my favourite's to shape your overall sexual experience. Different music will evoke different feelings, desires and flow between your partner and you. Sex is like a dance, and like a dance, it has flow and rhythm. You can choose romantic, sensual, arousing, fast paced, slow paced, erotic music. Or you can choose whatever you like! It's different for everyone, and that's great.

Join groups - There are plenty of meetup groups, community groups, social groups, networking groups, and spiritual groups all dedicated to the exploration, and satisfaction of relationships through sex. Many of them are safe and designed to be comfortable for any and all people alike. Some want to share experience, knowledge, and resources. And some want to share more, if you know what I mean. Be careful of those ones, only because you always have to take care of your personal safety. Look them up beforehand and always go with your partner or a friend.

Do your research – There are plenty of great resources, online, in libraries and bookstores. I don't claim to have all the answers. I just offer my perspective, my experience, my clients' experience, and many years worth of research and study.

Adult Clubs – There are plenty of places you and your partner can go. In your city, there are likely a couple of adult clubs that are meant for people to experience pleasure and feel comfortable in a place where they wouldn't normally otherwise feel comfortable... expressing themselves in public sexually. Some people go to partake, some go to watch, some go to learn. This could feel risky for some people, **but I can guarantee you, wherever the most risk, this is where the most growth occurs.**

Vacations – There was an LA Times articles which stated after a survey of 2,000+ adults, it was found that 88% of Americans are "somewhat likely to be intimate" when taking a vacation with a spouse or partner.

Only 12% said they are "somewhat or much less likely" to be intimate on vacation, (according to the survey conducted by Harris Interactive on behalf of Expedia). What's more, the study said couples who vacation three or more times per year are more likely to be satisfied with their love life than those who take two or fewer vacations per year.

Taking It Up A Notch

There is always room for more heat

An exploration into intimacy requires going deeper into your desires. You have to desire a deeper connection with yourself or your partner... or with life for that matter. Relationships are a place to experience more emotion. Intimacy is no different. I understand if it occurs to you as risky and scary. I can get that. If you are used to your blanket of security, you will have to give up a part of it. If that scares you, put that aside for now. Just become in touch with your desires. Your desires are about emotion. **Remember we are emotional beings.** You must look deeper into your emotions and become more deeply connected to your feelings.

I challenge you to push your boundaries. A deeper exploration into great sex and intimacy requires you to be uncomfortable, if only at first. Again, although it may seem scary, you can do this. You can push the limits past your comfort zone. It will be worth it. You are going to go somewhere you have never been before. I commend you for it. Why? If you take this on, and it is my sincerest hope that you do, you are going to go somewhere that people do not normally venture to and you will be rewarded.

This is so much more than just orgasms and getting off. You must discard that notion if you are to experience true intimacy.
It's not just about orgasms.

It's about a lot more than just getting off, people!

Great sex is about so much more than just the animalistic aspects of getting what you need and getting off. Animalistic sex which is satisfying yet immediate in nature can be very exciting but only offers a minimal level of fulfillment. A much, much deeper level of satisfaction and connection is possible, which gets into the heart and soul of human beings. There are moments when I have melted while looking into the eyes of my partner. There are moments where my partner and I have disappeared as separate entities and unified as one. There have been moments where we have transcended our physical bodies temporarily and come back only to experience such high vibration, such a highly positive state, it makes you question reality itself. I can look back on those moments with intense heat and passion of course… but they are some of the most memorable human experiences I have ever had. I don't really expect you to understand right away, but I want you to know that this is possible. You have to experience it for yourself. It becomes available when your focus is on more than 'just getting off.'
You wouldn't not use your eyes to see. You have a tongue to taste. You have your genitals to procreate, sure. But that's not all they're all used for. You can use them to feel good, to feel more, to connect deeply to feel your own inner being, and more (You're probably wondering, "What is this 'more' he keeps talking about?" I can't really answer this, as it is part of your journey).

We kiss with our eyes closed, not to avoid the awkwardness, but to go to a place, to disappear, to come away from reality, to feel the kiss more because it is natural to want to feel more. Emotion = energy in motion. Sex = high emotions. This partly explains why we're so obsessed with sex! We feel more.

Here's something to consider... a teacher of mine once said, (in no particular order) "There are 4 areas to sex: 1. Sex as fun, 2. Sex as spiritual, 3. Sex as procreation, 4. Sex as power." I am willing to bet most people are only familiar with 1 or 2 of these areas.

I have had a minor experience with Tantra, (what I did experience was AMAZING!) and I know many people that have taken a course, or met with an instructor and they have truly enjoyed it! It has added a lot to their relationship. For your information, the musician Sting and his wife Trudy are quoted saying, "Couples that Tantra together, stay together."

Regardless of what you do, you should know one very important thing,

Golden Nugget

"The health and well-being of a couple can be assessed by the state of the bedroom."

If it's not about orgasms, then what is it about? So much more! And it is up to you to discover it, find it, and play with it and see what happens. I'm still exploring it for myself, but I can tell you that it is all dependent upon your connection to who you really are and your partner.

I want to end this brief inquiry by quoting one of my favourite authors here. David Deida wrote, *"It's not time that kills delight, but familiarity, neutralization and lack of purpose."* In essence he's saying, take the time to make things exciting, keep things moving, and quit blaming time on the thing which stops your sex life and relationship from growing. Remember that sexual energy is a powerful driving force, and it is connected to your ambition. Your partner will not be attracted to you if you aren't moving anywhere in life. If you're sex life isn't where you want it to be, look at your desires and ambitions in life.

In her book, "*The Invitation*" Oriah wrote: *"Anyone who has ever made love knows that part of the pleasure is in anticipating both the familiar and the unknown. The pleasure of sex and intimacy of lovemaking are deepened when I am able to slow down and consciously savor the sharp taste of the moment in between, the second just before, the place where the breath catches in anticipation. I am aware of the scent of heat held in the air between two mouths, reaching for each other hungrily... the skin that tingles, waiting, fine hairs at attention, reaching, aching. There is anticipation in the places that have not yet been touched but know they will be. There is hope of being fully met by the one who can touch me without taking his eyes from mine."*

Notice that as a female she is looking for a man to meet her match. A male has a mission to meet and serve the feminine, to provide security, sensuality and ecstasy. And as the feminine, she shows the ability to savour the moments, the seconds as she tunes into that feminine energy. What is not important is who is doing what and how gender roles are defined. That's not what this is about. What is important is that both partners are partaking in an exchange, a dance if you will. No one person is responsible. Both are parties to the same outcome: Loving Sexual Expression.

Body language

Your body is a conduit for sexual energy

Like an electrical conduit, electricity moves and passes the electricity through the conduit and goes to other places. The electrical energy is available; it could be sitting still without anywhere to go, nowhere to move to unless it is channeled into a certain direction or outlet. If you have a body, it is a conduit to move the energies of love, sex, intimacy through you. If you don't use your body, the energy will go nowhere. It will remain dormant, unseen, unheard and unfelt. Your body is a tool to feel and experience more pleasure, emotion, and gratification than you could ever experience anywhere else. So you might want to consider opening up and stimulating the body, and allowing the body to express its natural sexual energy.

Most people in today's western world are not in tune with their bodies. Most people have their minds controlling their bodies and they listen to their mind, instead of listening to their bodies. However, there is a new movement of information coming out which indicates that your body actually has the power to inform your mind, as to what is best for you. What is being discovered is that your mind may play tricks on you (think of the Ego and the Id in Psychology). But your body will never lie to you. Yes, your body does speak to you. It has its own intelligence system and it sends messages through feelings and intuition to your mind and heart.

If you watch someone's body language, and study it as I have for many years, you will see that you can learn a lot about a person just through observing the way the body moves. I have come to the conclusion that the body, and how one carries themselves, everything from walking, posture, sitting position, gestures, and more, will demonstrate for you a complete reflection of the characteristics, attitudes, and beliefs of a person.
Sometimes the best intimacy and sex is careful, relaxed, and slow. Other times, the best sex is actually quite sloppy, messy and quick. It depends on the buildup, the setting, the mood and the state of mind you and your partner are in. Those who are experienced love makers will probably understand. Others may be interested or curious as to how this would work.

So how do you do it? Let it start with a kiss. Wait, it actually starts before the kiss. You see before the kiss, there is usually an energy exchange in the air, a mutual interest, a semi physical, semi emotional desire that gets translated between you. Whenever moving in for a kiss, you should know beforehand if there is something pulling the two of you together. How will you know? You will feel it. It takes time to develop a sixth sense, but mostly it will require you to be "out there" with the other person instead of in your head, wondering, pondering, worrying if this will go well or not.

Other things that run in people's minds while being intimate are the everyday distractions of work, family, friends, to do lists, cleaning, cooking, business etc. This is a problem in our western world today, that we are mostly living in our heads instead of in our bodies. The way to deal with that is to really feel the feelings and sensations between you and your partner, really see what you see in front of you and really hear everything that is going on around you. I know it sounds easier said than done, but trust me, it will make for an overall greater pleasurable experience.

Golden Nugget

Great foreplay is part of great sex! So build great sexual energy because it all equals sexual chemistry.

Build excitement, intrigue, curiosity, and anticipation! How do you do this? Talk in subtleties and ironies. Play and have fun! Bring a sense of fun and play to each moment and don't be afraid to test the boundaries, push the envelope and open things up a little with your dialogue. Be comfortable talking about sex. Ask questions, talk about what they like, or don't like, what are their thoughts or views on sex. What have they always wanted to do, or fantasized about doing? Everyone has fantasies, and it doesn't mean you have to fulfill them per se, but it would be great to know, wouldn't it?

As a side note, research and study has shown that 80% of a woman's orgasm is mental. What this does mean is that women can't be thinking, thinking, thinking, for them to mostly reach orgasm. No, it means a woman's state of mind is what is most important. What I have found is that the more present, comfortable, relaxed and feeling safe and secure, is where her true climax lies. For men it is a mostly physical nature, which is why for men, having an orgasm is incredibly easy. I believe it is because men are mostly active in their left brain all day anyway which is all about thinking rather than feeling. When men have sex, their mind naturally disengages because the physical and visual receptors are so active (men are typically visually stimulated).

Back to kissing, Kissing is a way to disarm your concerns, it reduces anxiety and quiets the 'noise' in your mind. It increases the levels of oxytocin, a very important and natural occurring hormone that promotes a feeling of calm and peace in the body. After first kissing, then you should begin to caress and touch. Caressing is so important. Why? Upon physical contact, the mind will disengage. That's very important! Physically connecting with someone will disengage the mind and also release beneficial and healthy hormones in the brain. That's why they say we need eight hugs a day to really feel happy and healthy. Happy is a big part of healthy.

How to make it all work

But there are so many distractions

The key to making intimacy work is to play and have fun. It's almost too simple I know, but it is an easy key. If you haven't noticed yet, the simpler you make life, the easier it works. Don't be afraid to laugh. In fact, laughing can be a great connecting puzzle piece to this whole intimacy thing! Some of the best most connected love sessions are when my partner and I are laughing a lot before a great love fest. Laughter really excites the senses, is a high vibration of energy and gets the blood flowing. Laughter also gets your mind off of concerns, which is why we love to go see movies or comedy shows when we have had a rough day or event occur in life. Laughter can open up the heart and soul and really let things breathe. Sex is supposed to be fun remember! You must be willing to try new things or do things differently. And you must communicate with each other. You can do this by using the tools in the next chapter (are you seeing how important communication is?)

Sex is all about feelings. This is not about being technical, or getting things right. Sex and intimacy is not about being perfect! If you feel you are bad in the bedroom, that's fine! This is a total opportunity to play and discover! Becoming a good lover is all about practice and learning. Like any skill or muscle, it takes time to build (unless you're Italian and the Casanova is in your blood! Yes, I am Italian and that was a very cheesy joke). However, it has taken me much practice and desire to get to know what feels good for my partners to actually be in the place where I can be referred to as "a great lover".

If you are in a relationship or dating and having trouble, try this. Discover your partner all over again. Pretend you are a child, completely curious and intrigued by this person, this body, this being before you. Pretend they are a new object in your life that you must explore and understand all parts of. No matter how much time has passed that you have been together, new is possible, and new is still available. Start with some small part of them, i.e. their toes, their belly, their hands and explore. When you enter the mental space and take this on and stay in it, you will naturally start to see things differently. You will see parts of your partner you never saw before.

I dare you to look at them with mystery, curiosity, and allow yourself to be amazed by your partner. Be amazed at what you may find. If need be, return back to chapter 1 on being and becoming curious. You can do this now, with your partner tonight. It is irrelevant how long you've been together or how much sex you've had.

You can come back to this chapter anytime, and you can do that in any relationship you are in. When you start, in whatever way you start, whether it's kissing, or straight sex, keep all distractions at bay, all of them. Turn the cell phone off and put it away, turn the TV off. The kids are away at friends or grandparents, if you have kids. You can have music on or off as long as its music that will add to the mood and love making session. If it's anything else, turn the music off. You can have lights off or on. Some dim lighting can be a really nice addition (if you're looking to add aesthetics to help the mood).

For those people who want to have sex with the lights off all the time, nuh uh. No pass. No way. That is so unjust. That is unfair to your partner. Don't do that to them. That is a mind case of body image and self-righteous concerns. I know I am deviating as this issue could be an entire chapter on self-image. But we don't have time for that. We want you to experience more love and connection in your life now. And because of that, it really is simple. If you insist on the lights off **all**

the time, listen up- this is incredibly selfish of you. You have made this entirely about you, which it is not!

Golden Nugget

Great sex and intimacy is not about how good you look. It is about how well you connect.

If you are with someone and you are enforcing a 'lights off' rule – stop. You are torturing your partner. It is their choice to want to make love to you. They want to make love to you. It is **their desire.** This is an act of expressing their love for you. This is about **them giving themselves to you.** Nowhere in this is it about how you look and feel. So take a deep breath and sigh. Good. Now take another. Isn't that a relief? Yes! If you think you can't do it, you might want to consider getting help. Otherwise, your partner has every right to leave you, since this is near torture for a person to have to put up with this. Can you imagine what it's like to be excited about something, like a kid in a candy store, and then be told you can't taste the candy you choose to eat?

If you are basing having sex on how good you feel you look, you are missing the point, severely. You are diminishing any and all possibility for true intimate connection, real pleasure and deep satisfaction for you and your partner. You should stop this now, and apologize to your partner and go surrender into some blissful deeply connected sex right now.

Communication

The second most important tool, next to your body

You can't have sex without your body, and you can't have sex without communicating. So although the next chapter is all about communication, let's spend a little time talking about communication in the context of sex and intimacy.

You have to express your feelings. You have to express what you want. How else are people supposed to know what pleases you? The silly thing about us humans is we don't really say what we want to each other. We aren't straightforward. We're afraid of hurting the other person, being too imposing or inconveniencing them (especially here in Canada). I know this well because I too did not express what I wanted. Now I can clearly see it everywhere. In the past, I would put aside what I really wanted in sex, even though it would be on my mind, stay on my mind and drive me crazy. Even while doing it! It would be in my head, while trying to enjoy what was happening. What do you think that led to? Only a partial enjoyment of what was actually going on.

I'm now proud to say that I openly talk about what my desires are. I know it sounds scary at first, but it is a muscle that gets built the more you use it-speaking about what is on your mind. In turn, I have better sex, I can focus more, I can be honest with my partners and they appreciate me telling them the truth. Why do you think they appreciate this? It's because they will know what to do to please me. Because in sex, we naturally want to please our partners!

Speak it! That's one of the main uses of your mouth. In a sexual context, talking to each other builds excitement. Tell them what you want to do with them or to them. Ask your partner what they want to do. Your homework is to do this. Practice this. Ask them what they want, and then close your eyes and wait. Conversely, tell them what you like. Whether they respond or not, your job is to be open to their response. Be free of judgment and then find out for yourself if you are comfortable with that, if you can do that or not. It might not be as bad as you've made it out to be.

In essence, you want to create a safe space in the act or in the conversation beforehand, where they will understand that there is no judgment on your end. How? Use a light, comfortable, sexy voice, speak slowly, prevent yourself from reacting, and smile when they say whatever they say. This can be done outside the bedroom or inside the bedroom.

If you're being kinky with them in the act, have a safe word. If it's going too far, then use the safe word. Establish trust beforehand. Make sure you trust this person before you interact with them in a sexual context. How do you know when you trust someone? You'll know. You'll feel it. You'll simply know that you can trust them.

It's important to have agreements beforehand. Obviously it's not necessary or 100% required, since there is an exciting element to lustful, passionate, adventurous and risky sex. If you can have some of the details worked out beforehand, that will allow you to focus. Consider talking about some items like birth control methods, how far you'll go together, what positions they like, what their favourite parts of sex are, how often they like to have sex – these are great items to have sorted out ahead of time. You can only get those answers by talking them out.

It is important that you talk to each other. Should you encounter things you don't want, or things that don't work for you, say so. It doesn't work to have it continue and say nothing, only to then feel bad about yourself afterwards.

One more small thing you can do to make sex and intimacy better is to shower each other with compliments. As humans we are starved for appreciation and acknowledgement. A great way to get the spark going, and arouse some excitement in your partner is to compliment them. Tell them what you like about them, their body, their technique, the way they feel, the way they make you feel and more. There is so much to use here. This is something that really excites me, and keeps the blood flowing (no pun intended). This could cause some really hot energy between the two of you. It is such a simple and small thing, but there is a cause and effect to it. The cause is the words you speak, which land in their ear, which move into their mind and then their body and heart. The effect is admiration, feeling appreciated, feeling understood, arousal, feeling safe, seeing you in a new light, hearing what they've always wanted to hear, or looked forward to hearing from you for some time. This will stimulate their senses, and cause attraction to build!

I have given you golden nuggets throughout this book. Now it's time to find your own golden nuggets for yourself, in your partner. They will thank you and enjoy you more because of it.

Now on to one of the most important chapters of this book, continuing on the topic of..... communication!

8
Communication

An entire chapter on communication?

Someone once told me, "*If you have the skill to really communicate with people, it can trump any other skill.*" I believe this to be true. The ability to communicate is such a special skill. It can transform conflict, turn negative situations into positive situations, it can drastically change the way someone sees and experiences the world and it can make someone feel at home, even when in a strange place or event. The skill of communication can stop someone dead in their tracks in the heat of emotion, it can cause a person to melt in satisfaction, and so much more!

I once heard a painter tell a story about a job he completed where he painted a living room for a customer in her home. After finishing the job, he called the customer to inform her it was completed and said, "It's all finished ma'am. I hope you like it." She said, "Oh thank you! I'm sure I will like it, as long as it's not burgundy, it will be fine. I will be over in a few minutes to see it." "Great, see you then," he said with his mouth. But in his head he thought, 'Oh crap! I'm looking at a burgundy wall in front of me here! What am I going to do?' He immediately began pacing around the room, looking at the wall, looking at the floor, looking at the wall again in panic. Until he realized, he had a nice glass of red wine last night. It was a Merlot in fact and when he realized that he shouted, "Hey! It doesn't look like burgundy, it looks like a Merlot!" The woman came over a few minutes later, and stood in the living room looking at the walls with the painter and said, "Umm, do you think that looks burgundy?" "No, no" he said, "It definitely is not burgundy. I would say it's a nice shade of Merlot." Immediately, she took a step back, placed her hand on her chest, gasping a fresh breath of air and said, "Oh! My gosh, you're right! It IS a nice shade of Merlot! I love Merlot!" Her phone rang in the next few seconds, it was her friend Joanne and she said "Joanne, I just painted my living room and it's a beautiful shade of Merlot! I love it!" And that was a very satisfied customer for the painter.

Language shapes our lives. Language shapes the way we live. It completely describes our experience. It governs so much of the way we live.
A great use of language can enrich your life, and the lives of those around you. There is really so much to the world of communication I could write a whole book on it, and I have to keep it to one chapter. This is one of the most important chapters in the book (I know, I've said this before, they're all very important). In this chapter, I will give you many of the tools I have used, helped my clients use and still employ on a daily basis to live a great life and have better relationships.

In dialogue, we create many of our agreements and expectations with each other. Usually, actions are not taken until they are created or agreed upon in language first. Think about it. There is much that lives in the air between us. Take a moment and think about what is said and what goes unsaid to the people in our lives. So much of our intentions go unspoken to the people we care about. What if we spoke those intentions? What if we put them into language? Would people understand us better? Would we understand ourselves more? The unfortunate thing is that most people don't know how to communicate, at least not past their basic frustrations, emotions and thoughts. What do I mean? Well, mostly people communicate from a very surface level, 'topical only' place. When someone speaks, you'll get the basics and only the basics, instead of the whole real issue, the deeper meaning, the underlying truth. We haven't learned how to communicate better yet. We communicate from a place of trying to get rather than give.

I firmly believe anything is resolvable in communication. I have been living this principle in my life and in my relationships since I understood this. There is a whole world of communication which you are likely unaware of. In this chapter I will do my best to share all the different tools, techniques, skills and abilities that I have gained and used over the years. It should be noted, to be a Master of Relationships, you must be a Master of Communication. Relationships are ALL about communication.

You'd better get used to it – You're doing it all the time

Are you aware of how you are communicating?

There is no such thing as 'not communicating' because you are always communicating. We do it every day don't we? Even when you think you aren't communicating, you are. How? Communication is more than just talking. You are communicating with your tone of voice, with your body language, with your energy and with your emotions. Remember that **emotion = energy in motion** and so your e-motion is moving. It's moving all around you, and anyone around you picks up on it. Also, remember that every single part of you is connected. Your mind, body and spirit are completely connected to each other. They move and react in unison. That is why you it is often hard to fake how you really feel and think from others, and being completely authentic is a great skill and asset. We'll come back to this in a little bit.

For now, I share this very important fact with you - the brain interprets communication on many different levels. Your unconscious mind does this automatically, and so while you may not be conscious of it, it is still happening. Check this out, the majority of your message is comprised of three parts: 55% of what you say is based on your body language, 38% of what you say is based on your tone of voice, and only 7% of what you say is based on your words. Wow! I love sharing this with people because it blows their minds!

I often conduct workshops on working relationships and communication skills for career or community organizations that support new Canadians and Immigrants. Many of them feel that their 'English is no good' and so they become fearful of how they will come across in a job interview or setting of that sort. Once I share this information with them and help them understand why the actual words they use are least important, they become lighter, more confident and clear on the spot. Communication is mostly a function of body language and tone of voice. Both of these will communicate your 'state'. You could call this your state of mind or way of being. It is totally congruent through your physiology and again consists of your thoughts, feelings, experience, and way of being.

If you are being hesitant, cautious and nervous, you will display a certain kind of body language and carry your voice in a manner which you would obviously recognize as timid, shy, and potentially uncomfortable. What is interesting is as you read this, you might have obtained the image in your mind of a picture of someone or yourself behaving in just this manner. Alternatively, if you are being confident, comfortable and relaxed, you will exude and see body language and hear tones of voice that reflect that.

You know what the funny thing is? You have almost no control over this. You unconsciously behave in the way your state reflects. You don't even get a chance to think about it. Since it happens instantaneously, you are exuding it before you know it. It's automatic, so don't blame yourself, don't hate yourself for it either, there is no point. For now, just be aware of it.

This can dramatically improve your life

How would you like to be heard?

This chapter is going to be thick and chock full of the essentials to creating a great relationship. Listen carefully and hang on every word and apply it to your relationships. If you apply this to your life, I promise you your whole life will change. For example, if you want your message heard, you have a responsibility to ensure it gets communicated in a way that others can hear it. Focus on this statement; you are responsible for how you communicate in the world. If people are constantly misunderstanding you, then you aren't communicating responsibly. If you constantly have disagreements and arguments with your partners, coworkers, and others, then you might want to look at the way you are coming across. Now obviously disagreements will happen and that is a natural part of life, however you have something else available, and that is to do your best to communicate in a way so that others will actually be able to understand what you are saying.

Something you should know is that after all the thousands of people I've worked with, and understanding my own experiences, I have to admit, people are stingy.

We don't communicate. We think we communicate, but we don't. To be honest, we think the other person should understand what we are thinking. It's crazy and it's true. We walk around thinking that everyone should behave the way we do, understand things like we do, and have the same beliefs and points of view. We think people should just know what we're talking about. People seem to feel as if we shouldn't have to put effort into the way we communicate, the other person should just get it. Normally when things don't go our way, the thought we're having is, "What's wrong with you? Why don't you get it?" If you think about how different we all are, what different backgrounds, experiences and points of view we have, this is crazy.

Golden Nugget

If you want a great relationship, you'll have to have great communication.

Guess what? To have great communication, you'll have to put some work into it.

Take a few moments, dust off that old notepad and ask yourself the question, "How do I want to be heard?" I know this is might be an unusual question, but it is very worth examining. Brainstorm some different ways that you would like to have your messages received by your partner. Remember that **you have a responsibility to communicate in a way that your partner can receive**. So you might say, "I want to be heard in a loving way. I would like my messages to be heard clearly. I want my messages to be received without judgment. I would like my partner to hear my point of view as valid." List at least 10 different ways that you want to be heard. Do that work now.

Now after you do that work, ask yourself the question, "How can I communicate in a way, to ensure my message is heard or received in that way?" Take some notes in respect to that question as well. The simple answer is to think about what you would need to say, or how you would need to say it, to actually have your message land in the other person's mind and heart the way that you want it to.

For example, if you want to be heard in a neutral way, you will have to listen and speak from a neutral place, where you are not triggered by a reaction. You would have to be unattached as to the outcome of the conversation (there's that word again, unattached!). If you want your message to be heard in a loving way, you'd have to speak from a place of love, rather than a place to be right or prove the other person wrong. Love has no right and wrong. Love is all encompassing. Love is forgiving. The need to be right or wrong can really, really get in the way of that. That's why there's a whole section coming up on right and wrong, for now just put it aside (since it dominates so much of the way we communicate.)

One of the easiest and best things you can do to improve your communication immediately is to have an intention in every communication. This requires some thought before you go into the conversation with others. It's very important because it means you are walking into a conversation knowing what ground you are going to take, or what place you are going to come from (I never liked that saying "think before you speak"). If you are in a relationship, consider communicating (which includes listening) from the place of, "This is my partner, this is my lover. This is my friend." When you listen from that space, there is no right and wrong. There is no trying to prove your point or prove how right you are. There is only love and a real willingness to work things out. If you can maintain your composure and avoid being triggered, you will have more successful communication. Why? Because in truth, this is your partner, this is your lover, this is your friend. Sometimes we forget that when we get lost in conversation. If you are dating and things aren't working out or you are concerned about something they have done, try and come from this place: "This is someone who is interested in me, this is someone who I am interested in. I won't know if it will work until I give them a chance to express themselves and be themselves." If you want things to work out with someone you are starting out with, then you will need to actually give it a chance and that includes giving them a chance. If you can't communicate well with them, what makes you think you will be able to communicate with anyone?

Anything Can Be Resolved in Communication

What's possible?

Why do all this work? Is it worth it? Is it actually going to work? Why do we actually communicate in the first place? We communicate to connect. But to communicate newly, you'll have to see communication in a new light. **Anything can be resolved in communication.** From here on out, I want you to take this approach, "I can resolve anything through communication." I promised you by buying this book that you would have great relationships. You won't have great relationships just reading this book. You will have to work at it, and communication ladies and gentlemen, is the key. Communication is so much of the meat and potatoes of why relationships either succeed or fail, why they're happy or unhappy, why they're 50 year marriages today or divorces tomorrow. Think about it as a way to connect.

I promise you, if you can communicate, you can completely resolve any conflict, issue, or problem. You'll need to take this position and take it now. Aside from solving problems, communication is brilliantly important for the other purpose of your relationship: connection. Connection = love. Connection = communication. Communication = speaking and listening. Speaking & listening = Connection. Connection = being heard. Being heard = what we all want in our relationships.

You will feel connected by being heard. Being heard = being understood.

How you can actually resolve upsets and arguments is by using the super power of being unattached! It's a superpower remember! How you can resolve upset and achieve resolutions is by letting go of the attachment of getting what you want, because mostly what you want is to win or have the other person lose. Most of why we argue and feel so defensive is because we feel so attached to being right or proving that someone else is wrong. Remember that, because this applies to all of us unfortunately. Everyone has been told no by someone, when they wanted to hear yes. Everyone has been rejected, denied, had their ideas, passions and desires obscured. It is a natural instinct to want to pay that person back who hurt us. Many of us become defensive around being challenged. We don't want to be wronged. We want to be right. We feel justified, righteous, and 'good' (better about ourselves) when we get other people to share our point of view. We unconsciously take it out on our partners if they don't see things the same as we do And you know what? That's not what they're there for. So you'll have to learn to let go of the attachment of being right or wrong and just communicate from a place without attachment. Communicate for the sake of communicating. Use the superpower by leaving your communication in the area between the two of you, and then allow whatever response to come out, comes out.

In a later section I will cover speaking honestly and truthfully in a compassionate way. Allow me to tell you about an experience with someone I was with named Estelle. Estelle and I started seeing each other shortly after she had gotten out of a relationship. We were only dating and hadn't made things official yet. One particular Saturday morning I was headed to a conference and she was out partying late the night before. She happened to run into her ex-boyfriend and he was flaunting the girl that he was now sleeping with. They made it very clear he and his new friend were strictly casual. Naturally, this upset Estelle and it didn't help that they were all drinking a little too much. On this phone call, she was venting and I was listening. I listened and listened and agreed with what she was saying, that he was being insensitive and insincere. Maybe it was the alcohol or the hangover, but she continued on. I noticed I was having trouble listening now as I was getting a little triggered. "Why is she telling me all this? Why is she pouring all of this to me? Wow, she is really caught up about this!" I caught myself. I knew why she was telling me this. She cared about me, she wanted to share, she needed to get it out of her system. It is having an impact on me however, and I realized this is a conversation that would be better for her to have with one of her friends. I politely interrupted her, "Estelle, can I just interrupt you for a second?" "Okay." "I don't mind hearing about this and I can tell how much this bothered you. I know he wasn't being sensitive and was insincere. However, I think this is a conversation that you might want to have with your friends instead. And I don't want you to feel like you can't talk to me, because that's not what I'm committed to. At the same time, if you put yourself in my shoes, and think about me hearing all about your ex and his new girlfriend, and what an impact it has on you, you might feel funny. You know what I mean?" She paused, and there was some silence. Then she said, "Yeah, you know what, I am so sorry. Like so sorry. I feel like such an idiot, this is not the kind of conversation I want to be having with you." I wanted her to stop beating herself up, so I said "No, It's okay. Don't beat yourself up. I get it. The situation really sucked. I just have to go, and I think the more we talk about him between us, the less it's about us." She was so grateful I said what I said, I mean she really appreciated it. She told me a few times in the next few days. And I'm just glad I trusted myself and was straight forward. It's important to make note of the fact thatshe did the other part, which was that she received it well. This really strengthened our communication and created a good pattern for compassionate, straightforward conversations afterwards.

Golden Nugget

Turn breakdowns into breakthroughs.

Golden Nugget

Great communication requires controlling your emotions.

Let me tell you another story. One day when I was younger, I was home in my apartment when my roommates Mary and Darren were walking in the door. I heard them arguing and could tell they were in the middle of some kind of disagreement. I felt the tension as soon as they walked into the front hall. They were making small comments to each other. You know the kind of comments. The short, cut, abrupt kind the way people do when they're in a tiff together.

I came out as it was getting louder and louder. I went into the kitchen to get some tea and they came over to involve me in the debate. They wanted me to settle an argument for them and I said, "Okay, on one condition. Before I do, I want you to know, what you are doing is dangerous." They said, "What?" "This," I said, "This is dangerous. As a couple, it's not a good idea." And they were kind of shocked. I said, "If I agree with you Darren, you will feel right and righteous and say, 'See I told you so.' And Mary will be upset at me possibly and she'll be mad at you too potentially. Meanwhile, if I agree with Mary, you Darren might feel slighted, stupid, that might impact our friendship, and how likely are you to show love to Mary for the rest of the day?" (I know I went on for a little bit of a coaching session. They are my roommates after all.) I didn't stop there, "And what I want you to know, is that my opinion is only my opinion. It isn't right or wrong. It's just my opinion and the same goes for you both."

They stopped and paused after that. It was funny. They paused and looked at each other. Their attitudes and reactions shifted in that moment. Needless to say, the tension disappeared. They told me about the argument they were having and their sides and to be honest, I saw both sides to the story. And I gave them my opinion on both outcomes and after that it didn't matter who was right.

What's the lesson here?

Both of them got to see the future. The road they were heading down. If they continued with their actions and their mission to "be right," they would have headed down an ugly path.

In a relationship, there is no winning when someone loses. If someone loses, and your objective is to "win" the argument or debate, then you've both lost.

We as partners should do our very best to always see our partner's point of view. And respect them for what they say. It will always end in peace and harmony, which will allow you to spend more time together that you enjoy.

That's the objective of the relationship anyway.

Acknowledgement

The world is starved for acknowledgement

Would you like to know how to elevate your relationship and your partners love for you within minutes? I want to teach you something so simple, but so important. It has the ability to bring your relationship to a higher level of love and understanding. It is the concept of acknowledgement. You could think of it as making compliments, however I assure you it is much more than that. I want you to think deeply about someone you care about - anyone. It could be a family member, a pet, or a person you are currently interested in. Just make it someone you know well and someone that you know matters to you. Now think for a second. Why do they matter to you? What is it that they provide for you? What is it that their being in your life, that contributes to you?

If you think about this long enough, you'll see that there are some specific things you gain from this person. There are specific things that you 'get', no? This could also be the case with someone whom you may dislike, or have some disagreements with. Because they also do something for you. So, what is that something?

It might be that they really understand you, or maybe they make you feel at home. Maybe they have this way of giving you the space to say anything want. Maybe they have a knack to make you feel simply happy and that just turns your day right around.

Whatever it is, this is what there is to acknowledge them for. It is a way of expressing deep gratitude. It is a way to thank them, for the hidden things that you may not always notice. This is special. This is more than just compliments. If you do this, they will usually be taken aback by this unusual action. Now here is the really interesting part - there are people who are apt to disregard such compliments, such displays of affection and gratitude. It can be normal for others to quickly defer or avoid accepting the comments that you make. Don't let them push this opportunity away. This takes courage for you to do. This takes stepping outside of your comfort zone to express yourself and how they make you feel this way. Pull them out of that behaviour by literally interrupting them and having them accept and hear your words.

Why go to all this trouble? The funny thing about acknowledgement is that giving it is a benefit mostly for the person who is giving it, and not for the person receiving it. Don't get me wrong, of course they will gain from this, and the idea is to have them hear the words. However it's mostly for you to release, express, and acknowledge all of the great things that this person gives to you. It is for you to recognize them. You can do this with anyone. This is a deep form of love, affection, and can really build attraction. How? Because it feels so great to receive! The world is starved for this. Commit to go out and do this now. Get in the practice of this loving habit. Put this in your day timer or calendar. I'm serious. Could you imagine both you and your partner going back and forth on this every now and again? Do you know how much love that would foster? There just isn't enough of this in the world. We are critical enough as it is on each other. Let's give this a break and acknowledge one another.

Bonus material: This is one great way to really shift the conversation – it clears the air. It gets you back to love. It gets something workable in the space. It interrupts the challenging aspects of your relationship. It makes things work. This will have you be more compassionate and filled with love for yourself and your partner. Because what you sow is what you reap. It will increase intimacy, as a way to add to what we talked about in the previous chapter. It can cause your partner to fall in love with you. It can cause them to see you in a new light. But remember, this kind of special acknowledgement requires you to look deeper, for what they add to your life, moment by moment, for what that does to you. What it does for you.

This is so much more than just positive thinking, it is positive living. Who said your life had to be the way it is? You are a creator. You get to create your life. Your life is governed by language as you can see in this chapter.

So how do you want to live?

Golden Nugget

The words that leave your mouth, the conversations you have, define your life.

A little moment that transformed my entire life

You'll never guess who I used to be

Most of the time when we communicate, especially in an argument, our objective is to prove a point. Right? (Funny how I just did that). We are trying to get the other person to agree with us. More than that however there is a hidden agenda running in the background to 'be right' or prove the other person wrong. (Similar to Darren and Mary's example above.) I know that I can speak for myself, as this is something I used to do obsessively.

Listen to this story. When I was in the second grade, I had a teacher named Mrs. Macdonald. She was a decent teacher in my books, until one day she asked us to do an assignment on dinosaurs. She asked each of us to draw our favourite dinosaur, so I drew a triceratops. I liked the triceratops a lot, especially with the three horns and the shield, all which made it great for offense and defense in the dinosaur world. I coloured in the triceratops in orange. Knowing that orange was not the natural colour of the triceratops didn't matter. He was my favourite triceratops and I was going to make him special and unique by colouring him in orange. Mrs. Macdonald came around shortly, checking over everyone's shoulders commenting on their work. "Nice job Matthew, Great T Rex Jonathan, lovely Melissa," were the words that left her lips as she walked around. This was until she came to mine when she said, "Michael what is this? No, no, no, this is all wrong." She picked up my paper and held it up for the class to see and said, "Look everyone, Michael did the assignment wrong!" and let out this big cackling, heckling laugh and the rest of the class laughed too. You'd think I would have retreated in my shell and thought, 'I'm not smart, I suck at life' and became saddened. But instead in that moment I looked up at her and thought, 'What you are doing as a teacher, and as an adult, is wrong. You should not be doing that.' I was aware enough at that age to notice that and make that assessment. Needless to say, I hated her forever after that. Anytime I saw her in the halls, I spoke nasty obscenities under my breath. On the day she retired I celebrated, "Goodbye you nasty woman! Never speak here again!"

Fast forward throughout my life until a few years ago and I'm in a transformative course called the (Landmark Forum). I became aware of this incident and how much it had impacted my life. What I really noticed that was so powerful was that I decided in that moment with Mrs. Macdonald that no one was ever going to wrong me ever again, and I would always be right. Who was that human being in the course? I was filled with anger, righteousness, and stubbornness. In arguments with anyone, I would fight them to the death. Worse, I would build up a case against someone throughout our time together, saving up all the little things that I felt they did 'wrong' and use it against them. I would build up a case where if you challenged me, you would regret it in the end. I was super defensive and could not take criticism or feedback on anything. I remember some of my supervisors would give me feedback (as was their job) and I couldn't take it. I would get mad at them, I would criticize their criticism. See to me, feedback wasn't feedback. It was an attack. So you can imagine the kind of arguments I would have with my partners. Wow.

When I discovered this, I did not like who I was. I became fully present to the impact that this had on the people in my life. I left them depleted, defeated and devoid of energy to try and contribute or converse with me about anything that I didn't agree with. I was disgusted at myself. I remembered moments where my girlfriends would break down in tears and just give up. And I would feel like I won. What an idiot I was… I vowed in that moment to completely change the way I looked at arguments, criticisms and feedback. I promised myself I would see people as unique. I promised myself I would honour people for what they see and create. I also promised myself to be coachable. I became aware of the huge opportunity that lay before me. Since I thought I knew everything, my world was rocked when I realized just how much I was missing out on.

That was one of the defining moments of my life and has no doubt caused me to do what I do, and develop my capacity as a great partner. And now I live to help others do the same.

When I tell people that story, they have no idea who I am talking about. They can't seem to connect the two. And yet, that is who I used to be. And I am proud of myself today. My partners today would call me a great communicator, a great listener, someone who makes them feel comfortable to say anything around.

There is no such thing as right and wrong

How committed are you to a great relationship?

Golden Nugget

Someone wise once told me, you can be right, or you can be happy.

You want to remember this because the desire to be right will overpower the desire for anything. The human desire to be right can be a nasty, overbearing force which is extremely unpleasant to be around. It rears its ugly head unconsciously and usually won't go away until one party gives way.

If you think about it, this is quite ridiculous. Right and wrong are subjective. They are a matter of perspective. They hold no real weight in the real world.

Take for example monogamy. In some cultures it is illegal or 'wrong' for one person to have multiple wives and multiple partners. In some cultures it is not. There are groups of people who are inside of the structure or society where this is considered wrong, and others do it anyway. In some parts of the world it is perfectly normal. In some parts of the world there is the death penalty, in some there is not. In some families you discipline your kids with physical actions, in others it is only verbal corrections that are made.

Now you may have been emotionally charged or judgmental by the things you just read. And that's okay. The point is to notice where you get charged up and start to freak out saying, "That isn't right! That is wrong!" Calm down there, because this is what you'll do with your partners. Rather than write that person off, think about it. If you do it with one person, you'll do it with everyone.

There is neither right nor wrong. There just 'is.' The point is for you to understand what is happening and avoid judgment. Judgment makes emotions runs high in your conversations and can lead you to fight to the detriment of your relationship about something that is really not that important.

In another section of the book I recommended a practice where you take on 'being wrong' for a day or for a week. We are going to revisit this. Why again? I promise you there is great advantage here for you. Here is where you can be free-free from your prison. Your prison is your reactions. You are imprisoned by your automatic responses to situations or perceived threats. And you really want to look carefully at this. We all have been 'denied', insulted or challenged at some point in our life, and that is where decisions get made to never be wrong again, and protect ourselves. And those decisions create thought patterns. And those thought patterns repeat throughout your life, until you interrupt them.

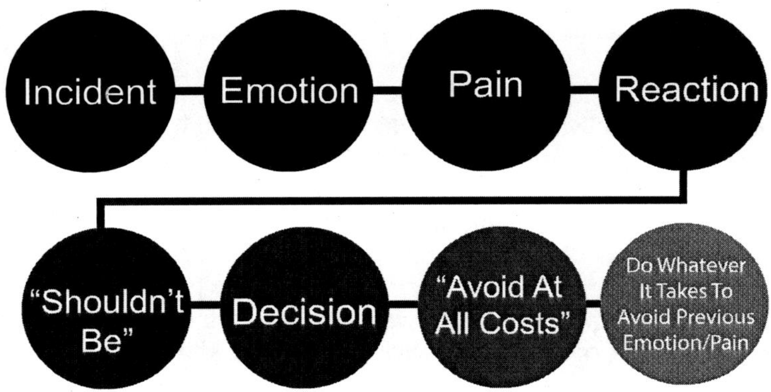

Now try to not react with, "But what Mrs. Macdonald did to you was wrong!" That is something I have heard often when telling that story. And that too is a matter of perspective. I am at the point now where I understand, Mrs. Macdonald did what she did. She did what she thought she should do in that moment, **because of her own decisions from her own past.**. My assessment of whether what she did was good or bad or not is irrelevant. Since she did it and it's done, I have left it in the past. What's the point in me holding onto a scorecard? Why should other people pay in my life, those whom I care about, those whom I love, and work with even at work on a daily basis... because she held up a piece of paper and laughed out loud 20 years ago?

You will have to give up the scorecard in your own life and in your relationships. Only do this if you want a life filled with more joy, happiness, love and connection. And you do. That's why you bought this book.

Mutual Understanding

The key to a thriving relationship

So what becomes possible when right and wrong becomes a concept? That is what it is after all. A concept, an idea, like most things in life, it is made up. You might be thinking, "This guy is crazy, I'm putting this book down right now" (If you haven't already). Okay that's fine. No problem. You can do that. And you can just hear me out, and then decide from there.

Imagine a world... a place... where this concept of right and wrong does not exist. Instead there is universal acceptance of everything. Now that is not to say that you don't get hurt, or offended, or win a game or lose a game, that still happens. But when someone says something or does something to you, you don't take it personally. You don't feel hurt, sadness, anger or guilt. Instead you keep your calm, and maintain a space of peace and acceptance. Better yet, when a disagreement happens you rejoice! You celebrate! You think, "Yay differences!" You have no blood rushing throughout you, your fists do not clench, your voice is not raised and you don't shut out their opinion as useless. Instead everything is a contribution, everything is an experience. You might shake their hand and say thanks. You might hug them, or buy them a gift (I know, what a crazy concept). This might seem quite farfetched for today's world. Sure we have a long way to go as a planet. However, you can start in your relationship, and you can have that relationship with ease.

This is an extremely powerful position to take in your love life. It takes time to master and it will test you. It will mangle your insides, and take some time since we are all so wired and programmed for reaction 99.9% of the time (It's the lizard, animal, or monkey brain which is still pre dominantly active in us from the caveman cavewoman days, the fight or flight mechanism). But if you can do this, even sometimes, it will dramatically change your relationships, potentially stun your partner and alter your communication, leaving you with more freedom, peace of mind and harmony.

But it has to start with you.

Men - imagine your woman says something that you are certain is designed to tear you up inside and cause you to freak out with frustration (Yes, ladies some of you do this). Now picture yourself having no reaction at all... at all!!! Imagine, you being a solid, immovable ROCK when she throws you a HURRICANE of criticism or demands... **see yourself as powerful beyond measure, un-activated by anything she says. You are that strong.** You know you can handle anything she throws at you because you chose her. And she chose her. And that is what matters. That is where you stand, and that is where you'll continue to stand because that is what she needs. That is what you can deliver.

Women - imagine your man does something you feel is stupid. Like pretty dumb, (We just weren't thinking clearly. We do that from time to time). He leaves dishes in the sink, or whatever really hits your nerve. And you are about to explode! You can't wait to hurl criticism and ridicule, and show him that the mistake he made is bad and how right you are. And instead, you breathe deeply... you relax your shoulders. You release the tension, you are calm. You are unwavering in peace and become present to love. You feel love. You recognize that you appreciate him for the man that he is, regardless of this mishap. Better yet you laugh or giggle! And you say, "You know, I was going to freak out... and instead, (giggle) I'm just going to say, I love you." And you **do** feel love! You don't have to fake it. You feel genuine love for this person, this possible gentle buffoon standing in front of you. It is actually genuine, and it feels great. This is what is possible if you are willing to let it go.

How do either of you achieve this?

Acceptance. Seeing their point of view. Realize they are **not** doing this consciously to upset you. Even though it may seem like it is.

Then communicate using the tools I'm giving you.

Listening

Do you listen well?

Listening is a skill which can always be improved. It is an incredibly important skill. Now I know you may have heard at school, in conflict mediation, or in your workplace during customer service training about the skill of listening, and that's great. What I am about to talk about, is completely different.

I frequently lead workshops on communication to new Canadians and landed immigrants here in Toronto. It's a privilege. The people that come to this country are so loyal, hardworking and hungry for opportunity. They feel they lack the communication skills and so they come to our workshops to improve their skills in the area of which they lack. One of the things I spend a lot of time teaching is listening skills. Listening is highly underrated and a very powerful skill you can master. Why? There are two reasons: 1) Most of the breakdowns in the world around us, whether global or personal are because of a lack of understanding. Listening grants understanding. Proper listening and understanding dissolves upset. 2) All people really want is to be heard. All people really want is to be understood. Usually we are so desperate to get our opinion across and shove it down someone else's throat we don't even think about listening. Most people can't wait to interrupt the other person and get our two cents in so much so that that we can't wait for the other person to finish talking, just so we can talk again.

Someone who listens is easy to love, because we all just want to be heard. That person can be a breath of fresh air in today's world. When you meet someone who just listens to you, it's very refreshing isn't it?

One thing I teach is what I call the three levels of listening:

1) Hearing: This is basic. You could be in the same room, and you can acknowledge that words are leaving their lips. You could even recall some of the words.
2) Understanding: A higher level. You hear them and have a conversation back and forth. You can paraphrase what they are saying.
3) Emotional Understanding: You can enter their shoes and be in their skin. You can re-create their experience for them. You completely understand what their experience was like as if they were you. You can replicate the feelings and how they came to have those feelings.

Remember that we are emotional beings and so this requires a higher level of emotional intelligence. How can you become a better listener? I will give you more tools. For now, practice as much as you can # 3. What will it take? It will take you leaving your body, leaving your concerns, worries, judgments and assessments behind and being in the other person's world.

If you practice #3 enough you can get to a place where having the ability to sum up one's life and experience in one sentence is completely doable. And here's the thing- right now you might be thinking, "I could do that." Or, "I do that already." I assure you, you don't. Unless you've taken specific training or have some innate natural ability, then I would be coachable in this moment. Why? Because what you're thinking and what they're thinking are two completely different things.

For example: If you think you can completely understand one person in their life and sum it up in a few sentences you might think, 'Yeah I did that, good job me.' And that is not what I am talking about. How you know you are a good listener is if the person you are talking with says the words back to you, "Yes, thank you. That is exactly how I felt. That is exactly what I was thinking. How did you know? It felt so good sharing that with you and telling you that, because I know you understood." Unless your partner or someone has told you those words, then you are not fully with what I am saying. So remain coachable.

Random Story Break

Listen to this…

I had an experience that was not pretty several years ago. It was one of those moments that was so impactful it caused me to vow to do something differently on the spot. I was living with my girlfriend at the time and I was sitting in the living room playing a video game while my girlfriend was in the kitchen making a snack. The kitchen was adjoined to the living room and was separated by a window. We were having one of those distant but audible conversations (those are never a good idea).

She asked me, "Are you meeting me at the restaurant for dinner after work or can you pick me up on Friday night?" I didn't know what she was talking about. "What dinner?" I asked. "The dinner with my friends Sarah and Benjamin" she said casually. "I don't remember that" I responded, realizing I really did not. "Come on, I told you about this Michael, remember?" she pleaded. "I really don't think you told me babe. I have no idea about Friday night. In fact, I know because I made plans and I wouldn't have done that if you told me." She began to get really upset, "But I DID tell you!" I felt her upset and thankfully stayed calm. I got up off my chair and headed towards her, "I don't know if you did though." She began to break down and cry. "You always do this, Michael! You never really listen to me! You think you're listening but you're not!" Her tears came hard and fast. I could tell they were genuine. She crouched down towards the floor as if in pain, "I told you about the dinner and I was really looking forward to it! You suck!"
I was shocked. I was stunned. I had no idea what was going on! I stood there

with my hands outstretched towards the floor. My mind went blank and my jaw nearly dropped. 'What the fuck just happened?' I thought. How could such a simple misunderstanding have affected her so much? I stood there dumbfounded.

Thankfully, it hit me. This wasn't simple. This was our relationship. This wasn't a misunderstanding. This was how I communicated. I felt like an asshole. I felt like a shitty boyfriend. It took a minute or two and then I got over myself. I left the self-pity there in that moment. I was clear this wasn't about me. This was about her. I vowed, I swore, with complete certainty that I would be a better man. I would listen. I would find out what it meant to listen. I would pay attention! I would know what it means to really hear and understand someone. I promised her that would never happen again. I am very thankful to say, that has never happened since.

I am intentional in my communication, both speaking and listening, and it feels good.

I feel pride as I have become the communicator, the listener, the partner and yes, the man I wanted to be those years ago. Better still, I teach other men and women how to communicate, because to communicate is to listen.

I am thankful for her and for that experience. I'm thankful for the way she reacted. If you must know, yes we went to dinner that Friday. You bet we did. I cancelled my plans and explained what I did to the other person, and my girlfriend and I had a great time at dinner.

What did I do between then and now? I put in effort. I took training, and courses. I spent a lot of time and money developing my ability to listen. I considered them all investments in myself. And I practiced what I was being taught. I am grateful to teach others because the value.... well, it is invaluable.

If you aren't happy in your relationship, why be in it? Great communication is a must have for a great relationship.

Here's a simple way of expressing what makes for a great listener: Compassion, non-judgment, keen interest, and undivided attention.

All of these qualities can't express enough why it's so important that you listen to your partner. However, there is one important reason why you yourself should pay attention to your partner as there is something for you to gain. When you say things like, "I know what you're going to say, or, I've heard this all before," you shut off your listening abilities. When you shut down your listening you also shut down all your learning abilities. You lose all hope of learning and truly being with your partner.
And when you do this in this with your partner, you do this in all areas of your life.

Golden Nuggets

How you act in one area of life, is how you act in all areas of life.

Several times in my journey of self-development, I heard the phrase "How you do anything, is how you do everything." So this will impact your working life, your home life, your love life, your social life etc.

Exercise:
I want you to earnestly ask yourself on a scale of 1-10, "How well do I listen?" After you do that, I want you to ask 5 people in your life, one from every different category- friends, family, ex or current partner, coworker, community member, boss. Ask them to rate you. Now here is the important part - DO NOT REACT.

This is key for all communication-DO NOT REACT. JUST HEAR THEM AND WRITE DOWN THEIR ANSWER. DO NOT GET DEFENSIVE either. Do not try to explain, rationalize, or deflect. And no matter what, be coachable. There is always something to improve.

The Other Person... again

Where are you?

Remember that whole chapter on the other person? Good. I hope you haven't forgotten it yet, or that would be a problem. Now remember, that whole chapter was about focusing on the other person and having the relationship really improve and work out because you know, 'it's not about you' remember? Well we're going to revisit that now because in communication, focusing on the other person is what really works well.

So here is a few things you can begin to immediately incorporate in your communication:

Use text messaging less: (Shocking I know). However, I am very serious about this one. Text messaging can be very frustrating for you and your partner and it is an easy way to put distance and a gap between you. You cannot convey emotion, tone, or intention over text. And those are what make up the majority of our communication. Make an effort to make phone calls more often. And if they ask, 'Why didn't you just text me?' Say, 'I'm trying to improve our communication and it's harder over text. I want us to be (fill in the blank – connected, able to understand each other, communicate well, have a great relationship etc.)

Stop interrupting your partner: Oh boy, this one's a doozy. People interrupt each other all the time. Especially in heated arguments. And it just doesn't work. It builds tension, aggression, frustration and impatience. It is not okay. Maybe here and there if it's playful, or comical, etc., but not in serious situations, arguments, and definitely not when your partner is expressing themselves passionately, i.e., having a bad day, a frustrating moment, etc.

Be responsible for your stuff: As I mentioned in chapter 1, everyone has stuff, baggage, past issues, crap, etc. No one is exempt. This is the nature of life. So when your stuff comes up, recognize it and be responsible for it (stuff is categorized here as your automatic reactions to words, phrases or situations which has a negative impact on others). Say the words to your partner, *"I'm sorry I just __________. I didn't need to do that. That was my stuff. That wasn't who I really want to be for you. I won't do that again."* And then promise and commit what you say you will do and when you don't, (you won't get it right every time, you aren't perfect) tell them you are working on it, and it might take a little time. You are human after all.

Talk about what matters to them. You will spend a lot of time with your partner won't you? Yes you will. Doesn't matter if you're married or in a relationship or not. Time is required for a relationship. The more you know about your partner and discover about your partner, the more you'll know if you are compatible. The more you will know if they are the one for you or not. The more you will know about them overall, which will really help in the long run. Because then you can use that information to make them as happy as possible with gifts, expressions, messages, and more. You want to be aware of their behaviours and their nuances. Everyone wants to be known. Remember, that all everyone wants is to be listened to, and no one ever does that. If you do that, you will have one devoted lover on your hands. It would do you good to constantly ask and talk about what matters to them, to constantly be in that inquiry.

No more mind reads, just ask the question: After a while you may feel like you really know the person. And you will after some time won't you? And yet there will still be more. As human beings, we are always changing. Every day and every year, we are different. We have different thoughts and feelings. You won't be the same person one year from now, and neither will they. Therefore, you must ask the person how they think and feel, rather than assuming and giving them very little credit. You want to encourage them and understand them, not predict and belittle them. Often times,that is exactly what assuming does.

I want you to read each of these bullet points, the bolded words, out loud to yourself three times. This will help you commit them to memory, and actually allow you to incorporate them into your physiology. You could think of them as affirmations, however, really they are creating new brain patters. The way to create new behaviours, is to create and enforce new brain patterns. And the way to do that is to say them out loud three times to yourself. That is the first and easiest way anyway.

Authenticity = Less Ambiguity

Be more authentic… That's it

One of the greatest ways to access getting what you want is to talk about it more often. Gee, that sounds simple, right? Yes! And that doesn't mean you're doing it. This is more of the onion, remember the onion? It's about being and accessing more of who you really are. Now listen, I myself used to be very concerned with being a nice guy. I never fell into the 'friend zone' because in dating and relationships, I was always able to make it very clear that I wanted to be with the person, and thankfully, I obviously know how to create and compel attraction. However, I often was unsatisfied in relationships in my early years, because I didn't get what I wanted. Why didn't I get what I wanted? Because I didn't ask for it! I didn't talk about it!

Now where did that come from? It came from a place called, 'I don't want to hurt, offend or harm people.' Do you have a little bit of that? A lot of us do. Most people don't want to hurt other people, it's normal, but it is a part of being nice.

Golden Nugget

Being nice is all about the fear of being rejected.

So we keep them in the dark. If you keep people in the dark, they will have no idea how to communicate with you, or give you what you want and need. If it makes more sense to leave things as they are for you, to keep hoping, wishing and waiting for someone to read your mind, instead of risking making it worse, than this is especially for you. You are not good at communication. And you need to work on this, badly. Being nice will not get you what you really want.

Remember, all you're doing is keeping people in the dark. And it is inauthentic.

Being inauthentic goes against who you really are. Being this way leaves others in a state of confusion and mystery. It leaves them having to work really hard to get through to you. And that is not okay.

Golden Nugget

Make your partners work less hard, and they will be able to love you more.

Otherwise, trust me, this will cost you happiness and harmony in your life.

Stop stabbing your partner

Ouch that hurts!

Again, think about the other person. They will never know what it is that you want, unless you know what you want and tell them what it is. They will stay frustrated when you aren't being straight with them, and that will tear you apart. So stop doing that. Be authentic. I don't recommend quitting anything, except being ambiguous. Resolve for yourself, "I will quit being ambiguous now." If you are having an argument or a breakdown with your partner, it is likely a breakdown in communication. And if it's not in communication, whatever the breakdown, argument or fight is, communication can resolve it. Say what's there for you. Refrain from believing, 'people should just know.' That is just ridiculous and arrogant. Everyone has their own concerns, their own desires, and their own way of life. If you feel they should just know how to understand you, you will be very disappointed. You have to teach them how you want to be treated.
After working with so many people, what I've come to clearly understand, is that most people don't know how to say what it is that is really going on inside of us. It takes practice.

Here is what you must understand about yourself and your partner:

We don't know how to say what we want to say without offending the other person.

We fear their reaction, even though it hasn't happened yet (which is crazy, because we can't predict the future. Remember, perception is projection.)
We spend **so much time in our heads, fearing the outcome, and envisioning failure,** without actually saying it and being out there in the interaction.
We don't know how to clean up any messes that we have made. We just don't have the tools or know how to make things right, after we've made a mess.

What normally happens is that you tell your partner what it is you want, and then they get upset. They get upset because you think it's enough to just tell them and then let them deal with it. This doesn't work. You have to talk about what you want, and have it be a conversation- a dialogue, or discovery if you will. You want to incorporate as much love into the conversation as possible. Have an intention and do your absolute best to communicate from that intention. Communicate in such a way that will have your partner actually feel loved no matter what comes up. If something slips up and comes out of your mouth that is off or not what you wanted, then clean it up. Otherwise you will create a mess. And messes can be cleaned up.

Here's how you do it:

Be responsible for the impact and upset it left them with, the emotions that they felt as a result.
Be responsible for their experience that they had after the event happened.
Your listening will heal the wound. This is sewing up the scar that you left.
Remember, the goal is to communicate in a way you want to be heard.
Allow yourself to admit you were wrong, that it is was irresponsible to let your pain, crap, stuff – whatever you want to call it, come out.
Accept responsibility for the part you played. Stop dropping hints, and beating around the bush.
Quit taking shots at your partner. Don't do that ever again. Ever. It does not work and will not get you to the happy, healthy, harmonious relationship you want.

Exercise:
When going into any conversation, focus on the 3 H's: happy, healthy, harmonious.
Understand the 3 P's you must stop immediately.
No poking
No prodding
No provoking

This means all judgments and 'better than' statements must go out the window. No more "I do this and you don't. I did this last time, I did this and you didn't. I'm better at this than you."

Happy, Healthy, Harmonious.
Surprise yourself

Allow yourself to be surprised

I really want you to have a transformation-a a transformative experience. I want you to have a moment in time where you wow yourself, where you really stop yourself and say, did that just happen? Did I just do that? Once you make a shift, and make a change in your communication, your whole world will change. I know, because I've had those experiences where I blew myself away and really wow'd myself! I've marveled at my partner's responses and I want you to do the same, because it is a wild, wild trip! You will be amazed at how much it can dissolve upset, and resolve issues in the relationship in no time at all. Plus, it makes way for so much more love, connection and intimacy, and I know that that is what you want.

If you aren't in a relationship right now, practice this with your family, your friends, or your coworkers. Listen from a place where you could see, if you had implemented this type of communication somewhere in the past, things might have gone differently.

One time, my sister and I were arguing about something. We were both home and living at our parent's house at the time. My parents were selling the family home and it was a big deal for all of us. They had been there for 31 years and so my sister and I went back there to help out for a few months. Well of course, we started to argue about something and it was getting ugly. It was reaching a point where she was getting louder and louder, trying to prove her point and I could see that my attempts at working around her point of view weren't working. Her style of communication was to get louder and louder and more in my face to get her point across. I realized I was fighting a brick wall and so I simply stopped arguing and gently said, "You're right Stephanie!" and she said, still yelling "Yeah and I know that this should go there because..." And I just gently said again, "Stephanie, You're right." And she stopped talking and instantly walked away.

And just like that, BAM! The argument is over! That's it. Done! Simple. Its over! Can you be with just how simple that is? Can you get just how long that argument might have gone on for? And it didn't. Not only that but it's all good from there on after. This worked because the meaning I placed on being right in that moment was totally insignificant. Most of us have the significance or the importance of being right so damn high. I know my sister did. She would have fought to the death for it. I've seen it. I was able to easily give it up because I saw what she was committed to. I saw that she was being a fixed position, unwilling to give up her point of view, and for me there was no point in interacting with that. She was being right. With every fiber of her being, she was so committed to being right and having me know that, it would be a complete waste of energy and time to interact with that part of her. So I dropped my guard, saw what I was doing and that I was perpetuating this experience for her, and decided to end it. I walked away calm, cool and collected. I maintained my composure and went about my day.

Remember that we are meaning making machines and the importance I placed on being right in that moment was very little. To me, if being wrong means less arguing and less drama, less pain and suffering in a relationship, then I'm all for it. I will be wrong all day. Now this is with my sister, but this is just as easy with your partner. You will surprise yourself with what happens. For me, I was so completely surprised with how easily, and **quickly** my sister walked away and the aggravation disappeared.

Who said being wrong is a bad thing? Have you ever seen someone admit when they are wrong? That shows character. That is a courageous human being. Seriously! Someone who can look another human being in the eye and say I was wrong, and you are right, is a powerful force- a force of love, a force to be reckoned with. It is wise, it is courageous, it takes something to say "You're right". Not everyone is capable of this, but you can do it. Your partner will deeply love you for it.
It's not the words, it's not the speaking of the words. It's not the admittance of guilt. It shows the admiration and respect that you have for your partner. If you do this, they will know it. They will feel it.

Golden Nugget

Say "You're right" more often. It shows that you value their opinion and that they are worth more to you than being right.

This can be used in so many ways. When you do it will reduce tension, and increase room for affection. It doesn't matter if it's a small discussion, or you messed up directions or instructions. It doesn't matter if this is a huge blowup and upset that lasts 20 minutes either. My sister may have just walked away, but in my intimate relationships, we have hugged, cried, laughed and shown more affection after this, than ever before. Since you are willing to let your guard down, they usually are willing to do the same in return. It might take a few minutes or a couple of different attempts, but when you do this, you two will come together in new ways like never before. If they are the kind of person who is open then they will open up too. And by the way, in due time, after you open up this way, they won't be able to do **anything but change!**

You know by now that I like going on tangents. If you think about this, this could be the solution to all upset in the world. We could celebrate every time we are 'wrong'. This could dissolve wars, and relieve countries in conflict. But let's scale it down and keep it down to our everyday lives for now, with you and your partner. Picture the look on your partner's face when they are fuming, upset, arguing, and

you just say the words, "You are right. I was wrong." And MEAN IT, without the snide, snarky, nastiness.

Why this serves both of you

Freedom on more than one level

Think about this from a physics perspective. If you hold a grudge, you are holding onto something-being right! The very words and meaning of 'holding a grudge' mean you are holding onto something, obviously. What are you holding onto? Emotion and energy. Remember that emotion = energy in motion. And energy = mass. All energy has mass. Mass can be measured no matter what type of energy, gas, heat, etc. So when you let go of holding onto something, i.e., a grudge or being right, you let go of energy that you have kept within you. And that energy holds mass inside where? Inside you! Inside your body! I have been in many programs, courses and seminars which are transformational. People throughout these courses literally come alive again. In many cases, you can see the colour come back into their skin or their face. These are very transformational programs which are highly effective. In these programs, years of tensions, frustrations, and grudges get released. It is beautiful. The release of these needless hindrances brings forth life, joy, and awareness. Physically, the years come off of you because of this. In many cases, the fat and the wrinkles are completely shed. Trust me. This happens. It makes sense. It is physics. Better still, there are many who are in the wellness industry that understand that these releases contribute to overall freedom from illness and disease. This is not what this book is about, however. This book is about increasing wholeness, and that includes mind, body and spirit. You may have noticed by now, this book is more about just than finding a great partner, it's about finding a whole and complete self. This will have you being more attractive, more appealing and likeable to others. It's simple physics. Please look up the wellness industry and the health benefits of releasing negative emotions.

When is it a good time to fight?

Is it safe?

Disagreements and debates are a healthy part of any relationship. They will happen, they will come up. And so will arguments. They are inevitable. However, how big or bad the argument gets is up to you. What if I told you that arguments did not have to be a necessary part of a relationship? What is your context? The power of context is a brilliant thing. We talked about context earlier in the book.

Golden Nugget

Your context is decisive

The context that you choose is completely up to you. I don't have a context of fights or arguments in relationships. When my partner and I are getting heated and hashing something out, it is in the realm of discussion and debate. My context is one of discussion and working things out. Sure, it might get a little heated, but it is incomparable by normal arguing standards. I am very proud of this.

Yolanda and I were having discussions about spirituality versus science early on in our relationship. We had a very strong and undeniable connection and we made each other very excited. She was an atheist and I am not. As you can see I am a little bit of both. In this book I've incorporated very science based information along with some spiritual based information as well. Although I am very spiritual, I don't see them as separate. I see them as together, two sides of the same coin. For Yolanda, they were completely separate. She would get triggered when we would have conversations about spirituality or when I would talk about some of the more 'out there' concepts which much of the world is waking up to and becoming more aware of.

People are amazed we were able to hold a relationship together when she was an atheist and I was a spiritualist. It just goes to show that religion does not have to dictate whom you can or cannot date. I wouldn't be able to do what I do if I wasn't able to see this. It was a test to who I am and who she is. And what is important is that you are committed to the person and not their religion or dogma. Are you committed to who they really are? Sure their beliefs are a big part of who they are, and beliefs change. What's important is who you are together, the space that gets created around you both when you're together.

If you want a great relationship, you've got to have this handled.

Here's a simple thing you can do to improve your communication with your partner. Stop exaggerating! It just damages the relationship and hurts the other person. Why do we do this? We think it can be harmless, we think it will add to our case and if it's a little white lie, its innocent right? It isn't. You think it will help them understand but it doesn't. It just confuses things and muddies them up. So stop exaggerating. It diminishes your credibility. Your partner will begin to see you as untrustworthy and not as a good communicator. Human beings are not stupid. They are more aware than you think. We know when you aren't telling the truth, and it just takes up more time and space. Be straight. Say only what is and not what isn't. It takes practice but if you can pay attention, you can do it. Better yet, if you do it, you can pull it back, retract the statement, take responsibility and apologize for it. That will take some courage, but you can do it. It will make you a better person, partner, and communicator.

Arguing early on in a relationship isn't good. Confrontation of any kind isn't good. Don't kid yourself. If you are arguing with someone early on, you know you need to leave. You do not need the drama. This is supposed to be the honeymoon period remember? Puppy love? In the beginning you should be really enjoying each other. This should be your foundation. So don't let arguments early on mess that up.

Now disagreements are different. Disagreements are healthy. You know it's a disagreement when you have differing views on topics. That's okay, but you know there's a difference between disagreements and arguments. When it escalates, walk away. And consider walking away for good if it gets too bad, too early. How do you know? Simple. You're already asking the question. That's the only sign you need.

If you're still in the dating period early on, watch and listen for arguments with others that they have and talk about. Are they always arguing with their family members? With their coworkers? With their friends? Are all the stories they are telling you filled with drama? Try to dive deeper a little. Why are the arguments happening? What is going on? Sometimes you can't help but be duped into a situation. But you want to build the awareness to read people well. Sometimes people lie and hide themselves. Their true nature comes out, some times six months in. That can get you into some sticky situations. But those are experiences to learn from. As I said earlier, everyone comes into your life to teach you something. Learn the lesson and move on. Otherwise the cycle will repeat, and it will keep coming up in your life, if you don't learn the lesson. And like most people, you'll wonder, "Why does this keep happening to me?"

Arguments are ordinary. Very ordinary. If you want to have an ordinary relationship, no problem. If you want to have an extraordinary relationship, then arguments are a part of that equation. However, extraordinary relationships require extraordinary communication. Above average relationships, require above average conversations. Have your arguments turn into conversations for growth and expansion. When you take this on, arguments simply become discussions. This is not about being 'perfect' or being the perfect couple. It is about working at it. It takes practice. So enroll your partner in this being what your relationship is about. When you have breakdowns, come from a place of wanting to work it out, nothing less.

Tools you can use

You need to be equipped, if you're going to win

Here are a few tools to aid you in your communication. I can promise you that if you incorporate them into your daily life you will have more of what you want.

HALT – This is a tool to remember. It is hugely beneficial for your relationships, not just at home but in other areas as well. If you want to get the most out of your communication with someone, remember it. This is a simple acronym to realize when you should avoid talking to your partner, especially about important topics. They can wait.
HALT stands for Hot, Angry, Late or Tired. This is when you should avoid talking to your partner, just so that you get the most out of your communication. When someone is hot (temperature, yes) angry about something, late for an appointment or event, or tired, overly worked, etcetera, then they are less apt to listen and converse in the way you want them to. Anytime other than this is the ideal time to communicate. You want to be heard, you want to be listened to, and they want to fully converse with you too. And these are moments when they need to breathe, get settled, or just have a moment to themselves to calm down. Maybe you'll need to reschedule the conversation. But it's just insensitive to converse when they are in one of those states, so remember HALT.

Have and INTERVIEW together – Yes an interview. I want you two to interview each other. This might sound uncommon but it is very powerful, I assure you. It doesn't need to be formal. No need to dress up and have official titles. Just sit down together, on the couch, in the bed, or across the table, and hang out. Ask each other the questions that follow, and be open to the answers. These are simple but important questions. They can be very transformative for your relationship and a great opportunity to grow if you tactfully ask and answer these questions with your partner. It could be a fun and playful thing to do early in the relationship (you don't have to ask all the questions, if you aren't comfortable). Don't spring it on them. Approach it like a thing to do, when you are spending a nice relaxing evening together. If you're already in a long term relationship, then this is a must. One of my partners and I did this every 6 months, and it was such a healthy thing to do!

Before you do the interview, set up some context for it. Make each other three promises: 1) Promise to be honest, 2) Promise to be coachable and receptive to the feedback, and 3) Promise not to hold grudges and leave it in the interview, and that you won't bring it up or use it against them negatively. This last one is very important. In other words, you aren't allowed to tease, insult, torment or mock the other person for some of the things you say in an argument or a fight. None of that, "Oh yeah, well you said this and that etc." You want to create as safe a space as possible for your partner to be honest with you. This is about learning and growing remember? This is about contributing to each other. At times, when I've done this interview process, I've learned vital things about myself that have made me stronger. They have made me a better listener, lover and a better boyfriend and business person.

Here are the questions:

What are my strengths?
What are my weaknesses?
What can you count on me for always?
What can you never count on me for?

What do you like/love about me?
What do I do that makes it hard to love me?
How do others in our circles see me?
What do I do that makes you happy?
What do I do that upsets or bothers you?
How can I be a better partner to you?
What is unique about me?
What else do you want to say to me?

ALWAYS VALIDATE EACH OTHER – This one is a biggie. (Aren't they all?) You and your partner are there for each other. You are a support to each other. You are building a relationship- a partnership. You are building trust all the time. You need to know that your partner has your back and you want to have theirs. It is a beautiful thing once you have it. So one way to do it is to validate each other. For example: If you feel your partner's point of view on something is a little off, then you can validate them and give them feedback at the same time. If you feel their approach on something isn't serving them, or that there is a better way of doing it, validate them and give them constructive feedback. It might sound like, "Yes, I believe you have the right idea, and there might be a better way to do it." It could sound like, just listening and saying yes and agreeing with them. And then a little while later, you might say, "You know I thought about it, and I think it's worth trying this."

Try this as well: Just hear them out, and reinforce that they aren't crazy. Especially when they have had a tough day. Agree with their world, even more so if they've just gone through a tough time.

The sister I mentioned earlier told me about a terrible experience she had in one moment she and her boyfriend went through. They were heading to the movies and as they were walking, she was telling him about a rough day and ugly experience she had that day. She was very frustrated and was telling him the story until the moment they parked. She was exasperated as she parked the car and sat for a few minutes finishing up the story, letting all her emotions out. He listened. She got to the end of the story and looked at him and said nothing, waiting and hoping for a reply. He looked at her and there was a second of silence until he said, "Can we go in now?"

Put the obvious judgments about him as a guy aside and lets just look at what was expected. Although he was innocently looking forward to going into the movie, he was not in her world and came across as very insensitive. In her world, she needed validation! In her world, she needed him to **agree, listen, and acknowledge her experience.** In his world, he just wanted her to finish so they could go into the movie. Well that was pretty insensitive and he was not being 'out there' in the conversation as I had mentioned earlier. He was more concerned about his own mind and needs being satisfied instead of listening or paying attention to her needs.

She was very, very upset, needless to say. She got out of the car and they went into the movie, but not before she threw up her hands in sheer disbelief and was left speechless. She was in a state of bewilderment. Why? Because she needed and wanted him to validate her. She needed to know he cared! That he wasn't just a wall with no emotion.

As she told me, I summed it up for her as to what was going on behind the scenes. I said to her, "If I were him, I would have said this. Lisa, I apologize. I am so sorry for making you feel like I didn't care about everything you told me. You were confiding in me, something that upset you deeply, and I was not paying attention. I was not with you in the conversation. I should have been present with you, listening to you, since you confide in and place your trust in me as your boyfriend. And you should. I am your boyfriend. I want to be that person for you. And in that moment, I wasn't. I should have cared for you and acknowledged the experience you had. I am sorry. I promise next time, to take the care, time and preciousness of your sharing with me, seriously. You **can** trust in me and confide in me. That's my promise to you. " And you can even leave it open to accept or deny your apology. But how could someone deny that?

My sister was moved by this to tears, and I know why. It was what she was looking for. It was exactly what she was looking for in him. You could say I re-created her experience. Her emotion disappeared when I did that. That's how powerful that tool is. Validate their experience. Unfortunately, he didn't do that and so they didn't stay together for long.

Put these tools to use in your relationship and you will notice a marked difference from where things were before. Communication is so important. Don't let it slip you by. Use these tools and improve it immediately.

9
THE L WORD AND 'THE ONE'

Those 3 little words – I love you

Why are they such a big deal?

You know that if we're going to talk about relationships, we're going to talk about love. Notice that this book has a flow to it. It began with you starting out and learning how to attract someone, and then knowing when someone really is great for you. Then you learned how to be great with them in different areas like intimacy and communication and have the relationship really work. Now we're deeper into the relationship and into your time together. So now you can understand why it makes sense that the first chapter wasn't about love. The 9th chapter is about love because it shouldn't be a factor or considered until later on in the relationship... normally, right? Well, sort of. But we'll get to that later. Here's a story I was told recently:

A group of women were at a seminar on how to live in a loving relationship with your husband. The women were asked, "How many of you love your husband?" All the women raised their hands. They were then asked, "When was the last time you told your husband you loved him?" Some women answered today, a few yesterday, and some couldn't remember. The women were then told to take out their cell phones and text their husband: "I love you, sweetheart." Immediately after this, the women were told to exchange phones with another person, and to read aloud the text message they received, in response.

Here are some of the replies:

1) *Who the hell is this?*
2) *Hey, mother of my children, are you sick or what?*
3) *Yeah, and I love you too. What's up?*
4) *What now? Did you crash the car again?*
5) *I don't understand what you mean?*

6) What did you do now?
7) ?!
8.) Don't beat about the bush, just tell me how much you need.
9.) Am I dreaming?
10.) If you don't tell me who this message is actually for, someone will die.
11.) I thought we agreed you wouldn't drink during the day.
12.) Your mother is coming to stay with us, isn't she??

Notice the responses. Some were confused. Some were bewildered. Some were automatically assuming the worst. Some were downright pissed off. Only one, maybe two of them were genuinely excited.

Let's look at why. All of the responses relate to one thing. It seems that the men hadn't heard "I love you" in a while. And if they did, it was usually in response to trying to get something, or receive something in return. So you can see there is an element of trust missing in the relationship.

This has got to stop. To avoid this, you need to say the words, I love you. It doesn't matter if you're saying it early in the beginning or later in the relationship. (I know some of you may be triggered by this right now, but we'll get back to that). Either way, say the words. Have your partner know those words well. This is just the beginning, be patient we'll get to all of it. For now, think of the reasons why we don't say I love you. Think of why those women in the seminar weren't saying it to their partners. And that goes for you too. Why don't you say I love you? Why haven't you said it?

In this chapter I want to demystify what those words mean. I want to deconstruct the significance we have around those words, and bring it back to what it is meant to be. Then I want to empower you, so that you can have the authentic, loving and fulfilling relationship you really want.

'I love you' does not translate to 'I want to marry you'

What is truly being said when I love you is being said?

I met a woman in an airport recently when our flights were delayed. We were talking back and forth and she started telling me about her relationship with a guy she has been seeing for 11 months. She told me he said, 'I love you' recently and she didn't say it back. She felt confused and concerned about the whole thing. I listened and I thought it was perfect that this came up as I was writing this chapter. I heard that she was not sure what to do next. I explained that she most likely felt the love for him however she probably had a fear around telling him. To my surprise, she actually agreed pretty quickly. I then inquired as to why she felt concerned around saying I love you to him. She told me that there was a man whom she felt very deeply for before the current man she was with, and it didn't work out. She was very hurt and it left her very emotional for a long period of time. I understood, and I shared a secret with her. This guy was not that same man from the past. And this fear that she has about getting hurt again is getting in the way of the actual love that she has for this guy now!

Golden Nugget

Refusing to acknowledge what is really going on, doesn't make it go away.

I instructed her to stop denying the feelings that she knew were there for this man, get in touch with them and reciprocate the courage this man displayed before her. Overall, I say you better love them, if you are with them for 11 months! 11 months is a long time. I had no doubt in my mind that she loved him by that time, just that she was afraid to come to terms with that. Let's face it. If you aren't in love, then you aren't on the same page. If you aren't on the same page, well.... you need to be on the same page!

What you're saying is I love you. That's it. You're not saying you want to spend the rest of your life with this person. You are saying I love you, now. I love you in the moment. That is what you (and they) are saying. Anything aside from that is what you are adding to the communication. This is something that you'll want to add to your communication tools. You need to take the communication as just the communication in the moment, and not add anything to it.

We add to the communication of 'I love you' all the time. And that's why there's all the fear around it. We add the stigmas which are entirely made up and are not real. Stigmas are made up around the significance that is added to the communication. The fear and concern around 'I love you' has nothing to do with what the words really are. It is all around the made up meanings you gave the words. The words to you are not just the words. To you they mean so much more. Well, that needs to end now. When you are saying I love you, that is all you are saying- I love you to another human being. And love is a natural part of life. It is not, 'I want to live with you. I want to marry you. I want to have kids with you. You are the one.' Those are all separate communications. Understand that they are separate communications! I love you means, "I love you," right now!

I love you needs to be more about the moment and less about the significance around it- the built up fears, the seriousness of it all. It's nonsense. I love you needs to be about the moment. What you are in touch with now. What you are feeling in your heart and body now. It is not in your head. Say this with me now: "**Love is not in your head.**"

I would love for the world to come to a point where we can say I love you, openly, and honestly, without fear of judgment or rejection. Love is the natural state of the world. If you can tune into it, you can feel it everywhere. It is a beautiful thing. I would love for you to say it because you want to. Because you would realize that you are free. Because you would realize that you can. Say it, 'I love you.' If you get to a point where you can say it to another person comfortably, I will be proud of you. I know it takes some courage to say the words. And still if you can say the words, and they still become concerned or turned off, don't lose out. Don't feel shunned, be who you are. You will meet someone new who will receive your words, who won't be intimidated by what you say. They will be totally able to 'be' with what you say. And if that's what you want, total expression free from judgment, since that's what love is, then you can have it.

I want to share a quote from Mother Teresa. She said, "I have found the paradox, that if you love until it hurts, there can be no more hurt. Only more love."
Think about the layers of the onion that she is talking about here. Imagine yourself coming to your core, finding your center and finding that an abundant fountain of love is what is there. Nothing else.

Timing IS Everything

Is there a good time to say I love you?

Unfortunately, we must deal with the way things are. We have been conditioned to think I love you is a significant step into a cautious and undertaking of the relationship. So we must pay attention, and have awareness to the current state of things out there in the world. We aren't there yet. We aren't in a world where love and the ease of use with that word is at a unified state all across the globe. So because of that, I have to go into what the current 'listening' of the words that are out there in the world. Why? So that you don't use it, get rejected, get disappointed, and give up. You did that once in one area or another. The truth is, "I love you implies a serious commitment." Remember the data from the match.com study in the 3rd chapter. This is not our fault. This is just due to the stigmas that are out there which we just spoke about. So because of this, it will take a little work to get things right, since for your sake, you'll want to say it when it will 'land' with the other person, in the way that you intended. Do this because I want you to have success. I want you to be a good communicator. I want you to make it work with the one you love. I want you to build your awareness. I want you to have what you want, because your partner, as amazing as they may be, may get scared or freaked out and take what you have to say another way. So we want to be responsible for our communication. (Remember that from chapter 8?)

The good news is, sometimes you don't even need to say I love you. For some time, it doesn't need to be said. It's a doing. It's an action. It's a demonstration, through living in love with your partner. That's why they say that saying, 'I love you'. Because at times, it isn't. The mere act of saying it, is not enough. Saying it is a big- deal don't get me wrong but if you can hear where I am coming from, it is something you can feel, especially in a long term relationship. It is a real giving of affection in different ways, that has love be felt and experienced by another.

Don't think of this in a 'prove it' kind of way. You don't have to prove anything to anyone.

But you should know that saying it would be part of things like:
Time invested – time spent together
Thoughtfulness – going out of your way at times
Sacrifices made – they happen, and they will come up
Acceptance of differences and points of views – without forcing
Actions – commitments made and upheld, gifts given
Expressions – Physical, verbal, non verbal,
Compassion – Giving space and relief for mistakes, misgivings, and misunderstandings.
Trust – Letting go of the need to have it all figured out, and have it your way. Granting your partner the ability to be comfortable with anything close to your heart.

Exercise: Take that notebook out and make a list of the ways you like to make your love known. Ask yourself the questions:
How do I like show my love?
How do I like to make it known to my partner that I love them?
In what ways do I like to express the love I have?
And a very important question, how will my partner know that I love them, without question?
After you have done this work, I want you to look at new ways you can express your love. Think outside the box.
Explore this question with your friends or family if you have to.

Sometimes you may feel like you give and give and can't give anymore. Maybe your partners in the past have made you feel like you have been sucked dry and you've hit your limit. No problem. I have been there. Love is a funny thing. It is abundant. It is beyond abundant, it is empty-less. So right now, all I want you to do is take the love you feel or have felt in your life, and multiply it by 6. See if you can imagine multiplying the current levels of love, acceptance, time, understanding, compassion, patience, trust, and action that you currently GIVE AND RECEIVE (yes receive). That is what is available to you if you can fathom that. Regardless, try to see what you can come up with.

When you are ready to say it you can do so in a variety of ways. You don't always have to be serious about it. You can be fun about it, and you can be cute about it. There are other ways to warm up to saying it as well so as not to scare your partner, (since the implied and possibly worrying commitment is inherent in them, and not their fault) you could say, "I care about you. You mean a lot to me. I love being with you." Notice that those words do not give you the same chest palpitations or concern as I love you does. Isn't that interesting? Did those words seem easy to say when you thought about them? Think about it. Isn't conditioning an interesting thing?

When you feel the need to say it

The agreement of love

The two reasons we don't say I love you are based on fear- fear of rejection and the fear of commitment. We're afraid of being shunned or rejected if we say it, and we're afraid we mean we will have to commit when we do say it.

Why are we afraid of being rejected?

In my study, research and through working with many people I can see clearly that we are afraid of rejection because we have it collapsed with labels like bad, unworthy, undeserving, failure, hurt, guilt, wrong etc. It is different for everyone but being labeled one of the above is a deathly fear many of us have, that can send us into a spiral of sadness and sorrow. I don't expect you to alleviate yourself of those fears in the next two pages as they have been with you your entire life. But what you need to know is that there is no truth here. If you apply many of the lessons I spoke about earlier throughout the book such as, **we are meaning making machines, or however they respond, it's not about you**, you will make your way through this with more ease if you are rejected. To really have power in this circumstance, it takes a lot of self-work. There are many resources on my website which are listed there because of the time it takes and the work involved in really letting go of the fear of rejection.

Why are we afraid of being committed?
We don't want to be held accountable.
We don't want to let others down.
We don't want to 'get it wrong.'
Once we feel we've committed to something or someone, we then have the concern of disappointing another come up.

Why do we need to say it?
We need to say I love you to release it, to acknowledge it and have it be outside of us; to have it and your feelings to be known. You want to release it because it is inside of you. Upon the realization that you love someone, you have this thing inside of you which you may feel compelled to express. This is great, no? Yes, however this is where you get scared, because a desire to speak the words also comes from needing and wanting agreement. This can be a tricky topic.

We have a desire to have agreement nearly everywhere in our lives. For us, the agreement of others gives validation. We feel validated when we get agreement. Pretty basic concept right? Makes sense? This is a big part of the reason why we argue or gossip (there's that need to be right again. This is how big the 'being wrong' is engineered away from us). But when you think about it, this desire gets in the way of simply giving and receiving communication. Usually for us, when we're saying 'I love you' what we're also saying is, "do you love me? Or I love you, don't you love me too?" To have real peace of mind, and to be okay with your partner not having to reciprocate the words right away, which will give them freedom, practice the **'superpower of being unattached'** because it will set you free. It will set your partner free as well.

I learned a lesson some time ago that these words although beautiful and powerful to express, should be taken with some degree of care. One can't just throw them around lightly. You must arrive at a place where you are ready to be responsible for the weight that they carry. This is where I want to insert a great quote I heard. It's an unconventional one, but it goes like this, "If you only love me when you like me, were going to have a problem." You can guess what this means right? The reality is, love isn't everything. And you can't just love someone solely when you like them because **loving them means loving all parts of them.** And that includes the potentially ugly parts, or the parts which may not be pretty all the time. It's about honouring the words and what they represent and in the process, honouring the person. You honour the agreements that get made in the relationship. It's truly about compatibility, which includes still being compatible when you aren't best friends. Woo hoo! I know this is a new concept of love, different from the sunsets, roses and cherries, we're used to. Why? **Because a great love grows when challenged.**

Let's take a break

And look at what love is

Listen, I know this book sometimes is heavy. It can be challenging at times and may contradict what you know and believe about love, dating and relationships. And that can be hard to deal with. I understand. And I greatly appreciate you reading this. So let us take a break for a second, from all the challenging stuff and I'll just share some facts with you right now okay?

Let us look at what is happening in the body when we experience love. In doing a little research online I found a great paper from the University of Rhode Island by a woman named Heather Chapman. The paper is a great exploration titled, "Love: A Biological, Psychological and Philosophical Study".

"Looking into a lover's eyes is like looking into a fire...Thanks to a shot of

adrenaline, your palms sweat, your breathing gets shallow, your skin feels hot, and your pupils dilate. Your amygdala, the center of the brain that processes emotion, blazes with activity. At the same time you produce dopamine, a 'feel good' neurotransmitter that is associated with passion and addiction, and oxytocin, a hormone related to bonding." She quotes someone named Pincott:

"Research has concluded, without a doubt that a person responds with their entire body when they feel desire. As stated earlier, when one is around an object of their desire, adrenaline is released, at least in the early stages. Adrenaline, also known as epinephrine, which is both a neurotransmitter and hormone, is released from the adrenal medulla during the "fight or flight response." (Sherwood, 188). This response, activated by the body's sympathetic nervous system, prepares the body for the decision to either fight the stressor, or "flight", to run away from the attack. During this reaction, the person's heart rate increases, the pupils dilate, the sweat glands are stimulated, and the brain becomes increasingly more alert. This reaction, the sweating, the dilated pupils, the increased heart rate, is exactly how people describe the feeling and energy of being "in love".

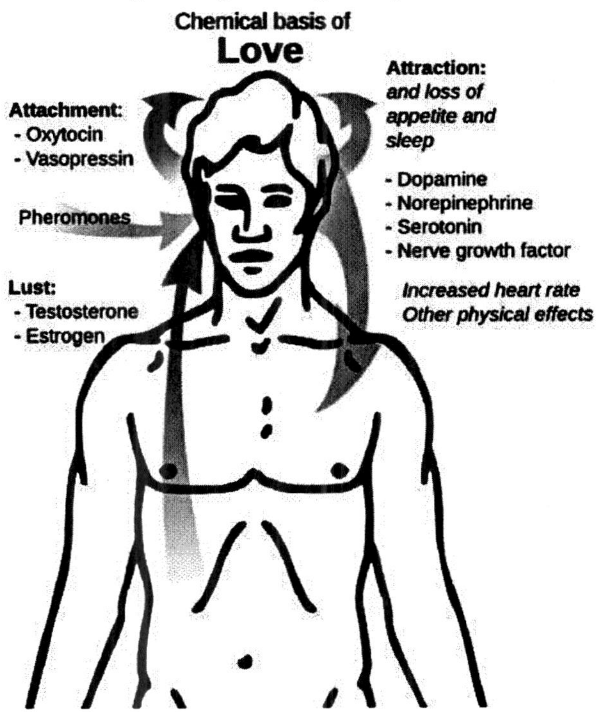

In addition to epinephrine, there are several other chemical responses

released when a person experiences "love at first sight." Endorphins, oxytocin, dopamine, and vasopressin are also important to examine when looking at the brain's response to love. Endorphins are peptides that are manufactured in the pituitary gland and the hypothalamus. These "feel good chemicals" act both as an analgesic and as a sedative. Endorphins are released during exercise, which is what many avid runners describe as a "runner's high". Eventually, the runner's body begins to crave the release of endorphins, which is why many exercise enthusiasts report the "need" to exercise. Endorphins are also released during sex; they provide the "feel-good, calming" effect that one feels immediately after orgasm. Finally, endorphins are released through touch, which is why a mother's touch can soothe a crying infant. "Endorphins, for instance, can create the sensation of euphoria and relief from pain." (Selhub, 33). It is that compelling euphoric feeling that couples describe when they say they have "fallen in love."

It should be noted that this is what is happening inside your body when you are in love. It's not game changing, and it is worth knowing. It might help you understand yourself in a deeper way.

You can't fight the power of love and you often don't get to choose whom you fall in love with. I've often said that to people and they always fully agree. It doesn't just sound like something nice and cliché. It is true. It's nearly completely biological as you can see. You can't help whom you fall in love with. So don't deny it when you have feelings for someone. I don't recommend trying to stop yourself from "unloving" those whom you are attracted to. You can make a conscious choice about who is worthy of your love. That is a different story. We will discuss this in the next chapter.

For now, I will add that for me, **love is trust. Love is when you trust another person fully.** It's letting someone in, giving them the keys, opening up and welcoming them into your heart. Although it might sound dramatic, love is the act of giving a person the fullness of yourself, abandoning concern and committing to the moment in front of you.

And here's the other tricky part: true love requires letting go. Surrendering to love is really where the beauty of love and life is found. Remember that there is so much more to love than what is just happening inside the body. Deepak Chopra talks beautifully about this. He says, *"The secret to communion is soul to soul connection. Communion is the basis of trust. The secret is to transform our awareness from separation to unity. In unity we perceive and express only love."*

For some of you, you must keep letting go. You must keep surrendering yourself to love and what is undeniable. Some of you have been denying love for a very long time. Surrender, not only will you develop thick skin, but you will also expand your ability to live fully and give fully.

There is also this quote by Mother Teresa which is one of my favourite's:
"**I have found the paradox**, that if you love until it hurts, there can be no more hurt, only more love."

What is love to others?

Different cultures have different versions of love

Love takes many forms.

I have no idea about your culture, but in every culture love can be expressed in different ways. I live in Canada where we have the most multi-culturally diverse place on the planet. The different cultures are everywhere and it is a beautiful thing. If you take a look at the dynamics within each culture, you can look closely and see that love is expressed in different forms. Love is shown, felt and heard in different tangible and non-tangible expressions. It might do you good to look at how your partner or partner's family expresses love.

Here is a small list of examples some cultures have, you'll notice some are unique and some are what you might call 'universal':
Making crafts for someone
Spending time together 'lounging around'
Cooking together with others

Cooking for others
Doing favours for others and volunteering their time
Writing notes, messages and cards
Working hard to provide a roof over their head
Going out and having experiences together
Teaching traditions, mentoring or training for activities

My Nonna was one of the most loving people I have ever known. And she expressed it in very subtle ways. She didn't often say too much, she mostly kept to herself. But she prayed for all her grandchildren every day. Every single day of the year, she would pray for the people in her life that mattered to her. What a selfless act! If that isn't love I don't know what is. She also spent a large majority of her day cooking. Yes I am talking about the same Nonna and Nonno as earlier who met in Italy and came to Canada. And of course in that old school, traditional European way, the women cooked and the men went to work. So my Nonna didn't work when I was growing up. She spent hours and hours in the kitchen in the basement, in the Cantina (cold cellar) and the upstairs kitchen cooking and serving. And let me tell you; that is one of the major ways she expressed her love, because she thought about you all day long when she was cooking. She thought about and focused on you eating her food, enjoying her food, and being completely nourished by her food while you were eating it. And that was love. And that loving energy went into her cooking and you felt it! You felt it when you ate it, when you were done eating it, and when you were on your way home, stuffed and satisfied.

Remember that energy is in everything around you, including everything you do.

My mother is also one of the most loving people I have ever known, obviously right? Yeah, but my mother doesn't like to cook! But she will bake for you! She will bake cookies, muffins, tarts, pies and cakes. And you know that takes time too. My mom actually oozes love. You can feel her love in her smile. My mom is always smiling. You can feel her love in her hugs, in her giggle, and her laugh. And she gives stellar advice. You can feel her love in her advice because it is objective, calm, well thought out, and presented from all sides. Her advice really is about what is best for you, and not about her.

Love is connected to emotion. In order to feel love you must be able to feel emotion. Unless you're a robot, you already feel emotion. You might experience it to different degrees than others, but know this, emotion encompasses all things. And all emotions are connected to love, because love is in all things, love is what created you and love is what creates everything. Everything is born from love. Here is an emotional scale for your reference. Note this is also a mood scale, awareness scale and an often referred to scale for the state of one's spiritual growth (take notice if you will that they are also the colour's of the chakras. Hmm… interesting that they are all the same thing). Also remember that everything is vibration as stated below. Take note of what you are 'vibrating.'

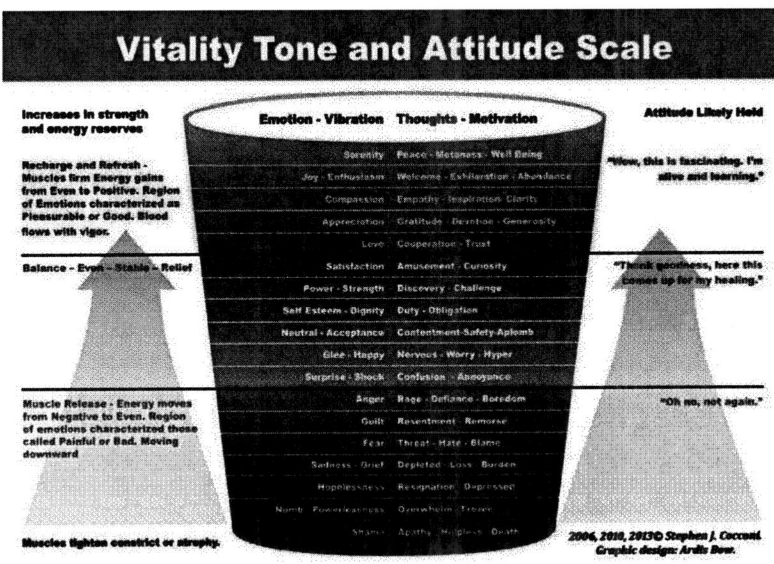

I met a man once, who openly said he could not feel emotion. His wife said it was a problem and wanted him to go to work on it since he was always neutral. She would often say, 'he feels nothing.' Can you imagine being married to someone who felt nothing? He wasn't depressed either, just neutral. There were no highs and lows, which is okay but that meant everything is a 'middle, mediocre, neutral only' response. ...everything! When we looked at the source of things and where this way of being came from (remember it's just a way of being), we traced it back to his dad. His dad never showed emotion. His dad was always neutral in every situation and laid on the couch, disinterested in life. After seeing it for years and years, he simply learned it from his dad. It wasn't really him, the man in front of me. It was not who he wanted to be. For him, it was a default way of being. Can you see where that was on the emotional scale listed above? He was stuck in 'neutral/acceptance. He had to work through those layers of neutral emotions and experiences over time. Once he worked through those emotions and cleared them, then created new behaviours and ways of being, then higher levels of emotion were possible.

The most important person you must love is yourself

You must love yourself before you love others

We first looked at loving yourself in the first chapter. Now we're going to look at it again from another perspective.

What if there was a law, *'The law of loving self'* that states, *'One cannot love another, no more than one can love thyself.*' I've created this law and I say it is true. It is proportionate. The amount of how much you love yourself is, equal to how much love you will experience and know in your life. The amount of love you feel and give for yourself, is equal to the amount of love that you can give and experience with another person. I myself have taken the journey of looking into what it means to love myself. I have taken on loving myself again and again. Why? Because when life hands you lemons it is incredibly easy to beat yourself up. I don't know about you but that's what I find. I can be really hard on myself, and so I have to come back to me. Knowing myself and having compassion for myself and my mistakes, my failures and my faults.

A lot of people that I work with can be the same. And so I recommend taking on different forms of self-love practice. Now there are a lot of self-love teachers out there and I happen to know a very good one! She is one of my friends and her name is Renee Mullings Lewis. She is a modern day wise woman, and a self-love expert. Renee says, "Self-love is love. It's the foundation. If you want to be more in tune with your partner, then practice self-love. You are going to have a better connection with your partner if you do because at any moment you can bring forth a **Tidal wave of love inside any conversation."**

Love yourself! It feels good to love on yourself a little. I know it might be a fairly new concept; however it is essential to good health and self-esteem. We are all human and we all forget how great we are from time to time so it's important to remember. And when you remember you feel awesome you are awesome! Tell yourself you are awesome more often. I do. I love myself and you should too. You are totally lovable, so you should love yourself.

Regardless of whether you are hard on yourself or not, I still believe you must love yourself in order to love another. How could you if you didn't? Let's go back to the law of loving self. How can you give what you don't already have inside yourself? Have could you show or display what you don't already feel and understand? It just makes sense doesn't it? Can you give what you don't have? You can't! You can't give someone $1000 if you don't have the $1000 to give in the first place. You can't love another person with all of your heart and soul, until you know what it's really like to have that love inside of your heart and soul! It's like having an empty jar and expecting delicious peanut butter to just fall out of it. It won't happen! The jar is empty silly!
So I say again, it is so important to love yourself, we could write a whole book about it. Because it is important that you understand, you must love yourself before you can love another person. So in order to have the kind of love and relationship you want, you have to fully love yourself.

How can you love yourself? There are many ways! You must discover what that means for you. For me, I love my alone time. It is so important to my health and well-being. You see, I'm very active, outgoing, and extroverted. I love being with people. I love bringing people together and I love my life the most when I'm on stage, sharing, teaching, and leading. I have a lot of love to give and those are some of the ways I enjoy giving it. However, I need to recharge on my own, by myself. It's one of the ways I feel grounded, centered and balanced. And that is self-love to me. So self-love is about self-care – taking care of yourself. Part of love is taking care of others, and so really, you can't take care of others without taking care of yourself. It's kind of like that oxygen mask on the airplane thing. Put your own mask on first, because you're no good to anyone if you can't breathe.

Something else you should know. Loving yourself is trusting yourself. When you trust, you can love. But you can't love without trust. The trust has got to be there to flow. I know right now if I tell you, you can't love someone without trusting them, you'd completely agree. And I'm glad you would.

Try to look at this simple equation:

If you have love and you subtract trust can that still equal love? Of course not.
Love – Trust = Love. No.
Trust + Love = Love. Yes.

A lot of people I work with avoid relationships and love because they can't trust. Usually trusting others is a common problem amongst people I work with as well as society at large, however a deeper rooted problem which they usually don't discover until later is trusting themselves. Here we come back to the past based hurt and problems that people experience and have yet to deal with which they may be unconscious of. So what happens is there is a lack of ability to trust themselves. Well guess what? At some point, this hurt has to be let go and the ability to forgive yourself and trust yourself will come back again.

It's just got to be done. If this is you, the only thing I can recommend is to learn to throw caution to the wind again and take on trusting the choices you make. Take chances, take risks, give up the fear of action and go after what you want. Trust yourself, leave doubt at the door and give yourself to another human being. By taking action you will find the love and relationship you desire.

Bring more love to your love

Did you know that love is limitless?

This piece is about how to increase the love you feel in your life. You see, as I've been mentioning, to elevate your relationships, you'll need to do things differently. One thing I'm very proud of is the amount of love that I can tangibly feel, sense, touch, and know in my life. I never knew this was possible until recently. But life is like a constant set of upgrades if you want it to be. You don't ever have to be satisfied with anything. Anything is possible and everything is interchangeable. What's fascinating is that it is always possible to increase the love you have in your life. The current level that you feel can absolutely be increased. Yes, this can happen with your partner, but also overall in your own life. Are you unhappy with something in your life? Bring more love into your life. Depressed? Bring more love into your life. Lacking creativity? Bring more love into your life. Sure it sounds easy, but how? Easy tiger, we'll get there in a moment.

You must understand something fundamental: **Love is abundance.**

The very nature of love is abundance. It is true what they say: love knows no bounds, it has no limits. Love places no judgments and makes no assumptions. Love discovers, and love is free. It has nothing to do with a scarcity mentality. So think about scarcity and think about love. It doesn't compute. Love is abundance. It is potential, further and further reaching, ever possible, never ending, just like outer space. That is how I would like you to think about love, just for the next few seconds. You see outer space is never ending, and ever reaching. It is unlimited and abundant. There is no end, it likely goes on forever. Think about your love like that. Maybe you can only see to the sun now, but soon you will be able to see past the sun, into the deeper reaches of space as we can now. We will see other stars, galaxies and planets that we can't even fathom.

Love is like that. If you can imagine it, everything that love is capable of right now

can be increased. There is always more- more patience, more forgiveness, more happiness, more thankfulness and more to give.
How do you bring more love into your life? First you must have an intention to do so. Declare out loud three times,, "I want to have more love in my life. I want to experience more and more love in my life. I am willing to do what it takes to experience more love in my life. If there's anything in the way of that I want to delete, uncreate and transmute it right now!"

Good for you! Here is a little assistance in helping you create that:

Break out that trusty old notebook! This one is one of my favourite's: Make a list of 100 things that you love. Take some time. Do this one because it's fun. Do this one because you will surprise yourself and you will actually enjoy this exercise. Here are 10 of mine to help get you started:

Banana and Limone Gelato
Warm Socks Fresh Out of The Dryer on a Cold Winter Day
The Matrix Movies
Massages in the upper back and shoulders
Vanilla flavoured tea with honey
My favourite navy coloured jeans
Seeing my breath in the cold winter air
Hot tubs and sauna's
The feeling when someone else is driving me somewhere
Christmas Time
Public Speaking
My partners kiss

I know I said 10 but I got carried away. See the good things that happen when you get on a roll?

Since you can be anything, (remember where we started, chapter 1) here are two ways of being that will increase your ability to love and be loved. They are simple (all the best things are) appreciative, and grateful. Practice these ways of being as much as you can, morning and night. It is simple and powerful. These 2 ways of being are so close to the vibration of love, they can't be denied. Also remember that

Golden Nugget

"What you appreciate, appreciates."

This means that what you recognize and give love to will increase in love and value and recognition.

Another way to feel more love in your life is to do things to feel more love. It's simple. Increase the sensory input and experience of love and you will know love at a greater level. You need to do more of what you love to feel more love. It's as simple as doing things that make you happy to be happy. So what do you love to do? Take from the list of 100 things if you need to. But think of actions, things that you love to do, and do more of that. Again, it's simple. But how many of us do it? I promise you if you do, you will feel more love and joy in your life. Joy is close to bliss and bliss and joy are both close to love.

This is how to make a great life even greater. This is how to make a great relationship even greater.

If you're still trying attract a great partner, no worries. By doing this you will become more lovable. Simply put, others will be able to love you more, and that will be attractive. Because being unlovable can repulse others who may want to love you away from you. Simple right? Yep.

As well, love is a very high vibration. Remember the chart from several pages ago (list page) and see that love is a very high vibrational energy. Loving energy is very high and thus, very attractive. People who are close or closer to the vibration of love will resonate with you and you will naturally attract them. Sweet!

Obey your heart

What does the fox say? I mean heart… What does your heart say?

My hope is that many of you reading this book are already familiar with the Institute of Heart Math. However, much of the world's population isn't aware of this incredible organization yet. This organization is doing so much invaluable research for humanity and is changing the way we understand ourselves.

They have done extensive research on the heart as a muscle and the actual connection to our heart and our world. They have over 20 years of research into our physiology, our brain, stress and our emotions and the relation between it all. Here is a summary of what they have found:

The heart has brain cells inside of it
The heart has more powerful brain cells than that of the brain
Where we once thought the brain was running the show, it turns out the brain is being run by the heart which is running the show
The heart is a generator of an electromagnetic field. As is the brain. (I am dropping some serious hints here!)
The heart is up to 100 times stronger electrically than the brain
The heart is up to 5000 times stronger magnetically than the brain
The heart is its own hormone generator. It creates, sends and secretes chemicals throughout the body for your health and well-being. Essential hormones are generated here, like oxytocin which cure's depression
The heart's electromagnetic field is so powerful it can affect others around you (Hello attraction! Hello magnetism!)
The heart has its own central nervous system, which means it can identify and process information, all on its own, separate from the brain.
Our hearts have a connection to the earth. Yes the earth, this planet we are on. The is mutual resonance from the earth's natural tone and vibration to our hearts as well.

I want you to take a moment and consider this. Consider how you are living and how you have lived your life. Consider what this information means. Please consider what this could mean for your life and if you lived in your heart what that might do to the world. Do that now.

It is fairly simple. You can think with your heart. If you are feeling low you are not connected to your heart. If you are upset, distressed, agitated or frustrated for no reason, you are not connected to your heart. Connect to your heart. It is simple. There is plenty of amazing information on their website which I highly recommend. www.heartmath.org

We spoke earlier about detaching from the mind and hearing your heart. I know it might sound cheesy but if you can't make up your mind, or can't make a decision, tune into your heart. Your heart will guide you and give you the answers. This can be done on any subject. The answer, your best answer, lies in your heart.

Golden Nugget

Guide yourself from your heart. Especially in finding and keeping the best partner.

Aside from the institute of heart math, there is other amazing information you should also know about the heart. Did you know that the heart is the most selfish organ in the body? It takes all the most oxygenated blood in the body, and uses it for itself. Obviously, the heart is essential to the body. Your own love and heart is the key to living a happy life. If the heart dies, all other organs go with it. There is a name for a condition upon dying of a broken heart. It is actually possible and real, and it is called "Stress Cardiomyopathy." Ouch.

Your assignment for the moment is to reflect on this question: How in tune am I with my heart?

Mad love

Can you tell the difference between love and lust?

To have a great relationship, and to really be in love, you need to be able to tell the difference between love and lust.

Let's start things differently. The definition of lust is 'very strong sexual desire.' Yes, lust could be connected to love. When you are with someone, it is normal to feel strong sexual desire for someone when you feel you're in love. However it is usually a separate feeling from love in terms of time. I see lust as fairly temporary. And love is a place in your heart that is there after lust has passed. A sense of loyalty is present in love. And lust has no loyalty. Lust is primal. Somewhere they will find that love is probably connected to that need to procreate that we all have. However, I had to some good research for this one and here is what I came up with:

A great online resource – www.psychologytoday.com - Judith Orloff, M.D. wrote the following:

"Pure lust is based solely on physical attraction and fantasy--it often dissipates when the "real person" surfaces. It's the stage of wearing rose colored glasses when he or she "can do no wrong." Being in love doesn't exclude lust. In fact, lust can lead to love. However, real love, not based on idealization or projection, requires time to get to know each other. Here are some signs to watch for to differentiate lust from love.

SIGNS OF LUST

You're totally focused on a person's looks and body.
You're interested in having sex, but not in having conversations.
You'd rather keep the relationship on a fantasy level, not discuss real feelings.
You want to leave soon after sex rather than cuddling or breakfast the next morning.
You are lovers, but not friends.

SIGNS OF LOVE

You want to spend quality time together other than having sex.
You get lost in conversations and forget about the hours passing.
You want to honestly listen to each other's feelings and make each other happy.
There is a feeling outside of yourself, almost in the space between the two of you that resembles affinity and 'caring for' this person.
He or she motivates you to be a better person.

For me and my partner, we have established,

Golden Nugget

"Sex is the deepest and most profound way to connect with your partner and give and receive love."

My partner and I teach this to singles and couples in The Sensational Sex Seminar.

You can learn more about The Sensational Sex Seminar and how to experience a deeper connected experience through sex at www.TheSensationalSexSeminar.com

The one

Is there a 'One' for you?

I don't believe in 'The One.' Not in the way you might think. I don't believe in 'the one' in the traditional sense. As in, there is only one person for you. I don't think it works to think there is a soul mate, only one soul mate that you are destined to be with. I don't believe it makes sense to spend your life looking for one person and believing there is only one person out there for you. Remember what I said earlier, I believe in compatibility and commitment.

There are multiple 'ones'. Changing and realizing that this is a limiting belief could be the thing that sets you free. It could be the thing that is the piece you have needed to hear. There is no ONE person and if you miss them that's it. Think about it. If there was one person, one soul mate, and if you aren't at the train station at 1pm, three Wednesdays from now you'll miss them. And it's also important to remember that you can't expect them to be perfect. This one, the one, your one, is not going to be perfect. He isn't going to be a perfect knight in shining armour, and she isn't going to be a total and complete innocent princess. They will still have faults, they are still human. However, they will be perfect **for you** as I have said earlier. I bring this up because many people confuse the one with love. Many people believe they will only love the one who is perfect. Bologna. You must love them for who they are. This includes their differences and weaknesses. We will cover this more in the next chapter, the final chapter. But **know that love is not perfect. And in its imperfection it is perfect.**

A word on couples. Great couples co-create. In other words, they create their lives together. You will create a sum of traits, habits, and experiences together. You know this, as this is what we look back on fondly or negatively. If you've ever found that you and your partner have swapped habits, ways of speaking, thinking, even right down to the words you use, you're right. Remember that quote, "You become the average of your 5 closest friends?" You become a reflection of them and they become a reflection of you. Your partner is the same, and so the two of you have separate dynamics. And when your dynamics interact, they will change. One of my teachers said, "You're partners are reflections of your unconscious mind. When you shift yourself and your unconscious mind, your circles will shift. The theme will repeat through other areas of your life and with other people." Be ready for this. Since we are moving towards the end of the book, and you are soon to be having new experiences after reading it (and you'll see changes even quicker if you did all the work), I have to tell to you be ready for the shift. When you find someone and commit, things will change. So here's a little tip on how to prepare yourself for the change.

Think ahead. Contemplate how you can sort through the tough moments when things aren't working out and use your tools to work it out. I gave you many suggestions in the communication chapter, amongst others. Whether you are deeply in love or just starting out, things will become rocky from time to time. It's up to you to ask yourself, "Who do I want to be when I am in love?" Remember, you are capable of taking on any way of being you wish. And just because you are in love doesn't mean you won't screw up from time to time.

You may fall out of love for a moment, and that is normal. So do this work and figure out the following, you will be thankful later. Ask yourself this question and then go from there - "If I find someone great, and I'm totally in love, how will I know how to work through it?"

-What will I do to come back to love when I fall out?
-What will we do, if unloving thoughts start to arise?
-Who will I turn to, that will truly, truly have my best interests at heart?
-Why will I come back to love?
-How will I come back into love?
-What practices will I engage in that will lead me back to love?
-Where will I turn if I don't know where to go?
-When will I know if I should come back to love or not?
(More on this in the next chapter)

Just because you fight, doesn't mean you aren't in love.
Just because you don't always agree, doesn't mean you can't be together.
Just because you get on each other's nerves, doesn't mean you can't make it work.

Now get ready because the next chapter is all about making it work. Congratulations on making it this far. You're almost there! I believe in you! I want to hear from you at this point too. I would love to hear from you! Do you have any questions for me? Is there anything you want me to clarify? Is there anything you need my help with? Please let me know!

Email me at Info@TheRelationshipMaster.com – It is important that you get everything you need before you continue on to the last chapter.

10
GREAT! I'M IN A RELATIONSHIP! NOW WHAT?

I've found someone and we're in it together.

Now, what do I do?

If you have noticed during our time together, I have been preparing you to be in a relationship. The first half of the book was about attracting someone and preparing for the relationship. The latter half was about being in the relationship, and how to make it great when you're in it. This chapter will be all about the other stuff, like how to make it work, what to do if it doesn't work out, and more.

Most relationships fail because people are not prepared to be in one. Throughout this whole book, I have prepared you to be in a relationship. I believe keeping yourself in the relationship, and being in the relationship will be easier and more likely. This is because you know how to be secure in who you are, you know how to listen, you know how to be happy regardless of the circumstances, you know how to be a good lover, and you won't depend on your partner to make you happy. Now that you are self-sufficient, you can focus on making your partner happy.

Relationships are a place to experience more emotion. My ideal for you is that you come to a place in your relationship where you are so fulfilled, so happy, and so in love that it will be indescribable. It will be beyond puppy love, beyond what you currently understand to be real, beyond simple excitement and joy, and more than a special feeling. My dream is that your relationship will be able to touch something deep inside of you. You may not know what I mean right now. I have taught you everything I know and I hope that's what you experience- that the words 'I love you' will be insufficient to describe the richness that you feel.

I hope you've made it to this part of the book. If you have, you will be heavily rewarded with more of the keys, the gold, the missing links that trouble people.

You can avoid the confusion that causes people to spend all kinds of time, money and energy for years and years trying to sort out their relationships.

The hard work is over, mostly. Let the games begin. From here on out, it's simple maintenance. I am proud of you. This is a different ballgame now. We are going to spend this last chapter looking at what we have to do, and who we have to be to make all our hard work pay off. This is because if you can't enjoy the time spent with someone, then why did you put all that effort into attracting them in the first place? For now celebrate. Do a little dance. Smile at yourself in the mirror. You made it through this far so reward yourself! And then set a reminder to reward yourself again one week from now, because you deserve it!

Get ready for some upsets

How do I avoid breakdowns?

Ask your grandparents or your parents, (if they are still together) "How do you stay married or happy for so long?" I bet that they will tell you one thing: "It takes hard work, and a lot of sacrifices." And they are right. However, they may not have had the tools that I have given you. You see, tools are a way to lighten the load. That's why they are designed aren't they? Mechanical tools, electrical tools, and relationship tools; all designed to make your lives easier and your workload lighter. So here's how to make life easier on you when things get rocky between you and your new partner.

Firstly, understand that issues are going to happen, and they are unavoidable. Call them what you will: fights, arguments, debates, discussions, accidents, breakdowns, they will happen. So there won't be any use in avoiding them, (I set you up with that question, I know) in fact I recommend that you face them head on. Now I don't mean take them on like a bull in a china shop and going straight for the jugular. Do not raise hell. That is not what I am talking about. I am talking about dealing with what is there. Be vocal and upfront about issues that come up (this was in the communication chapter and there were tools provided to do this). You should never placate your partner in way that is false, that does not serve them. Refrain from ignoring your problems. Sweep nothing under the rug. If you do, you would be doing a disservice to your partner.

The good news is that how these breakdowns or upsets occur to you, is completely up to you (remember from earlier in the book, the way we react is perfectly correlated according to how an event occurs to us). It is up to you how you view your partner when you are inside of an argument. You could see it as an opportunity to grow. You could see the whole thing as a moment to contribute to them. Or you can have them be as toxic, justified and dismal as you want. I know this transfer of perspective won't happen overnight, it will take some practice. We'll cover this in a few pages.

The other way to deal with breakdowns is to be prepared for them by doing that work earlier. Ask yourself, "Who am I in a relationship? Who am I in a feud? Who will I be when times get tough?" Review your notes from earlier in the book and add to them now. Will you fall to the wayside, and let your partner walk all over you? Will you be a force to be reckoned with? Will you be a partner, lover and friend? Will you side with them and tell them where you think they can improve? Will you listen to their suggestions to help you improve?

Breakdowns can be your best friend

Would you like to be the master of your own relationship?

Golden Nugget

If you become better at dealing with breakdowns in your own life, when it comes time to deal with breakdowns in your relationship, they too will be a piece of cake.

If you had a skill on your resume that said, 'breakdown handler' you would be a very worthy person to an organization. This is more than just problem solving. Problem solving is scratching the surface of the level of completion and integrity

I am talking about. Now, organizations don't realize this yet. However, having the ability to deeply deal with breakdowns in a timely and efficient manner, will make you invaluable and priceless. Why, because it leads to happier customers, vendors and partners and means less interruptions in business operations. If you have this skill in your life, what do you think you'll enjoy as a result? Fewer distractions, more happiness, better relationships and more time to enjoy the good things in your life, to name a few. The same goes for your relationship, so handling breakdowns is something you want to master. The way to do it will be illustrated here, but first, say this out loud three times:

Breakdowns = Breakthroughs

At the end of every breakdown is a breakthrough, an opportunity for you to expand and grow. So be mindful of every breakdown you encounter in your life and with your partner. Get excited about them!

When an upset happens with your partner, realize they are not doing anything 'to you'. Unless they are attacking you physically, they are not attacking you. Often we think the arguments we have are personal and we react to them negatively to our own detriment. It is all in how you take things. You can control how you react, it is 100% up to you. However, breakdowns are not personal. You want to remove yourself from the meaning that you give the breakdown. Take it for what it is; a breakdown. It can be that simple. You would be at the effect of the breakdown if you reacted in a hasty and harsh way. What you want to do is find a place of power (power is the ability to make something happen without the use of force). You agreed to this relationship, you attracted this person, so what can you do to help? What part did you play in this breakdown arising? The fastest way to end a breakdown is to see what part you played in it, what you could have done differently, and then explore that. Communicate with this in mind, and let the breakdown dissolve. The meaning shift when you accept responsibility, not with guilt, but with honour. Honour what you said you would do or didn't do that you said you would.

Stop reacting to your partner. It is not them doing anything to you. They aren't hurting you physically (unless they are, then get out of there fast!). They aren't making you do anything you don't want to do, so you don't have to react the way you feel you have to. You always have options. Always. The exploring of those options inside of a breakdown is what will save the day, and potentially save your relationship.

On one Saturday in the fall, my girlfriend Sophia and I made plans to spend part of the day together. We wanted to spend a lazy Saturday morning and afternoon in each other's company as this was something we never really made time to do. We're usually both very busy and on the go quite frequently. If we do stay overnight together, it is usually a rushed morning to get ready, get dressed and get to work on time. So on this day, we planned nothing for the first half of the day, but we agreed to go and do some work in the evening. A had a client meeting at 5pm and she had a meeting with one of her business partners at the same time. At around 330pm we started into a good conversation. We were working through something in one of her past relationships. A previous partner was giving her some trouble and she asked for my help around the issue. I knew the conversation would take some time, but I was sure that she could benefit from working through it (and so could we). It was 415pm when we were wrapping up. I told her the time (we agreed to leave at 4pm so yes we were late) and by the time we left the house it was 430pm. I had to drop her off to her meeting before going to mine. Surely cutting it close! Here's what I want you to know: When I told her the time she nearly freaked out! Immediately, she said, "Why didn't you stop me?" I explained why (somewhat harshly), in that I was more committed to her having the peace of mind she was looking for in the long term, and in the short term we would figure out how to make this all work. Even though I didn't let it show, I was concerned too! I didn't want to be late for my client meeting as I pride myself on being on time, and respectful of others time as well (I do my best of course, but breakdowns do happen). I immediately made the following suggestions to make it all work:

1) She could call and ask her business partner to pick her up at my place and I could leave her the key. This would be a favour from her business partner, but one that he may be willing to do, since they bail each other out from time to time

(sometimes being unreasonable is a good thing).
2) She could ask her business partner to pick her up from the bus station nearby, where I could drop her off. We would both be closer to our destination and finish this conversation in the car. I could be on time or just a few minutes late.
3) I could drop her off on the way to her meeting at the bus station and then she could take the bus from there. It was only a 5-10 minute bus ride.
4) She could take a cab from my place and I would give her money for it, or we could split it 50/50.

I already planned out the trip and the travel time and knew the details. Her destination was in the same direction as mine, and only a few minutes away. We opted for number three and I ended up calling my client to say that I would be a few minutes late as I was only a short distance away (people love to have communication with small details such as these. It is important that you do this, since it is part of respecting their time. It does not cause them to wait, wonder and consider leaving or cancelling on you). She picked up the phone when I called and said she was going to be a few minutes late and sincerely sounded like it was no big deal. PHEW! Thank heaven! I got there just two minutes after 5 pm and sent my girlfriend a text as I was getting out of my car to share the good news. We were both relieved! She was just as committed to my success as I was hers. I had a great meeting with my client and she had a great meeting with her business partner. Even still I apologized for being harsh with her and it was done. The whole mess worked out and everything was cleaned up.

There is an opportunity for you to practice demonstrating your love, communication and your commitment in every breakdown. Because it will take practice to build those muscles, allow it to take time. Realize that you will mess up along the way and with practice, you will develop great problem solving/ breakdown handling skills.

As always, it is up to you. And you get to stop having the person in your life if you don't like what they're doing to you or how they themselves react to the situations. But that is your choice. And you will want to be careful about this. We will look at this in the next few sections.

Your only job is to enjoy this!

How can I have fun and be responsible at the same time?

During my time in relationships and being with different partners throughout my life, I have learned a thing or two (enough to fill a book, haha!) One thing I have noticed is the happier I have become, the greater the partner I have attracted. The more I have constantly redefined and inquired into who is right for me, the more and more my partners seem to be 'right for me.' What is the connection behind that? Well it is quite simple.

If I am more and more happy, I find someone who makes me more and more happy. The more and more I pursue what it is I want in my life, the more I am personally satisfied with what I have. Is that odd? No its not. The keys to a great relationship are the following: if you want a great fulfilling, loving, honest relationship, **you have to be great, fulfilled, loving, and honest yourself!!**

Remember you can be anything you want to be!

One woman I worked with wanted to attract a man who knew his worth, was confident, successful and who honoured himself. I simply explained that a man who knows himself and honours himself, will want to be with a woman who honours herself and knows herself as well. At the moment, my assessment was that she did not honour herself very much. I was right. It quickly became apparent that she allowed people to take and take and take from her. Once we discovered this, we worked on her boundaries. We looked at where and with whom she needed to establish boundaries to set a new condition of respect from others and respect for herself. Once we did this, things started to happen for her.

There is a book on this topic all by itself. I haven't read it however it has been recommended to me by a few people. I believe in this practice as I have mentioned it a few times. It is called 'being the person your partner wants to meet.' This makes complete sense in terms of physics and the law of attraction since one fundamental principle in both is that 'like attracts like.' The actual book title is, "Be the Person You Want to Find: Relationship and Self-Discovery" by Cheri Huber.

Therefore your job is to be happy in life, regardless of whether you are in a relationship or not (easier said than done? No. Say it and you can do it). Remember that people want to be happy, it is an intrinsic part of our nature. Practice being happy! Practice being the person your partner wants to meet. And you will attract them, if you haven't already.

Let's look at having kids, for a moment. If having kids is something you want for yourself and even if it is not, consider this wise advice. **The best thing parents can do for their kids; is love their partner**. This needs to be said again, 'the best thing a parent can do, is love the heck out of their spouse.' Why? You and I, as children, watched our parents all the time. We listened, we felt, we saw, we paid attention. Our parents are our first example of a relationship in our life. They were the demonstration, the teaching of what love, relationships and companionship should look like. By osmosis we inherited whatever it was that they showed us. Chances are, when you read the statement I made above, part of you said, "Yep, uh huh. That's right." Because you can remember what it was like for you growing up. Children that I have met who have parents that did not display the affection and love that should have been there have completely agreed that this is true. As I mentioned in an earlier chapter, my parents were and still are very loving towards each other, and it's incredibly healthy. When love is in the air, everything is taken care of, is it not?

Be happy and loving in your life, be happy and loving around your kids. Your kids will pick up on this. Other experts would likely agree, if they could understand the simplicity of it. Wouldn't you agree, the simplest things are often the most effective?

Sharing is caring

How can I keep love present?

How can you make this relationship last? How can you keep the love going? I want to give you an unconventional perspective for a moment. You can keep the love alive and the relationship working by being proactive. That's right, proactive. You do that by sharing when things come up (and they will) you need to share them. You need to get into the habit of addressing any concerns before they come up, but **especially before they fester and build up**. You want to have any and all concerns handled by checking in, and preventing them from building up and blowing up. Agree to communicate as much as possible.

Golden Nugget

Transparency is a highly valued attribute which leads to a highly successful relationship.

Without erring on the side of pestering, constantly check in with yourself and your partner. It's the only way to maintain a state of mind where you are focused on what is actually going on inside the relationship, instead of what is going on in your head. Inside your head you will make up things, which aren't necessarily the truth. Remember we are meaning making machines.

Ask yourself, "Is this important? Or is it nothing?" "Does it matter if I bring this up? And will I let it go if it is nothing?"

Ask your partner, "Is this something I should be concerned about, or is it just me, worrying and being concerned?"

Understand that concerns are just concerns. And they are valid and really, they arise every day. So while they might be valid, are they real? Not necessarily. It's a thought, a worry, for only a moment. It is normal to have them. And if you think about it, you'll notice that they happen nearly every hour, don't they?

What you want to do is create something with your partner, where you can just check in with each other. Heck you could even call it 'a check in' if you must. And explain why you are doing this. Make it brief. Tell them you want to create the most harmonious relationship for the both of you. Blame it on me. It's a tool you read about it in a book. And you want to try it out and see how it works. Share your concern and then stop talking. Let them answer. Leave it at that. If it's something, it will create more dialogue. If it's nothing, let it end there. Trust them. Take their word for it. Open it up for more dialogue if it is necessary.

You will share and hear the concern so that you can both be free. You share it so that it does not get pent up and buried, hidden away in some cave, only to resurface when they spill your ice cream on the floor. Speak it and share it so that it is released, so that it does not live inside you. Then you can focus and get back to what you are committed to; a healthy relationship filled with nurturing and supporting each other. The sooner you bring it up the better. To practice, bring it up with a friend if you must. I myself used to do this all the time. You will realize that most of the stuff you come up with isn't about them, it's usually about you. And remember from Chapter #5, the less it is about you, the better.

When you realize this, you will be free.

This chapter is a summary of everything we've covered so far, arranged to reinforce your learning and support you as you move forward.

Interdependence

The difference between a great relationship and a good relationship

Interdependence is the holy grail of a great relationship. I know many couples that have too much independence or too much dependence inside their relationship. It places a limit on the level of greatness that is possible and attainable for both people. A great relationship has a balance between both, which I call Interdependence 2.0. I will share this with you and explain what these concepts mean.

Independent: Free, not influenced by control or others, self-sufficient.
Too much of this leads to fickle behaviour, lack of connection, and carelessness.
Dependent: Relying on someone else or something for aid and support.
Too much of this leads to obsession, repulsion, and disinterest.
Interdependent: Mutually relying on each other.
Interdependence 2.0: The ability to be free from neediness and dependency, while involving your partner in all necessary matters simultaneously. When you are together you are completely together. When you are apart, you are apart and focused on other important matters.

It is obvious interdependence is the healthiest choice of them all. It connects with the saying, 'absence makes the heart grow fonder.' And it can be hard on the ego. Keep that in mind and it will keep you in check. Time apart is healthy. With this, you will maintain your attraction. You won't adopt all of each other's habits. You will not become sick of each other either. These are all very healthy aspects to a great relationship.

Interdependence can be tough for people. Although it is an ideal state, not everyone can accept the concept. It is a very advanced idea that not everyone is practicing. It can be very humbling to a person as it incorporates into other parts of the relationship. For example:

Golden Nugget

Rather than fighting obstacles with 'my way your way, or the highway,' using interdependence, you would build a third way;

a way that works for both of you. Interdependence also utilizes synergy. You are much more powerful when you are together, focused on your goals. In this way, you are that 1+1 = not 2 but 5. Your combined power makes your goals more attainable when you are operating inside of interdependence.

More goodness for you to consider- I have come to understand that true love and trust requires interdependence. To be fully dependent on someone is not even love. It is something else. It is more akin to infatuation. **Love can be blind, of course, but if you are blind then you are caught in love's trap. Love should illuminate you, it should not blind you.** To be completely independent does not create love either. To be without connection, to feel no remorse, means to be independent. Love will have remorse; love will have connection, deep, deep connection.

That is why, at some point, once you are in a loving and committed relationship, the superpower of being unattached may be a superpower you will have to let go of. Superhero's eventually give up their superpowers, abilities and tools. What do they give them up for? For love; for a new chapter in their lives; for someone whom it is worth hanging up their hats for. They realize that someone else will fight the good fight, so that they can focus on being a lover. **Because you can't be a lover and a fighter at the same time.**

Break ups and what to do if it isn't working out

What do I do and how do I deal with it, if it isn't working out?

Sometimes you stay in a relationship because you are comfortable. That's bullshit. Don't do that to yourself. What a waste of time and energy. Plus, as much time as you spend inside of an unnecessary relationship, the more time you are losing out on precious moments where you could be experiencing joy filled, pleasant, enthusiastic experiences. The impacts of you staying in a relationship you know you shouldn't be in are measureless. Time, energy, money, emotion, habits, practices, thoughts, love, sex- it is hard to count and add them all up. You are doing a huge disservice to yourself if you stay in a relationship that you know you shouldn't be in. It is never a good idea.

Sometimes breaking up is necessary. **If it isn't working, you may be able to fool everyone else into thinking it is working, but you won't be able to fool yourself.** One client and friend of mine said this about his marriage, "We both knew within one year it wasn't going to work. We knew we were not right for each other. You could see it in our eyes. But we stayed married for 11 more years. What a waste." You mustn't do this to yourself. Promise yourself you won't waste your life and waste your time. Promise me you will get into dialogue or get into action if you know it isn't working.

How do you know if it isn't working out? You'll know. If you are asking questions, you are in the beginning of knowing. If those questions persist and go unanswered, you'll know. If you aren't answering the questions because you are avoiding them, you'll know. Either it isn't the right person or it just isn't the right time. Sometimes it's the perfect person, but it isn't the right time for you. If you are doubting yourself, then you are not ready. I recommend you do not waste their time or yours. Time is precious. It is the something we cannot make more of.

Respectfully breaking up, and ending the relationship with integrity is possible. It's something I've been able to do by practicing it my entire life. Some went better than others, but I used the tools that I had, and the training that I'd received to put it into practice. And as a result, many of my relationships ended harmoniously, peacefully and with integrity. We honour each other, and we treat each other with gratitude and love, even on the way out. Revisit the communication chapter and the values chapter and use the tools I gave you there. You and your ex-partner will be better off for it. The #1 thing you must do is actually communicate what is ACTUALLY GOING ON inside of your heart. Not your head, but your heart. Remember that your heart communicates differently from your head.

Dust off that old notebook and pen, and break it out. Do this work and answer these questions:

- If it doesn't work out, who will I be?
- Who do I want them to know me as?
- How do I want them to speak of me?
- Why should I care?

Doing this work is essential because you should care. You should care because you had experiences together. You learned things from each other. You shared things together. And all of that is precious. You should care because

Golden Nugget

"Your next relationship will begin only as good as your last one ended."

It is my strong belief, that every relationship should be better and better. Your next relationship should be a damn good one. Every single one should be, obviously, however, your next one should be a better one than the last.

I have a constitutional belief that every relationship should be an upgrade from the last. And since you are a creator and a powerful human being, and you create your life, you can make your next relationship better than the last. Use **what I taught you earlier:**

- Realize what it is that you don't want,
- Acknowledge that this is what you don't want.
- Then use that to focus on and identify what you do want.
- Then completely focus on what you do want.

Every single time you enter a new relationship, you can be a better human being, a better partner and lover. You can be the kind of lover and partner and person you've always wanted to be. So expect and create the next best thing. The bar should move higher.

How should the bar be measured?

Not materialistically, not financially, and not based on looks, not based on job or social status… those are fickle and superficial. In the end they don't matter. Base the bar on your experience, base the bar on your happiness, your level of positive emotion, base it on your sexual ecstasy, and base it on your level of love, overall satisfaction and fulfillment.

Don't worry about always having to be in a relationship. Don't fret and concern yourself with feeling like you are a loser if you aren't in a relationship. That's crazy talk. It doesn't mean anything if you aren't with someone 24/7. You will be fine. In fact it will be healthy for you. Remember, I always recommend after a relationship that you be with yourself for a while and no one else. It's so vital that you have a cleansing period after a long term relationship. I do not recommend bouncing from person to person, or relationship to relationship. Take time for yourself. Have no rebounds after a break up. Do yourself a favour and have a relationship cleanse. Again, this is something I have always done, and has always served me well. It allows me to clear my head, and heart, and be ready and available for the next person to come in. A few months break is something you would benefit from. I am a serial monogamist and it's always worked well for me. It also allows me to appreciate the next person that comes into my life. You want to give some space to yourself, in a period of singleness. This is a time to reconnect to yourself and who you are.

Sometimes someone leaves you. Sometimes you get broken up with. Sometimes it isn't about you. Sometimes they leave because they aren't ready. Sometimes they are dealing with things that you aren't aware of or they aren't willing to communicate. Sometimes you don't get an explanation and sometimes the explanation isn't the real one. Not everyone is willing to have the courage to express what is really happening inside of them. Not everyone has the courage to look into themselves and dig into the deeper reasons why one does what one does. Some people don't have tools like this book, or other tools that you have access to, to understand what is really happening inside of them. It takes a high level of awareness and self-understanding to be able to see your blind spots and where you are blocked. To see inside of what is going on inside of you and get to the heart of the matter is often no easy task. That is why I have all the love and compassion for you for reading this book. Because my intention was to stir you up at times, and I know you may have experienced heart break and frustration in your life, and some of that may have been revisited while reading this book. Heart break is part of the entire process. And heart break is only temporary. Thank god.

If and when the relationship is ending, it is super important to take out 'what's wrong' from the situation (review this from Chapter 6 to support you). Remember that nothing is wrong here. You will have to be 'that nothing is wrong and all is well' here. No one is to blame. You are both human beings, simply doing the best you can. You have your own issues, and your issues do not go away. You are doing your best as human beings. There is no fault. You are both there to be responsible and be there for each other. No make wrong.

Should I put everything I have into it?

Is it safe?

At some point you will have to be fully invested. You will have to throw all caution to the wind and throw yourself into the relationship and the person 100%. Now, I'm still talking about interdependence of course, however I'm not talking about half in half out type of behaviour. I am talking about giving yourself, committing yourself fully to making it work. On my journey through relationships I discovered at one point I hadn't really experienced a long term commitment. I'd never had one before. It was getting to that point in one particular relationship that it was either stay or go, and my natural tendency was to go. I saw that I was avoiding something and wanted to do things differently. I didn't feel my partner at the time was for sure the one. At least I didn't have that undeniable feeling. But because I'd never felt it before, I decided since I did care about this person a lot, 'I'd better stick around to see if I'm just fooling myself'. I chose to stay. I chose to commit to a long term relationship. And in particular, I told her 'I commit to making it work with you. I want to really give it 100% and see where we can go together.' She was ecstatic and overjoyed. She felt I was the one for her. I was nervous, but I was excited. I was excited to see where this would really take us. We were together for two years and it was a great two years! That feeling didn't really change, and I didn't feel compelled to spend the rest of my life with her. If you think this was a waste of time, you are missing the point. I needed to go through this. I needed to have that experience. I needed to know I really put my whole self into something, to see what would develop. You might need to do the same, if you are interested in walking down the aisle for example. That is what walking down the aisle will take.

And it's never safe. There is always risk. Unfortunately, there are no absolutes. But that's the game of life! Heartbreak is always a possibility. It's never not a possibility. There is always a risk in getting hurt and especially in fully giving your heart to another. Anything can happen. But what a thrilling rollercoaster ride that will be! There is no fairy godmother that will wave her wand and say, "Nothing will happen my dear. You can trust this will go perfectly." It doesn't work that way and you know that. Something could always happen to you, your partner, or the relationship. You should just give it your 100% all the time. This way you'll have no regrets. How do you know what to do? When should you give it 100%?

Simple:

Golden Nugget

You've got to go after the ones that light you up.

Remember the process itself. Revisit chapter 4 if you need to. This is something that my friends Hannah and Marshall, went through. They were happy together, they looked great together and spent several months deeply in love. One day they surprised me and started talking about getting a ring and spending the rest of their lives together. A few months later they had a very ugly break up. Eighteen months later they are both very, very happy, in separate relationships with other people. They are now both with people who complement them much better. They are in long term committed relationships and there is harmony. But they might not have met or found those people if they didn't find each other and go through that experience first.

Remember that manifestation means that the form of the manifestation must be released. The attachment to the form or the outcome must be completely released for it to show up and for it to show up in the way that is best for you. It will look different, sound different, appear different, and the timing might be off too. It never goes how you think it will. So put your whole self into it anyway. Why do anything less than 100%?

Help me, it still isn't working!

Have you implemented everything I said?

If you've followed what I've said and done everything I've recommended in this book and you still aren't getting what you want, you missed a step. It's that simple. You missed a step and that's likely. Come back and reread the chapters anytime. Alternatively, you may actually have something in your blind spot that is preventing you from achieving what you want. It is likely in your unconscious mind, where a certain program may be running (remember what my mentor said- we are hardware, running software). You may have a program running that has a primary objective to protect you which is preventing you from getting what you want. This program really thinks it is protecting you. However, if what you want is a relationship, and a great one at that, you've got to tell that part of you or your unconscious mind that it isn't protecting you any longer. You don't need it. It isn't serving you any longer. You must let go of it. How will you know what it is? You might have to call me and we might have to find out together. I'm able to help in that area. You can email my team at info@TheRelationshipMaster.com or you can find my contact info on my website at www.TheRelationshipMaster.com. It is usually one of three things and they're all based around a limiting decision, such as "I am unloved, I am undeserving, I am unworthy." Chances are as you read those words, one set of them jumped out at you or resonated with you. We never think these things consciously. It's funny, we image we think great things of ourselves. However, we all think some version or some extent of one of these three.

If you are stopped, or get stopped at any point in the process, know this... It might be due to fear or anxiety. Both fear and anxiety are a warning from the unconscious mind to focus on what you want. All it means is that the amygdala has fired. If you stopped because your amygdala has fired, you'll have to go through it and do it all over again. Anxiety is the body getting you ready, warming you up, and preparing you for something new. You cannot have anxiety unless you are doing something new. The way to get past it is by doing the new thing. Surrender to the feeling, acknowledge it as being there and let it go. Let the anxiety indicate that it is new. Thank it, and then take the action. That is it.

Congratulations for getting to the end of the book. Here is the last golden nugget:

Golden Nugget

You can have anything you want.

Any kind of life you want, any kind of partner you want. Trust me. Even if you don't believe it, trust me. I have done it. And I have helped countless others do it too. You are no exception.

Commit to 100% growth

Have zero regrets

Remember when I said in the beginning of the book, 'Relationships are the best place for us to grow and learn in our lives.' I really meant it. I have shared myself and my experience as well as the experiences of others, in the hopes that you will learn a thing or two. That's why we share stories; that is why we love stories. Because we learn, we see ourselves inside them and receive wisdom from them. There is something to learn from every person and every relationship. Make a promise to learn from every person you are with and have no regrets. You would not have met them if you weren't supposed to.

If you take on the perspective that there is something to learn from everyone, you will learn from everyone. And you will be the person you want to be, because you will bring forth in your life, the events, circumstances, and people who will need to teach you what you need to know, to be the person you want to be.

The only way you can have regrets is if you wished you did something differently or you wished something didn't happen. And there is no point to wishing something didn't happen, because it happened! Like my good friend Jeff Marx says, "How do you know it was supposed to happen? Because it happened!" He is a great guy. Remember that the simplest learnings are the best ones. Do what you feel you should do every single moment, as best as you can. And if you cannot do that, then fine. Make peace with it, leave it in the past, let it go, and do something differently next time.

Remember you are like an onion. (More beautiful and attractive, I promise.) I touched on the walls in previous chapters. What you don't know you don't know is that you have a shitload of walls. I do too. **I have peeled back so many layers, broken down so many walls, and you know what I find? There are more walls and there are more layers!** The walls just keep going! And now it has become a game! It's a journey, and an exploration of fun for me. I look forward to finding out what walls I have, so that I can walk around them, use them, and deconstruct them so that I have more freedom to move. Consider that even if you consider yourself to be an open and honest person, you still have walls, more than you know. Even if you consider yourself 'smart, aware, transformed, healed etc.' you still have walls. How do you know? Because you are a human being! Remember what another mentor of mine said, "When you're done, you're dead!"

Now consider this... consider the best relationship you can imagine. Consider the bliss, the happiness, and the ultimate intimacy you can create. Close your eyes if you need to and give it a moment. Go as far as you can. Make it look as good as you can, better than the last romantic movie you saw. I will give you a minute.

Exercise:
Take some paper and write it out. Everything from the looks, the sounds, the sights, the feelings, the smells, the tastes... Good. Now, take that and imagine it times 10. Can you see that image? Can you picture it in your mind? I say this because I myself thought I knew what a great, blissful, loving, connected, intimate, relationship was when I was 23 years old. Then I did a WHOLE LOT of

self-development, personal growth, and transformational courses from different organizations. Then my view of the ultimate relationship changed. It became bigger, brighter, more enhanced and more beautiful. It looked different. It felt different in more ways than one. And it was more fulfilling and juicy and lively than I could ever have imagined. Then... I expanded my awareness and took down more walls with my spirituality. And the picture changed again. And it wasn't before long, that I held it in my hands. I touched it and felt it and smelt it and experienced it along the way with my partners. So not only did the image change, but the experience of it actually on the court, while being in it did too.... and it kept getting more and more magical as time went on. My experience is beyond words often times. My hope is that you get to experience this and that one day, you email me and send me a message saying, "I'm here! Wow! It is magnificent!"

Making it last and making it work

What's the point in finding great partners if you can't keep them?

If you're attracting great partners that is just amazing! You are focusing on what you want instead of what you don't want! I am so happy for you! (I would love for you to share your success with me via email!) If you want to be in a relationship at some point with one of them, then your focus will have to shift from finding them to making it work. Which will in turn, 'keep them.' They will want to stay with you because you make it work. If you make it work, they won't want to leave because they've been with other people who make it difficult to be together, and so have you. And nobody wants that's. Do everything in the name of harmony, and it won't even feel like 'work.' Instead it will be seamless.

It's true what they say. The little things count. The little things matter. They are all little pieces, that add up to make the overall big picture, 'the big things'. This is what you ought to focus on. If your feeling isn't right, then your feeling isn't right. Your feelings are something you can't deny. Your thoughts will betray you. Your mind will play games with you. But your feelings will never lie.

Trust your gut, trust your intuition. It will guide you to what you need.

Our last moments together

This is it – No more Questions

This is my first book ever written. So what do I want to say to you in our last moments together?

If it were up to me, you would have exactly what you want in your life. What can I say in these last pages to give you the most benefit, of how you can have everything you want in a person and a relationship? In the end, all you have to do is accept responsibility for your life. Be "at cause" rather than "at effect." I can't say anything more than at the end of the day, it is all about you being complete. Being whole and complete as a way of being means to be perfectly at peace with everything in your life. This includes all of your past partners and relationships, successes and failures. When you are complete with everything that has happened in your life, you will be able to create anything newly. When you are being complete, you can be with any situation or person. When you know who you are and what you are worth, you will enjoy your life that much more. You will have fewer questions, more clarity, and more certainty. You will be present to the greatness and beauty in your life. You will appreciate people and places like you never have before. You will be able to succeed and have it all. You will be able to do anything you want. And you will actually go after the things that you want. You will find the people you want to be with, and they will come forth with ease. People will be who you need them to be, because you are who you need to be.

When you can be that way anywhere, when you are with your partner... wow! You will enjoy those moments so much more. Those beautiful moments, those little things that they do, will be like stars exploding in magnificence. You will appreciate every person that comes into your life. You will recognize them and all of your time together so much more.

At the end of the day, the right partner is up to you. It is whomever you choose. The right partner for you is anyone and everyone. In the end, you must understand you are responsible for yourself and your life. You are the one who is in control. The right partner will be the one you choose. Plain and simple, the one you choose. But when you get to a place when you know yourself so completely, and you love yourself so completely... it will be the right person, and it will be great. It may take time, but it will be the right person.

Let's look at the title of this book, *'Find 'Em & Keep 'Em: A Guide to Attracting the Right Partner.'* It is a guide (something I have learned which I am sharing with you) for you to attract (pull into your life and allow) the right partner ('right' is based on perspective and choice). Remember that right is based on perspective which is connected to choice. Right is about making it right. You need to continually maintain and choose that it is right. This requires constantly making your partner right, instead of making them wrong.

Your love life and relationship is your responsibility and is not a burden. It is a gift. Appreciate the saying, **'If it is to be, it's up to me.'** You have so much to give and share with another person! They want it! Will you give it? Will you share it? The law of attraction is real. It is more so the law of creation, not so much the law of attraction. You are creating it, first, before attracting it. You create it, no one else. You are sending out the signals, the thought waves, the vibrations, to people and to the world. Every desire and every action is your creation. You are a creator and a creative human being. You can have exactly what you want in a person and a partner. And you deserve it. You can have a great relationship. It is my intention in writing this book that you do.

I honour you. I appreciate you for reading this book. Thank you from the bottom of my heart.

Michael Santonato

PS: If you need more, I am happy to help. You can find me at www.TheRelationshipMaster.com

ACKNOWLEDGEMENTS

With immense gratitude and appreciation I thank:

- Andrea Ivanka; for introducing me to GR and his weekend book writing workshop and supporting me on this journey.
- GR and JG; for showing me the method, giving me the forum, taking a stand and making it appear completely possible for the first time in my life.
- James Macneil; I don't know how you did it man. But you believed in me, pushed me, supported me, and encouraged me. You also made it look possible, doable and achievable. And here we are and here it is. Thank you for this. Thank you for being the person with the job I strive to have.
- Landmark and the staff and those who assist; What a transformation, I can't believe what I've accomplished and who I am sometimes. I owe a lot of it to you. There is no way to measure what I have done and how much you have contributed to it. But this book is a big, big part. It really expressed what is possible for humanity.
- Adam Wieckowski; If you didn't get up and share about creating a writers group in a course I wasn't even in, I never would have joined the writers group, went to Gerry's seminar, and taken Andrea up on the invitation to attend. I never would have written this book. You are more powerful than you know my friend.
- Vicky; Woman, you have no idea the immense difference that one conversation had. It just goes to show the power of one conversation. If you weren't there in that moment, and said those words to me, picked up on my mood and made that invitation... I wouldn't have done any of this. That conversation is what started EVERYTHING. Thank you!
- Every mentor and teacher over the years; Brandon Ling, Julian Love, Iffy Love, Mony Vital, Robert Chun, Piero Palmerio, Greg Chow, Dan Harrington, Kim Redman, Lana and Max, Kam Singh, Renee Mullings Lewis, Damian Reid, Ken Trinh, Ana Rosenberg; Wow. Words can't express the difference you've made for me. The guidance you've given me, and everything you've taught me has been indescribable. I thank you so much and I love you for it. This book is a reflection of you. I have learned so much from all of you.

• Every woman that has ever graced me with her presence and beauty; Every single one of you whom has taken a chance on me, trusted me, and allowed me to contribute to you. Thank you, Thank you, Thank you. You have given me everything. The purpose for this book is in the time we shared together.
• Mom; For being a writer, an artist and a teacher first and foremost. For being completely inspirational and the first example of a woman I ever loved. For being so nurturing and loving. For showing me what a mother could be to my children, and what a woman could be as my partner.
• Dad; For being a romantic, a charmer, and a goof all at the same time. For being a fantastic husband, man, and father. And for so willingly putting up with my 'stuff' for so long. I hope one day you understand what a big part you played in showing me what it looks like to be a great man and have a great relationship. You have no idea what a great job you've done.
• To my brother and sisters, my brother in law and my nephew; thank you for helping me figure out who and what I am. Thank you for putting up with me. Thank you for allowing me to observe our lives, our relationships and all of our interactions. Thanks for not taking it personally. (*wink) Thank you for being beautiful demonstrations. Thank you for the support and the encouragement and inspiration. I love you.
• To all my friends that completely have my back; See you on the boat! In the stars and in the skies! I can't thank you enough for being there with me, for me and even at times, against me. For allowing me to contribute to you and your lives and for greatly, abundantly contributing to mine. PS: Thanks for buying the book, haha!
• To Alison MacMillan, who edited this book and helped be the one to get it done. Thank you for being on my team and for being there for me, willing to take this project on and help get it done. I don't know if it ever would have been completed if it hadn't been for you.
• To my love and my partner, Jessica: Wow. Babe. You are it. You are what this book is all about. It's all for you. I've been waiting for you, and I've been creating you since I was a child. Every action, every letter, was to bring you into my life. And now that you're here. I need nothing else. You are the one, my everything. I love you.
• To anyone that I forgot; You are with me and you are in this book too. I couldn't

be happier that we've met on this journey! Thank you for everything we've ever done together. It means the world.

The End

RESOURCES

www.positiveintelligence.com

https://www.landmarkworldwide.com

www.psychologytoday.com

www.therelationshipmaster.com

www.thesensationalsexseminar.com

www.drdewit.com

http://reneemullingslewis.com

http://www.rscbusinessgroup.com

www.heartmath.org

http://thespiritscience.net/

www.theorganicmethodofdating.com

Enjoy a Free Gift for reading until the end of this book at:
www.findemkeepem31.com